THE
EVERYTHING
GUIDE TO
HOMESCHOOLING

Dear Reader,

You've made the decision to homeschool your child, or you're taking your child's education in new directions. Congratulations! One of the most precious experiences of a lifetime awaits you and your family!

But where do you start? What if you're concerned about your ability to teach your child? What if your current homeschool method isn't working for your child? No need to worry! With *The Everything® Guide to Homeschooling*, you'll never be at a loss.

Over the years, I've helped thousands of families make decisions on homeschooling their children. I've helped families determine their children's learning styles, to choose the home-education path that works best for their children, and to learn through activities that are intriguing, challenging, and fun.

In this book you'll find ways to provide a well-rounded education for your children, keep your homeschool interesting and stress-free, and keep children learning and happy on their road to a successful life. Let's begin this wonderful journey together!

Sherri Linsenbach

Welcome to the EVERYTHING® Series!

These handy, accessible books give you all you need to tackle a difficult project, gain a new hobby, comprehend a fascinating topic, prepare for an exam, or even brush up on something you learned back in school but have since forgotten.

You can choose to read an Everything® book from cover to cover or just pick out the information you want from our four useful boxes: e-questions, e-facts, e-alerts, and e-ssentials.

We give you everything you need to know on the subject, but throw in a lot of fun stuff along the way, too.

We now have more than 400 Everything® books in print, spanning such wide-ranging categories as weddings, pregnancy, cooking, music instruction, foreign language, crafts, pets, New Age, and so much more. When you're done reading them all, you can finally say you know Everything®!

QUESTION

Answers to common questions

FACT

Important snippets of information

ALERT

Urgent warnings

ESSENTIAL

Quick handy tips

PUBLISHER Karen Cooper

MANAGING EDITOR, EVERYTHING® SERIES Lisa Laing

COPY CHIEF Casey Ebert

ASSISTANT PRODUCTION EDITOR Alex Guarco

ACQUISITIONS EDITOR Hillary Thompson

SENIOR DEVELOPMENT EDITOR Brett Palana-Shanahan

EVERYTHING® SERIES COVER DESIGNER Erin Alexander

THE EVERYTHING®

GUIDE TO HOMESCHOOLING

All you need to create the best curriculum
and learning environment for your child

Sherri Linsenbach

Aadamsmedia
Avon, Massachusetts

An Everything® Series Book.
Everything® and everything.com® are registered trademarks of F+W Media, Inc.

Published by
Adams Media, a division of F+W Media, Inc.
57 Littlefield Street, Avon, MA 02322. U.S.A.
www.adamsmedia.com

Contains material adapted from *The Everything® Homeschooling Book, 2nd Edition* by
Sherri Linsenbach, copyright © 2010, 2003 by F+W Media, Inc., ISBN 10: 1-60550-135-2, ISBN
13: 978-1-60550-135-2.

ISBN 10: 1-4405-9069-9
ISBN 13: 978-1-4405-9069-6
eISBN 10: 1-4405-9070-2
eISBN 13: 978-1-4405-9070-2

Printed in the United States of America.

10 9 8 7 6 5 4 3 2 1

Library of Congress Cataloging-in-Publication Data

Linsenbach, Sherri.
  The everything guide to homeschooling / Sherri Linsenbach.
    pages cm
  Includes index.
  ISBN 978-1-4405-9069-6 (pb) -- ISBN 1-4405-9069-9 (pb) -- ISBN 978-1-4405-9070-2 (ebook)
-- ISBN 1-4405-9070-2 (ebook)
  1. Home schooling--United States. 2. Home schooling--Curricula--United States. I. Title.
  LC40.L563 2015
  371.04'2--dc23
                              2015012538

Cover images © Kanate Chainapong/123RF.

This book is available at quantity discounts for bulk purchases.
For information, please call 1-800-289-0963.

Contents

Dedication

Thank you to my son, Devin, who kept our homeschool interesting, fun, and educational; to my husband, Don, who provided research assistance and support; and to the many faithful readers of our online homeschool site, *www.EverythingHomeschooling.com*.

Top 10 Benefits of Homeschooling

1. Children can learn and excel in the comfort and security of their own homes.

2. Homeschooled children receive a well-rounded education that's suited to each child's particular learning style.

3. One-on-one attention provides instant feedback and quick assessment of the child's strengths and weaknesses.

4. Homeschooling allows time for creativity and hands-on learning that makes education fun and memorable.

5. Children have freedom and flexibility in pursuing topics and areas of interest that truly matter to them.

6. Homeschooled children are self-motivated, self-confident, self-reliant, and eager to keep learning.

7. Homeschooling leads to proper social skills, high maturity levels, and the ability to interact with people of all ages.

8. Homeschooled children benefit from "real world" learning experiences, preparing them for life and the world beyond school.

9. Many colleges and universities are impressed by the knowledge and skills of homeschooled children and actively seek out and welcome them.

10. Homeschooling draws families even closer together, creating special times and precious memories that last a lifetime.

Introduction

IT'S A GREAT TIME for educating your children at home! You're understandably excited about the prospect of homeschooling your children or exploring new options for their education. You're not alone. Over 1.5 million children are currently being educated at home.

As more families commit to educating their children, you'll find an abundance of resources, materials, and options available to you. Sometimes this can lead to confusion or information overload, making you wonder which resources or materials you should choose for your children. This book will help you sort through the many options available today and determine which ones will best suit your children's learning styles and educational needs.

One of the most important aspects of educating your children is to understand that homeschooling is a lifestyle, rather than a teaching style. Yes, homeschooling is about helping your children achieve a quality, well-rounded education. But it's so much more. Homeschooling is a natural part of living and learning each day, blending seamlessly into life's daily routines within your home. It's a lifestyle that meshes perfectly with your family's values and your educational goals for your children.

Some parents might worry that they cannot "teach" their children at home. But homeschooling isn't "school at home." A classroom, student desks, textbooks, and test materials are not requirements for your homeschool. Those items are used in school facilities that must serve hundreds of students. Your home simply needs a comfortable area for you and your child to spend time together, learning together.

In addition to a quality education, homeschooling provides other benefits, too. Children feel safe and secure in the comfort of their own home. They can learn at their own pace, their days are less stressful, and their self-confidence grows.

Homeschooling can often bring families even closer together. Each member of the family takes an active interest in learning and sharing new information, brainstorming together on ideas or themes to study, and having extra time and opportunities throughout the day to engage in discussions on a wide variety of topics. Homeschooling is the common thread woven throughout their lives that pulls the family closer together.

As you read this book, you'll find curriculum suggestions and learning activities for language arts, social studies, math, and science, leading to a quality education for your children. You'll see how to determine your children's unique learning styles, and how to use materials that best suit their style. And you'll see how your children will regain joy in learning when they realize that homeschooling isn't just school at home.

Here, you'll find everything you need to make the homeschool experience easy, affordable, and fun. Even if you are a veteran homeschooler, you'll find fresh ideas and techniques that help keep home education interesting and exciting. If homeschooling is more of a challenge than you had anticipated, you'll find ways to eliminate stress and make learning at home more enjoyable for everyone.

If you are a single parent or working parent, you can still homeschool your children. This book provides the tips and guidance that will help you succeed. If your children have already entered a conventional school, you still have time to change directions and educate them at home, whether they are in the first grade or tenth grade.

Every child deserves a quality education, one-on-one attention, and guidance in finding the road that leads to his or her happiness and success in life and work. Every child benefits from learning in a safe, caring, stimulating environment surrounded by those who love and value him. Never doubt that you are the best teacher your child could have!

Come along on this amazing journey called homeschooling. It will be one of the most precious and rewarding experiences of your life. Enjoy the adventure!

CHAPTER 1

Home Education Expectations

Yes, you can homeschool your child! You needn't be a professional teacher to educate your child at home. Children are natural learners, and parents are natural teachers. You've seen your child learn and grow with your guidance and love since the day your son or daughter was born. Homeschooling is similar to parenting your child and just as rewarding! As you begin your homeschool adventures together, you'll find an exciting, new world opening for you and your children.

Understanding Home Education

Homeschooling your child is not difficult. In fact, a home-based learning environment often removes the stress that many families face each day. You're able to create a schedule that works for your family, and you also have flexibility to rearrange your schedule when the need arises. Take time to consider a homeschool lifestyle that best suits your family. But if you find that it's not working as you'd hoped, don't worry. Simply try a different approach until you find the style and schedule that flows for your family.

If you're considering the idea of homeschooling, you already possess the most important requirements: concern over your child's education, interest in your child's future, and love for your child. With these three essentials, you're well on your way to a successful homeschool experience.

It's also helpful to remember that homeschooling is not school at home. This is a theme you'll see repeated in this book and throughout the homeschool community. Why is it so important? Because it's the one area that causes the most frustration—and often failure—for homeschool families. Misconceptions and unrealistic expectations trip up even the most well-intentioned family. The information in this book will help you avoid this pitfall.

A brief look back at the beginnings of public school shows why the education of children migrated from the home to the schoolhouse. You'll also see why the education of children is returning to the home in record numbers.

A Look Back at Education

From the earliest days, a child's education took place inside the home. Children learned from parents, from a large extended family, and from everyday life. They learned to read books on their own or from older siblings. They practiced their alphabet, penmanship, and math problems on slate with a slate pencil. Families made sure their children learned important life skills; reading, writing, and math skills; and socialization skills. They taught their children morals and values, proper manners and etiquette, how to get along with others, and how to respect their elders.

Public Schooling

In 1642, the Massachusetts Bay Colony passed a law that required parents to make sure their children could read. Just five years later, they passed another law that required towns with fifty families or households to establish an elementary school. Towns with at least 100 households were required to establish a grammar school. The first public school, the Boston Latin School, opened in 1635. By the mid-1600s, schools began to crop up in other New England towns. Many of these were plain, one-room schoolhouses.

Public school did not become mandatory in the United States until individual states began to enact compulsory attendance laws in the mid- to late-1800s. Even then, it was difficult for every child to attend school. Some children were kept at home by inclement weather, snowstorms, or floods. Not every child could walk the distance to and from school, and mass transportation was not yet an option. These children continued to be educated at home by parents or taught by a tutor, while others received instruction in a nearby church.

Modern Homeschooling

As the Industrial Revolution swept the country, school transportation improved and so did attendance at public schools. However, in the 1960s and 1970s, some families, disappointed with the public school system, began teaching their children at home. Early homeschool pioneers and advocates broke new ground in the homeschool territory. Family-centered education began moving to the forefront of society once again.

Internet-Age Homeschooling

Years ago, it was difficult to find information on homeschooling or to locate resources. Public libraries were the main source of information, and they're still very helpful to homeschoolers today. But most families also have Internet access today, which makes it much easier to obtain and use a wide variety of educational resources. The challenge today is sifting through all the information that's available online, to find the resources that are right for your family.

The number of homeschooled children continues to increase each year. More parents are homeschooling because they feel they are best able to pass morals and value systems on to their children, and because they believe they have more time for their child, as well as a better understanding of their child's educational needs.

In the mid-1980s, approximately 150,000 to 200,000 children were being homeschooled in the United States. By the mid-1990s, the number had grown to approximately 500,000 to 600,000. As of 2012, about 1.7 million children were homeschooled, according to the National Household Education Surveys (NHES).

Number of Homeschoolers Today

Today, approximately 1.7 million children are homeschooled in the United States. This indicates a growth rate of about 7 to 15 percent per year, as determined by Dr. Brian Ray, president of the National Home Education Research Institute (NHERI). Parents cite various reasons for their decisions to homeschool, ranging from dissatisfaction with academic programs, to concern about school environments, to religious and moral reasons. The concern over school environments is one area that has grown over the past five to ten years, according to NHES.

Parents Make Great Teachers

Rest assured that, as a parent, you are the best teacher your children could have. No one knows your children better than you. No one knows their strengths and weaknesses as well as you. No one has seen their successes and failures, their ups and downs, their joys and despair, as you have. And no one loves them as much as you.

When you're considering homeschooling, you might wonder about your capabilities as a teacher. You might be concerned that you "don't know how to teach." But you have already been and continue to be your child's teacher. You are the one who cared for your child as a baby, and you are the one who taught your baby to walk, to talk, to eat the right foods, to cross a street safely, to treat others kindly, and much more. Those first few years of your child's life are some of the most precious and the most delicate. And through it all, you were your child's teacher, and you did it well.

You'll be pleased to know that the key to a sound education for homeschoolers doesn't rely on the formal educational background of the parent or on the parent being a state-certified teacher. Rather, it relies on the parents' natural ability to nurture and raise their children and to instill a love of learning within them.

Research has shown that the keys to a good homeschool education rely upon the ability to do the following:

- Learn through hands-on activities and projects.
- Take advantage of learning opportunities whenever they arise.
- Learn together, discuss topics, and seek answers together.
- Design a curriculum best suited to each child's learning style.
- Interact one-on-one with each child.
- Pinpoint a child's weaknesses and work to help improve those areas.
- Exhibit patience and good humor.
- Share love and close bonds with each child.

Most of these points come naturally to parents, and they no doubt come naturally to teachers in traditional schools, as well. Unfortunately, in traditional schools, teachers aren't always awarded the luxury of having only two, four, or six children in their classrooms. Consequently, they can't always provide individualized instruction one-on-one with each child or design different curricula to best suit each child in the class.

The Homeschool Lifestyle

Homeschooling is a lifestyle, a natural part of each day's routine. Therefore, the term *homeschooling* hasn't been the best description of what your children do each day. It's not actually *school at home*. Some families prefer to use terms such as *home learning*, *life learning*, *family learning*, or a *learning journey* to describe what they do. Regardless of the term used, it involves understanding and connecting with your child.

Think about the terms *teach* and *instruct*. These can take on harsh implications within the home and seem out of place there. Rather than teaching or instructing a child, consider homeschooling as *guiding* a child. Homeschooling or the educational process should be a learning journey that you and your children share, rather than forced instruction.

Reconnecting with Your Child

Some parents who have withdrawn children from school might find that they need to reconnect with their children. Former U.S. Secretary of Education Richard W. Riley, concerned over the gap widening between parent and child, stressed that there is a need today for parents and children to reconnect. He stated, "There is a disconnection here that demands our attention . . . a disconnection so pervasive between adult America and child America that we are all losing touch with one another." He encouraged all adults to take a special interest in young people and to "guide that child's education."

You can reconnect with your children by simply sitting down with them each day and talking, or by going on walks together, or for a ride around town or through the country. Many homeschool parents who have withdrawn their children from school suddenly wonder what they will talk about with their children all day. They may sit down together and find that the gap between them has grown wider than they had anticipated. Other than the basic "How was your day today?" or "What would you like to do this week?" they're not sure what to say or even where to start. By suggesting a walk to the corner store or a drive to the lake, you and your child can find room to breathe, share a different environment for a while, and encounter new experiences together.

After an outing with your child, you'll find yourself talking about many little things on the drive home or later that day. You may remind him of the osprey you saw at the lake, or the funny conversation you overheard between an elderly couple at the café. At the dinner table, you may talk about the biography you read together on Albert Einstein, the surprising facts you both learned about the ancient civilization of Mesopotamia, or the spectacular erupting volcano your son created that day. By sharing daily experiences, you and your child quickly reconnect with one another, bringing the entire family closer together.

Bonding through Learning Together

By being a part of your child's education, you naturally connect. By learning together, reading together, playing games together, and going on simple, relaxing outings together, you build experiences that bring you and your children closer. When your children are in school each day, the opportunities to connect are diminished. But when your children are in the home, opportunities present themselves throughout the day. The learning experiences that are woven into each day are like threads of yarn connecting you and your children, forming a strong bond that unites the whole family.

You can enhance your child's learning by applying the following tips in your homeschool:

- Choose something new to learn about each day.
- Use artwork or music to complement learning activities.
- Engage in lively conversations and discussions.
- Play a variety of strategy or "what-if" games each day.
- Provide a creative, stimulating, hands-on environment.
- Encourage experimentation, explorations, and problem solving.
- Demonstrate ways to seek answers to questions.
- Explore neighborhoods, businesses, and cultural centers together.
- Read together every day.

Listening Instead of Instructing

The parent who listens to his child is a wise parent. Keep in mind that *listening* does not mean *taking orders from* your child. When you truly listen to your child's conversations, you hear what's on her mind, where her thoughts are, where her interests lie, what she would like to do in her life today, and what she would like out of life tomorrow.

Children experience thousands of thoughts and feelings each day. Some are more important than others, yet none is inconsequential. It's these types of daily thoughts and feelings that lead to further discussions, questions, explorations, and, ultimately, to greater learning.

Your child feels valued when you listen to her. Here are some ways to truly hear what your child has to say:

- Stop what you're doing and look at your child while asking her to explain what she thinks or how she feels about something.
- Keep your hands still and retain eye contact with your child while she explains her thoughts and feelings.
- Avoid busying yourself with other things or becoming distracted while she is talking. Give her your undivided attention.
- Avoid the temptation to interrupt, fill in her sentences, place your ideas over top of hers, or hurry her along. Remain silent, and allow her to speak and think through her feelings.
- Respond with short sentences, such as "I see" or "That's interesting," to show that you follow and understand what she's saying.
- Encourage your child to elaborate by suggesting that she share more about her experience or ideas, and how they make her feel.
- Ask questions appropriate for your child's age, such as, "What do you think?" or "How do you feel about it?" Questions for older children could include, "What do you feel you've learned from that?" or "What do you think could happen as a result of this?"

When children are able to speak about their thoughts and feelings—and know that parents are listening—they feel that their thoughts are valued. When they can discuss their thoughts and ideas, they also gain a better understanding and a greater ability to learn.

Teaching Time Requirements

Most traditional school days are approximately six hours long. However, you and your child won't need to sit at a desk in your home for five or six hours a day. Some states might require you to keep a daily schedule and attendance record, showing that you homeschool a certain number of hours a day, 180 days a year. But in most cases, the hours and days can be flexible.

If you work outside the home, for instance, your child's "homeschool hours" might include the learning hours in the morning, plus time spent learning together in the afternoon or evening. When you add weekend homeschool adventures, projects, and fun lessons, the "homeschool hours" add up quickly.

The actual time required to focus on core skills (language arts, reading, social studies, math, and science) can be broken down per age group as follows:

- **Preschool and kindergarten:** 30 to 60 minutes per day
- **Elementary-school ages:** 60 to 90 minutes per day
- **Middle-school ages:** 1.5 to 3 hours per day
- **High-school ages:** 2 to 4 hours per day

This timeframe includes one-on-one time with the parent, focusing on required skills for a particular age group. While younger children may require more of your time, older children are usually more in charge of their study time. For most homeschoolers, the rest of the day is spent on other educational activities, such as reading, art, music, hobbies, strategy games, educational videos, and researching and exploring special areas of interest. For many parents, these activities provide additional opportunities for individualized one-on-one time with their children as they explore and learn about topics together.

Scheduling Strategies

One of the most important keys to success is flexibility in the homeschool schedule. There will be days when things don't go smoothly or according to schedule. You might even find that several weeks go by in which the learning process simply isn't progressing as planned. Don't worry or allow yourself to panic or become stressed. This is merely an indication that you need to look more closely at your child's learning style and your family's lifestyle, and try a different approach.

Every family has its own homeschool style, and you'll find the one that works best for your family, too. In upcoming chapters, you'll see several different types of homeschooling discussed. They'll provide ideas or inspiration for developing a unique home-education style that could be helpful in your family.

Free Time

Allow "free time" each day for kids to explore their own areas of interest, before or after the main homeschool activities. Free time provides time for arts, crafts, games, reading, hobbies, and other creative projects. Some families cover the core skills and busywork in the mornings, then the afternoons are free for exploring other activities of interest. For some families, the earlier part of the day is free time, then the family gathers together in the evenings to spend time studying the core skills. This schedule works well especially for two-career families or single-parent families.

When unexpected situations cause the family to miss out on their normal study times, many make up for this by spending a few hours catching up during the weekend. Sometimes, events arise to upset the normal homeschool schedule by several days or weeks. Remember that flexibility is your friend! You can take spring break a little earlier than planned, or you can take a midwinter break. Then spend a couple extra weeks in the summer, catching up if necessary.

Have a backup plan in mind for unexpected situations. Pick up an armload of books from the library that you know your children would enjoy reading. Keep a few puzzles, games, or models stacked in the corner of a closet. Your kids will be thrilled to get what they consider to be new toys, and they'll stay busy, having fun and exercising their minds during this unexpected free time.

Decompression Time

If you decide to homeschool a child who has been in school for some time, he will need some decompression time, or time to adjust to his new lifestyle. Nathan had begun homeschooling after attending a traditional school for seven years. He had been accustomed to moving through his school day in time to the ringing bells. He was conditioned to focus on one subject for forty minutes, then put that topic aside, and immediately switch to studying another subject for forty minutes. Then he had to backburner that topic, and switch to another subject for forty minutes, on and on, throughout the day. For Nathan, education had been a fast-food compendium of information quickly ingested to the tune of ringing bells, with little time left for him to think in between, let alone absorb knowledge thoroughly.

At home, though, the day stretched out before him, undivided by forty-minute classes marked by ringing bells. At first, he felt at a loss. He wasn't sure how to go to class without the warning bells. He wasn't sure when to stop studying without the sounding of the bells. Even though he had looked forward to homeschooling, he wasn't sure how to make the transition from school to homeschool.

Being at home during the school year had previously meant vacation time, holidays, summer break, and freedom for Nathan. As a new home-schooler, he felt a little guilty about not being at school. Doing schoolwork at home during the day felt strange to Nathan. It took a while for him to adjust to the new routine and find a learning schedule that felt right to him.

This is a normal reaction for children who have spent time in school. This is why they need to decompress and be provided with free time for them to adjust and become comfortable in their homes on a daily basis. You can help them by letting them know it's okay to do nothing for a few days. Let them get used to the idea of being at home and doing some of the things they've been wanting to do but haven't had the time. If they begin to feel bored, you can suggest some things to do, such as a field trip, a nature walk, a trip to the library, or going through some old toys they haven't played with for a while.

QUESTION

How do I know what to teach?
Curriculum guidelines for kindergarten through grade 12 are available at *www.EverythingHomeschooling.com*. Just click on "Curriculum Guide-lines" to see the topics that are generally addressed at each grade level.

Soon they'll be learning new things on their own, just by getting back in touch with themselves and with their surroundings. Then, gradually, you can begin incorporating your homeschool plans into their lifestyle as, together, you work out a schedule they are comfortable with.

Cost of Homeschooling

Homeschooling costs can vary, depending on your budget, age of children, and current needs. Some parents spend $200 to $300 per school year. Others spend more, while others spend far less. Some families purchase more items initially as they begin homeschooling for the first time. They might want to collect supplies to last several years, including microscopes and chemis-try sets, in addition to writing materials, art materials, and other supplies.

Others prefer to wait until a microscope or chemistry set is needed. The average amount spent per child per year, according to research conducted by the NHERI, is about $500 to $600. The money you would spend on back-to-school clothes, book bags, special binders, gym shoes, and other must-haves could easily cover your first year of homeschooling.

It's tempting to overspend in the beginning. You might think you need to purchase a curriculum package or enroll your child in a correspondence school, yet you aren't sure which would be the best for your child. Take time to observe your child's learning style first, before committing to a particular program. You might also check the type of curriculum packages other families use.

In lieu of a packaged curriculum, you might feel that you need lots of textbooks, workbooks, science equipment, and so forth. In reality, you don't need to spend anything before you start homeschooling. Consider using free or low-cost ideas before you begin spending.

FACT

For help with your homeschool lesson plans, curriculum ideas, and homeschool activities, visit *www.EverythingHomeschooling.com*. You will find hands-on activities, weekly challenges, virtual field trips, unit studies, and more to assist your homeschool endeavors.

Free Library Books

A world of information is contained within the walls of your local public library. And it's free! Nearly any book you will ever need to use in your homeschool, from the preschool years through college preparation, is available free of charge at your library.

From library books, you can create your own lesson plans and design worksheets, rather than purchasing workbooks. Public libraries also have a wide selection of educational DVDs on history, nature, science, math, and travels to foreign lands. They have CDs of music, literary works, biographies, and foreign languages. Children can spend hours at the library with educational magazines, puzzles, chess games, and software. Most libraries have a dedicated computer room and educational DVDs for children to use.

Programs offered by libraries include story time, sing-alongs, kids' clubs, reading and artwork contests, game nights, and special holiday events. If necessary, you can even enlist the help of tutors provided by the library. Watch for library book sales, too; you can pick up some great finds for only a few cents each.

Free or Low-Cost Resources

Keep homeschool expenses to a minimum by setting a realistic budget and sticking with it. Wait to purchase items until you absolutely need them. By acquiring free resources first, you limit your costs before you even begin. Although some purchases are unavoidable, such as paper, pencils, and crayons, you can usually find great deals on these items in July and August, during the back-to-school sales.

ESSENTIAL

Find free educational materials on the Internet by using search engines such as Google, Bing, or Yahoo! Or check out the free worksheets, games, software, and activities at *www.schoolexpress.com*. Try *www.abcteach.com* for more free worksheets, word searches, puzzles, theme studies, research projects, and more.

Teacher supply stores usually offer discounts or special deals to teachers, and they often extend these specials to homeschool families. When visiting the store, present a copy of your homeschool registration paperwork and find out the type of discounts they offer to homeschool families or groups. Take your children to the store, too, and see what books, games, science projects, or construction sets catch their interest.

Consignment shops are good sources for used educational items. You can find microscope sets, planetarium sets, telescopes, globes, games, puzzles, books, and more, all at affordable prices. It's also a place where you can put your used homeschool items up for sale when you no longer need them.

Buying in Bulk

Your local homeschool group might purchase educational supplies in bulk at reduced prices. If your group has enough members, this can be an affordable way to stock up on notebook paper, construction paper, folders, rulers, pens, pencils, and other items.

Check with your homeschool group to see if they offer a book loan program for members. This is a good way to acquire reference books, teacher books, or textbooks, which can be expensive. Borrowers will be able to use the books for several weeks or even a semester. And loaners will be able to clear their bookshelves of used books, while making room for more immediate needs.

Homeschool groups and state organizations often hold curriculum fairs once or twice a year. These are great for purchasing used books, software, and supplies, as well as used curricula other families have outgrown. At these fairs, you are able to look over the books and curricula firsthand and ask the sellers questions about the products.

Benefits of Homeschooling

The benefits of homeschooling are many. Not only do homeschooled children receive a broad and well-rounded education, but the entire family is brought closer together through the homeschool experience. Parents and children get to know each other better, they share experiences they otherwise would have missed, and their homeschool years provide a myriad of memories that will last a lifetime.

Above-Average Test Scores

Studies on the academic achievement of homeschoolers continue to demonstrate that they consistently score at or above average on standardized tests. In a 2009 study of standardized academic achievement tests (conducted by Brian Ray, PhD, with the NHERI), homeschooled children averaged at or above the eightieth percentile. The national average for traditionally schooled children on standardized tests is the fiftieth percentile.

Homeschoolers also tend to score higher on SATs and ACTs, especially in the areas of English, reading, and vocabulary. In math and science reasoning, they scored at or above national averages. A study conducted by Dr. Rhonda Galloway and Dr. Joseph Sutton, *College Success of Students from Three High School Settings*, showed that homeschooled college students ranked higher than other students in the following areas: academic, affective-social, cognitive, and spiritual.

The College Experience

In the 2006 article "Homeschooled Students Excel in College," Christopher Klicka reported that various colleges had seen increased admissions from homeschooled students. In many cases, those students performed as well as, or better than, traditional high schooled students and had higher grade-point averages.

Aside from test results (which is a controversial subject in itself for many people), homeschoolers are welcomed—and in some cases, actively sought—by colleges and universities today. And many now offer scholarships to homeschoolers. College professors continue to speak out on their experiences with homeschoolers in their classes. In many cases, they have found homeschoolers to be more mature (emotionally and socially), better prepared academically, strong in class participation and leadership skills, high achievers, self-motivated, and creative.

As Jay W. Wile, a university professor with a PhD in nuclear chemistry, says, "I experienced thousands of students. By far the best students that I had were the homeschooled ones. They were serious about learning, they could teach themselves, and they were far more likely to be able to think critically than any of their counterparts."

Social Skills

Homeschooled children often have opportunities to socialize with a wider group of people as they run errands with parents during the week. Or they attend homeschool gatherings and events where children and adults of various ages help one another. Since their learning takes place in the real world, away from the confines of a classroom or institution, they develop social skills that are applicable to everyday situations.

On the whole, they socialize more often with varied age groups, as well as with people from all walks of life, rather than the same age group in a classroom, day after day. They have more opportunities to interact with businesspeople, community workers, group leaders, volunteers, neighbors, and friends.

Reduced Stress

Sometimes the morning rush of trying to get out the door and to school on time can result in chaos and stress for school children. And the evenings are not much better—pages of homework to do, confusion over not understanding assignments, extracurricular activities to attend (after an already long school day), and basic chores to do.

When children receive their education at home, the morning ritual is far more relaxing. There is more time for preparing and eating breakfast together, and enjoying a less-stressful start to the day. Children are usually calm and relaxed in their own homes as their learning day begins. And all the while, parents and children are talking, interacting, laughing, playing, learning, and generally sharing their days and their lives.

By evening, homeschool lessons have been completed—and there were no misunderstandings regarding assignments on either the children's part or the parent's. Extracurricular activities are woven into the day's normal routine, and chores are often completed earlier in the day. That leaves the evenings open for family time together, a relaxing dinner, and free time for reading, game playing, and other enjoyable activities.

FACT

A relaxed child learns more easily than a stressed child. Some studies show that stress inhibits the formation of new neurons in the brain. Dr. Carla Hannaford, biologist and educational consultant, states, "Chronic exposure to stress inhibits full brain development." This can result in learning problems, such as ADD (attention deficit disorder), ADHD (attention deficit/hyperactivity disorder), or behavioral problems.

The benefits of homeschooling continue to make themselves well known. When studies on homeschooled students—as well as firsthand knowledge of homeschoolers—clearly demonstrate the students' academic abilities, social adeptness, leadership skills, concern for family and community, and well-adjusted attitude toward life and learning, the results speak for themselves.

CHAPTER 2

Learning Styles and Teaching Methods

Your child could be a visual learner, auditory learner, kinesthetic learner, or a combination of these learning styles. When you understand your child's learning style, your job will be easier, your child will be happier, and homeschooling will be a joy for both of you. This chapter will help you to enhance your child's learning experiences by incorporating the information-processing methods that come naturally to her.

New Learning Experiences

The brain is a complex organ, composed of billions of neurons, or nerve cells. By age three, a child's brain has approximately 1,000 trillion synapses (learning connections or pathways), which is twice as many as an adult. The synapses connect the neurons in the brain, enabling the advancement of thought processes and learning.

As a child seeks and acquires new experiences, new synapses will grow and strengthen in the brain. If the number of stimulating, new experiences drops off, the number of synapses will diminish and be lost, breaking some of the learning connections. Those synapses that are not used regularly are pruned off in the second decade of life, and they are lost forever.

ALERT

To strengthen synapses, the brain requires frequent new stimuli. This is why bonding, nurturing, positive interactions, creative stimulation, explorations, and new experiences are encouraged in the learning environment from birth. They provide crucial reinforcement and strengthening of neural pathways that are important for acquiring, processing, and applying knowledge throughout life.

Though much about the brain remains a mystery, scientists, psychologists, and behaviorists continue to learn more about the way it functions and processes information and intelligence. The findings of the following educational theorists can help you better understand the learning process and your child's individual learning style.

Active Learning Styles

Swiss educational theorist Jean Piaget found that quality learning took place when children were actively involved in their own learning process. Through exploration and discovery, children turned their experiences into learning patterns that provided foundations for further explorations and subsequent learning.

Piaget found that children's cognitive skills, or the way they process information, were enhanced through physical experiences and perceptions.

He believed in active learning environments where children could discover, absorb, and build on new experiences and information. Much of his research focused on the developmental stages of children's intellect and learning readiness.

Learning Environments

Maria Montessori believed that the child's learning environment should be endowed with simple manipulatives, or tactile materials, that hold the child's interest and promote exploration and learning. She felt that teachers should be guides who encourage children to freely explore the learning materials in their surroundings.

After working in the psychiatric clinic at the University of Rome, she opened her own schools for children, incorporating methods she had used at the clinic. Her style eventually became known as the Montessori Method, a self-motivated learning style that is intended to enhance a child's self-confidence and self-discipline.

Multiple Intelligences

Educational psychologist Howard Gardner, proponent of the theory of multiple intelligences, believes children develop their own learning and thinking patterns (intuitive learning) between birth and age five. When entering the school system, a different educational style is introduced (academic learning), which is not necessarily in line with the child's style. This contradiction in learning styles (intuitive versus academic) can create confusion for the child, making the learning process even more difficult.

Gardner suggests implementing varied learning methods and environments that allow children to use, and benefit from, their individual learning styles. In providing a wider range of learning activities and experiences, he believes that learning can be enhanced.

Common Learning Styles

Learning styles and multiple intelligences are based on in-depth research and scientific studies, which are fascinating. For the purpose of homeschooling your children, however, you'll want to be aware of three general styles of learners. Observe your children to see if they exhibit any of these learning styles:

1. **Visual learners.** These children prefer to spend time poring over pictures and graphics, and respond to bright colors and visual stimulation. They tend to learn best through visual presentations.
2. **Auditory learners.** These children enjoy listening to music, CDs, or audio tapes, and to people reading aloud or talking. They can learn best through discussions and verbal information.
3. **Tactile-kinesthetic learners.** These children like to move around, touch things, and talk, plus they have a difficult time sitting still. They learn best through an active, hands-on approach.

Even though a child may appear to be a visual learner or kinesthetic learner, it doesn't exclude him from possessing qualities of the other learning styles, as well. And it doesn't mean that approaches used for another style of learning cannot be incorporated into his lifestyle. The key, however, is to help your child learn in the way that makes the most sense to him, while still providing a well-balanced learning environment that includes visual stimulation, discussion times, and physical activities. Even when you've determined your children's best learning styles, provide a variety of learning styles to help them process and retain what they've learned.

Visual Learners

Visual learners learn through seeing and visualizing images. Whether they are looking at words on a page, the person who is speaking, or a presentation mounted on the wall, visual learners need to see something in order to fully absorb it. When thinking and processing information, they see pictures in their minds. Even if it is a word, in their mind's eye they see an image of that word.

Visual learners also like to take notes, even if they already have written material in front of them. By writing down bits of information, they are able to see it on their notepaper and inscribe their notes in their minds' eyes.

Here are some tips to help your visual learner make the most of his learning style.

- Create posters, artwork, or colorful pictorials to accompany lessons.
- Hang educational charts, displays, illustrations, maps, and mobiles.
- Use attractively designed flashcards for various subjects.
- Use flow charts, pie charts, and diagrams to illustrate math and science concepts.
- Design colorful cards for spelling, vocabulary, and English concepts.
- Read nicely illustrated reference books or picture books.
- Make eye contact while explaining lessons or concepts.
- Encourage note-taking, illustrating, or diagramming of topics.
- Use computer applications for learning topics.
- Allow educational videos on topics studied.
- Provide a quiet area of the home for studies, free of distractions.

Auditory Learners

Auditory learners learn through hearing. They may read information or texts, but they don't fully grasp what they've read until they hear someone read it aloud or summarize it in their own words. The tone, rhythm, and inflection of the voice are important to the learner's comprehension. When recalling oral instructions or information, auditory learners hear the speaker in their mind, as they replay the tone and rhythm of the voice as it stresses this point or that. The way in which a speaker conveys her message helps the auditory learner glean the important facts and details from the information.

Here are some tips to help your auditory learner make the most of his learning style.

- Read material aloud to auditory learners.
- Use rhythm and voice inflection when reading and talking.
- Record lessons for playing and replaying.
- Encourage the reading of books or information aloud.
- Present material in an interesting storytelling format.
- Engage in lively discussions and debates on various subjects.
- Allow CDs, audio tapes, or recorded books relating to topics studied.
- Create musical presentations of topics studied.
- Include and encourage speeches and verbal presentations.
- Turn off the television and radio, and limit distractions.

Tactile-Kinesthetic Learners

Tactile and kinesthetic learners learn through touching and moving. This learning group is sometimes broken into two separate categories: tactile and tactile-kinesthetic. Both groups are similar, with the tactile-kinesthetics enjoying hands-on experiences as well as lots of movement in their learning styles. They process information through physical sensations, and they learn best when participating in activities and actively applying fine-motor and gross-motor skills.

Where the visual learner is distracted from learning by noise or commotion, the tactile-kinesthetic learner is negatively distracted when remaining quiet or sitting still for too long. In order to learn, the tactile-kinesthetic learner must keep moving, exploring, and experimenting.

Here are some tips to help your tactile-kinesthetic learner make the most of his learning style.

- Understand that movement and touch is imperative for learning.
- Provide a variety of manipulatives for hands-on learning.
- Incorporate games, construction sets, geoboards, and Cuisenaire rods into lessons.
- Invest in lab equipment for reinforcing science and math concepts.
- Put on dramatic plays that bring social studies and literature to life.
- Create colorful, textured cards for spelling, vocabulary, and English concepts.
- Read or study while swaying to and fro, or in time to tapping feet.
- Create lesson plans choreographed to dance music.
- Encourage use of computers and electronics for learning.
- Devise brief time slots for sit-down study times.
- Allow classical music during study times.
- Take frequent field trips related to topics studied.

Your Child's Learning Style

By now, you've probably recognized your child in some of the learning processes described here. Even though she may practice some learning styles from each of the three groups, as you observe the results of her learning, you might realize that she comprehends concepts better as a visual learner, auditory learner, or tactile-kinesthetic learner.

When you've determined her optimal learning style, you can help your child by incorporating the previous tips. In addition, you'll want to provide the basic materials and create the type of environment that will keep her motivated and learning. Inspire her to use pictures, graphics, artwork, and color if she has visual-learner tendencies. If she has auditory-learner inclinations, encourage her to read aloud, make speeches and presentations, and discuss things that are on her mind. If she's a tactile-kinesthetic learner, allow her more freedom to move, dance, touch, and explore as she learns about her world and her place in it.

FACT

You give your child an advantage when you adapt learning and activities to suit her natural style of processing information. However, your child benefits even more when she's aware of other ways of assimilating information, so avoid focusing *only* on one style of learning. Remember that new experiences result in new synapses in the brain.

As the years pass and your child grows and changes, her learning style may shift as well. She may encounter situations where familiarity with different learning styles will be helpful to her, perhaps in sports, music, college, or career changes. By staying in tune with your child, you'll be able to provide the basis and variables that will result in optimal lifelong learning.

Your Child's Strengths and Weaknesses

In observing your child's learning styles, you'll also gain insight to his strengths and weaknesses. When you're in tune with your child and the work he is doing, you'll see how quickly he grasps skills, as well as determine where difficulties lie in other areas.

Writing Challenges

Some children have difficulty with fine motor skills, which results in disinterest or stubbornness when it comes to writing assignments. In actuality, the process of printing or writing can be very painful or at the least, uncomfortable, for these children.

At eleven years of age, Kyle was bright, quick, and witty. Math came naturally to him, and he had a knack for creating gadgets out of electronic parts and motors. He could tell jokes and riddles, aptly describe movies or books he had read, and he could focus on 1,000-piece puzzles for hours. But when it came to writing a two- or three-paragraph paper, he grumbled and resisted the assignment.

Kyle's mother began to observe him carefully when he was absorbed in close, detailed work. Although he enjoyed drawing and artwork, his was a free-flowing, abstract style, taking up a large expanse of paper with few intricate details. She also realized that assignments he completed were printed in short sentences or phrases, usually with large letters touching each other. His math papers also contained letters and numerals that were printed large but close together, one against the other.

As she watched Kyle work, she noticed his cramped style of printing and the way he often laid down his pencil and stretched his fingers before picking up the pencil again. She also noticed that he labored over the writing of his name at the top of his pages when she asked him to use cursive writing.

She soon understood that doing paperwork with pen or pencil was not comfortable for Kyle. After further investigating, she found that boys are often later than girls in developing fine-motor skills, such as gripping a pencil, making it move in the proper directions, and creating fancy letters or intricate artwork.

When Kyle's mother allowed him to type his three-paragraph paper on the computer and print it out, it turned into a four-page story. She realized that typing was easier for him, so she allowed him to use the computer more for writing assignments. She also helped him improve his fine-motor skills by allowing him to build the small gadgets he enjoyed, put together puzzles, use scissors for cutting shapes for artwork, thread berries and popcorn onto strings for the birds, and to use a slanted easel or board while drawing or printing.

Observing Children Closely

By homeschooling your children—and observing their learning styles and work habits—you'll be able to pick up on weaknesses before they become a larger problem. You can also ask your children if there are things they do each day that are somewhat difficult for them. Ask if they find a particular lesson or activity difficult, and follow up on why it might feel that way for them.

In Kyle's case, he might have said that his hand started hurting after writing four or five words in cursive. His mother might have thought it was a convenient excuse to get out of writing the paper. Or she might have paid closer attention, as she did in Kyle's case, and found that it was indeed something more.

Individual Patterns

When homeschooling your child, you are tuned to his rhythms, his sleeping and eating patterns, and his biological makeup, which has been a part of who he is since he was a baby. You can see when he is widest awake, when he is most alert, and when he is better able to focus and to learn. You can also provide him with more nutritious meals and snacks throughout the day to keep his blood sugar normal, eliminating the highs and lows that can result from improper eating habits. And you can ensure that he gets a good night's sleep to fit his homeschooling patterns, as well as rest and relaxation time when needed throughout the course of the day.

You will be better able to work with his weaknesses, take advantage of his strengths, and provide a more balanced day of educational activities. As a result, he will respond and react more positively to his natural peak learning times, which are in tune with his particular lifestyle and learning patterns.

Peak Learning Times

Some people are morning larks. Others are night owls. Some prefer to get right to work first thing in the morning, then enjoy their afternoons with a clear conscience of a good day's work already done. Some savor the relaxation of quiet morning hours, then rev up for excitement and activity in the late afternoon and evening hours.

Children also experience peak hours throughout their day. Some are still groggy and sleepy-eyed at 10:00 A.M. Others are bouncing on the beds and throwing balls around the room at 5:00 A.M. Some can't seem to focus well until late afternoon, while others are ready for lessons at 7:00 A.M.

ALERT

Research has shown that a good night's sleep is critical for alertness, learning, and retaining information. When sleep is limited or interrupted, the mind's ability to focus or to recall information is limited. Some researchers have recently found connections between sleep problems and ADD or ADHD.

You can see what a difficult time these children would have focusing and learning if they were in school between 8:00 A.M. and 3:00 P.M. Peak learning times are also influenced by sleep habits and by food that is consumed.

Sleep Patterns and Learning

Your child's particular sleep patterns can affect learning and the ability to focus. Some children simply will not fall asleep before 11:00 P.M., no matter how hard you've tried. Some fall asleep before 8:00 P.M., even though you'd rather they stayed up later (because you know they'll be up at the crack of dawn!).

Some children never took naps when they were young; others took morning and afternoon naps. This is all a part of who they are. Changing children's sleep habits can be done over time, but it can also go against their natural biological makeup, never quite setting well with them.

Nutrition and Learning

When children go off to school without a nutritious breakfast, their blood sugar generally falls around midmorning. This creates the midmorning slump, resulting in tiredness and a reduced ability to focus. If math class was held in school at 10:00 or 10:30 each morning, and your child was not doing well in math, the midmorning slump could be part of the problem.

ESSENTIAL

Studies on nutrition and brain function have shown that poor nutrition or meal skipping can impair a child's mental and physical performance. As you prepare nutritious meals for your family, educate children on the importance of a well-balanced diet and healthy snacks—lessons that will ensure a long and healthy life.

The same effect occurs around 2:00 or 2:30 in the afternoons. Depending on what the school lunch consisted of, your child could experience a mid-afternoon slump. She would be especially affected if she were an early riser, had missed out on a good breakfast, had a less-than-nutritious lunch, and had little time to relax between classes. With her body running low on fuel by the 2:00 class, her level of alertness and learning receptiveness would be dramatically diminished.

In the homeschool, these issues can be observed and corrected quite easily. You can take advantage of your child's peak learning times and be flexible in scheduling learning activities. If your child needs to rest or needs a quick, nutritious snack, you can accommodate her. If she needs some fresh air or a walk around the block to help energize her, you both will enjoy the opportunity to take a break.

Your Teaching Style

As noted previously, homeschooling is not "school at home," and you do not need to be a professional, certified teacher. As a parent, you are already qualified to teach your children. You won't need to take on the persona of a traditional classroom teacher in your home, or stand at a chalkboard and jot down instructions, or sit behind a desk and grade papers.

Chalkboards can be fun and desks can be handy, but when homeschooling your child, take advantage of the *home* and don't worry so much about *school*. Relax on the couch, and pull your children close to you as you read to them, work on math problems, or discuss the American Revolution and recite "Paul Revere's Ride" together. The warmth, love, and closeness of a mother or father is a powerful learning conveyance in itself.

Your teaching style should not be something separate from who you are. Your teaching style is a part of your innate parenting style. It's the part of you that is concerned about your children, cares for your children, and wants the best for your children.

Positive Attitudes

Remind yourself each day that your duty is to guide your child, not force instruction upon him. Your role is to help him learn how to learn and to encourage him to seek answers to questions, find materials and information that will help him learn, explore the things that interest him, and find new and challenging ways to learn. You will want to have patience and a positive attitude as the guider in the homeschool. Adopting a relaxed, easygoing, humor-filled frame of mind is also helpful.

Teaching Tips

First and foremost, you should homeschool in a manner that you and your child are comfortable with. Try some of the following tips to see how they work in your homeschool.

- Use resources around the home to help children learn basic skills.
- Take advantage of every hands-on learning opportunity.
- Make connections from one subject matter to another.
- Ask questions, and encourage use of reasoning and thinking skills.
- Brainstorm together on new or better ways to learn.
- Provide positive feedback on daily activities.
- Read a variety of books, together and separately, every day.
- Engage in interesting discussions throughout the day.
- Stress the values and qualities you feel are important in life and learning.

When a child learns about a subject in several different ways, he learns it better and retains the information longer. Therefore, incorporate aspects from various learning styles into your lesson plans to widen your child's experiences and sensations.

Your Strengths and Weaknesses

Just as each child has her own strengths and weaknesses, so do all parents. You may have a great grasp of the English language, but you may be slipping a bit in the math department. Fearfully, you wonder how you will ever be able to teach math to your child. Don't worry. Some homeschooled kids grasp concepts quicker than parents, and soon they'll be explaining it to you. But what if they don't?

No one said you have to be an expert in every subject in order to homeschool your child. When you don't have the ability or resources to teach a subject or two, there is always someone else who does. There are tutors at the library, college kids down the street, or retired teachers in the community.

Another helpful resource is your local homeschool group. There you can find moms and dads who have a special knack for math, science, art, or music. While they help your child in areas you are weak in, you can help their child in an area you are strong in.

Older homeschooled children are especially eager to help younger ones learn, so don't overlook them for helping with math or reading skills. Sometimes, a child finds it difficult to learn something from mom or dad, but put her with a study buddy and she picks it up in a flash.

Together, you and your children will be able to pinpoint and improve weak areas as well as build upon strong areas, culminating in a solid learning environment that works for the whole family.

Resources on Learning Styles

For activities to enhance learning styles, see "Games Support Multiple Learning Styles" by Andrew Miller on *www.Edutopia.org*. Learn more about Howard Gardner's work at *www.howardgardner.com*, and about his work on multiple intelligences at *www.multipleintelligencesoasis.org*. For more on the Montessori Method, visit *www.montessori.edu*. Try incorporating suggestions from each into your own homeschool, and see how your children respond.

CHAPTER 3

Start Homeschooling Today

You can start homeschooling today or take the first steps toward setting up your homeschool. You might wonder about legal requirements for homeschoolers, or procedures for withdrawing your child from school. Each state has its own protocol to follow. You can determine your state's requirements by contacting your state department of education or homeschool support groups in your area. With the information they provide, you'll be able to move forward with your home education plans.

Legal Considerations

Homeschooling is legal in every state, but each state has its own set of requirements. Some states require homeschools to operate similar to private schools. Some ask to see an outline of your educational goals, and others require that a form be filled out and submitted to your superintendent's office. A few states require that a certified teacher observe your child's progress periodically, some require you to keep a portfolio of schoolwork and projects, and others require standardized testing.

Most states offer one or two options, so that you can abide by the law that will work best for your family. For instance, in some states, you may have the option of establishing a home school, operating as a private school, or using a private tutor. You may opt to have your child's progress evaluated by a certified teacher, have your child take a national standardized test, or participate in testing on a local level. Some states are more lenient and do not require testing, evaluating, or record keeping, while others are more stringent in varying degrees.

If state regulations seem too confusing or unfathomable, don't be intimidated. If there's language you don't understand, such as "operate a home school as a public school," "be supervised by a certified teacher," or "file a notarized affidavit," don't let the legalese deter you! The wording of the laws is usually more confusing than the actual regulation.

Your State's Homeschool Laws

To find homeschool laws and regulations for your state, visit your state's department of education online. Many states have their laws posted on their website, while others have a homeschool packet of information they can send to you. Your state's homeschool association can also provide the regulations for home education in your region.

The Home School Legal Defense Association

If you have any concerns, questions, or problems regarding legal aspects of home education, contact the HSLDA. This nonprofit organization defends parental rights to homeschool, represents families who may experience legal conflicts over homeschooling, lobbies Congress on homeschool issues, and monitors laws and conducts research on home education.

ALERT

The website for the HSLDA, *www.hslda.org,* includes the latest information on homeschool laws, parental rights, legislation, and legal news affecting homeschoolers. You can sign up for their free electronic news alerts, which cover national and international issues, proposed bills, or changes in state homeschool laws.

The HSLDA also encourages homeschoolers and homeschool groups to work together to better educate the public and legislators on the benefits of home education, to participate in homeschool legislative issues at local and state levels, and to involve state representatives and senators in homeschool organizations and conferences. Through sharing personal successes with legislators and the public, families can continue to communicate the educational benefits and moral outcomes of home education. This, in turn, helps to promote public awareness of every family's right to educational freedom and the right to a quality education for their children.

State Education Departments

Each state's department of education can assist you with homeschool requirements. In most cases, your state's department of education will have their requirements listed on their website. Simply enter your state's name, plus "department of education," in a search engine online.

If the homeschool rules aren't clearly stated on their website, make a phone call to your department of education or to your state's main homeschool association. They should have the answers to your questions.

Homeschool Support Groups

Homeschool groups have played a major role in clarifying homeschool laws, bringing homeschools and traditional schools closer together, and helping to educate the public and the media on homeschooling philosophies and principles. Not only do the groups monitor laws and legislation at local, state, and national levels, they also provide the contact that homeschool families need with each other.

Even parents who have supportive friends and families often find that they need time with others who are in their shoes, who understand what homeschool days are like, and who share similar concerns and goals for their families. This is the role of the local homeschool groups.

ESSENTIAL

If your community does not currently have a local homeschool support group, you can always start one yourself. Place notices in community centers, public libraries, parks and recreation departments, educational supply stores, and children's consignment shops. Advise the homeschool division of your local school district of your intent and ask the administrator to direct interested parties your way.

Local Homeschool Groups

Nearly every town, county, or community has at least one homeschool group. Many have several, with each group serving different needs within the community. Yet all local groups share the same goals: to provide information, support, and a gathering place for homeschoolers.

Some groups have specific religious affiliations, while others are open to all, regardless of faith or philosophies. Many groups produce monthly newsletters, convey information to the local media, set up an information hotline, arrange field trips and educational activities, establish book loan programs, share curriculum ideas, and otherwise help families with homeschool and socialization needs. They may also hold curriculum fairs, co-op classes, sports events, skating parties, musicals or theatrical presentations, and much more.

State Homeschool Organizations

State organizations provide information on state laws, are aware of proposed changes regarding home education in their state, and work with legislative bodies. They may produce homeschool guides that answer questions on homeschooling within their states, as well as newsletters that are distributed to local homeschool groups. They also arrange state conferences, curriculum fairs, and workshops. In addition, they may participate in state and national surveys on homeschooling, provide statistical information on homeschoolers within their states, and keep databases of state-certified teachers, testers, psychologists, or special-needs therapists who enjoy working with homeschool families.

National Homeschool Associations

Some homeschool associations focus on specific areas or concerns, such as the Home School Legal Defense Association or the National Challenged Homeschoolers Associated Network. Others may have ethnic, cultural, or religious affiliations.

ESSENTIAL

Listings for local, state, and national homeschool organizations are available on the web. Use search engines such as Google, Bing, or Yahoo!, or call the homeschool division of your local school district, the public library, or an educational supply store. They often keep lists of homeschool groups or contacts.

In general, these national groups provide a contact point for state groups. They gather and report on homeschool news across the nation, and they also maintain websites or databases with links to resources concerning their special interest groups.

Removing Your Child from School

You can begin homeschooling in the middle of a school year by following your state's protocol. Some states could allow you to remove your child from school at any time during the year, as long as you file a notice of intent to homeschool within thirty days of establishing your homeschool. Others require you to file a notice of intent several days prior to withdrawing your child from school. Still others do not require a notice of intent to be filed at all, but they may have other regulations you'll need to follow.

Some parents prefer to let the child finish the current school year; others make the transition during semester breaks. Some can begin homeschooling their children in the middle of October if they'd like, or the latter part of February. Just be sure to check with your state's requirements before proceeding with your plans. As a parent, you don't want to be the one who is uninformed where homeschooling laws are concerned. Determine what your obligations are in advance, and plan accordingly.

Registering Your Homeschool

Once you've determined your state's homeschool requirements, you can take the necessary steps to register your child. If you prefer to establish a homeschool environment based on creating your own curriculum, you may find that registering with your school district is the way to go. Depending on your state, you may need to file a notice of intent to homeschool with your superintendent's office. You may also need to keep a portfolio of your child's projects and school achievements and to have your child's progress evaluated or tested at the end of each school year.

In addition to the notice of intent, some states require that you include a letter listing your reasons for wanting to homeschool and why you feel qualified to teach your children. They may also require a description of your goals and objectives for the coming school year, the type of curriculum you plan to use, or a list of subjects you plan to teach.

If you plan to operate your homeschool under an umbrella or satellite school, or through a private school or distance-learning program, you might not need to register with your school district. However, you will want to have the pertinent documentation on hand if any questions should arise.

Determining Educational Goals

When registering your intent to homeschool, you might need to submit a letter listing your reasons for wanting to homeschool, as well as your qualifications. This letter need not be difficult to write. Simply look inside yourself and jot down all the reasons that come to mind. You won't need to include all your reasons in your letter, but this free-thinking, free-writing method will help you get them down on paper.

Your Reasons for Homeschooling

Think about your own children and why you feel homeschooling is better for them than traditional schooling, then create your own list. Here is a list of possible ideas:

- Your children learn better when they can move about and explore.
- Your children need more creative-thinking activities.
- Your children learn better in quiet surroundings.
- Your children need more opportunities to direct their own learning.
- Your family enjoys learning and discovering together.
- Your family enjoys taking educational field trips together.
- Your family enjoys reading books and discussing events together.
- Your family prefers to take an active role in the education process.

Educational Philosophies and Goals

Educational philosophies focus on what you feel your children should learn to prepare them for their lives today and for a happy, successful adulthood. Since you are the children's parent and you understand them better than anyone, you might feel that you are the most qualified to pass these philosophies on to them. Your educational philosophies and goals for your children could include any of the following:

- Caring about family and their place within the family.
- Having a sense of duty within the home and family.
- Caring about the community and their place in it.
- Having a sense of duty within the community.
- Learning how to get along with others.

- Learning proper manners and respect for others.
- Appreciating the environment and beauty of nature.
- Living healthfully, happily, and responsibly.
- Understanding and reflecting family values, morals, and religious beliefs.

Educational Objectives

Educational philosophies can remain fairly constant throughout your family's homeschooling years. However, educational goals may change and expand as your child grows and matures. Your educational objectives should go hand in hand with your goals, supporting your overall philosophy of what you believe your children should learn in preparation for life. You should review your goals and objectives at the beginning of each new school year. The following are some basic educational objectives.

- Acquiring proper social skills for real-world interactions.
- Improving self-discipline and self-control.
- Improving speaking and writing skills.
- Reading quality literature and classics.
- Improving mathematical and scientific abilities.
- Enhancing musical, artistic, and creative skills.
- Learning how to access and apply information.
- Understanding world and national history and politics.
- Functioning responsibly as a citizen and respecting cultural differences.
- Strengthening understanding of right and wrong.
- Learning and applying good decision-making skills.
- Developing a good sense of self-worth and self-confidence.
- Developing life skills and skills critical to career goals.
- Practicing healthy habits, emotionally and physically.

You can create your own curriculum for your child based upon your educational philosophies, goals, and objectives. Apply your family's mission and goals to each subject area (such as reading, writing, math, science, and social studies) and weave your objectives into the daily lessons. You'll quickly see how well your child is learning according to your family's philosophies and desires.

School Support for Homeschoolers

Schools today have a better understanding of home education, thanks to increased media coverage of homeschool families and the opportunity to view a broad cross-section of the homeschool population.

This all leads to better acceptance on the part of school officials, and, in many cases, to their genuine interest in working positively with homeschool families. As a result, many public schools provide support or assistance with homeschoolers' needs. Some allow homeschooled children to attend public school part time or to enroll in individual courses, such as science, chemistry, home economics, or shop classes. Some schools even allow homeschoolers to participate in band, drama, or school sports.

Sports and School

Sports can be a tricky area, since maintaining passing grades is imperative for sports participants, particularly at the high-school level. Homeschoolers who are allowed to take part in sports programs may be required to provide proof of their grades and follow the same rules that apply to all students enrolled in school sports. At the high-school level, some schools must abide by the rules of their state athletic association. Check with your local school, and ascertain what rules would apply to your child in relation to its sports program.

QUESTION

How can my child participate in team sports?
Start your own homeschool sports team! Get other homeschool families involved, arrange to use local ballparks or basketball courts, and designate practice and game times. Allow kids to take turns being cheerleaders, team assistants, and to operate refreshment booths or sell homeschool bumper stickers to benefit the team and your homeschool group.

Sports are also offered in a variety of ways within the community. Check with your parks and recreation department or community colleges. They often hold organized sports events or have volleyball and softball teams, tennis, golf, bowling, skiing, martial arts, gymnastics, choreographed swimming, and other recreational activities for all ages.

Educational Materials

Educational resources and materials are often available from your local school districts. Establishing a line of communication with your school district is helpful. Or contact the person who acts as your district's home-school liaison. She can arrange meetings for you with the school officials and help you obtain the resources you need.

Even if your school district does not provide the materials or support you would like to have, remember that homeschool groups and associations are there to support your homeschool endeavors. They can help you find the type of homeschooling or curriculum you need, help you comply with state laws or explain the laws to you, and demonstrate how easily and successfully homeschooling is working for their families and children. You need never feel as if you are in this alone. Hundreds of thousands of other families are homeschooling, too!

Resources for Getting Started

For more help on getting started in your homeschool, see "Start Homeschooling" at *www.EverythingHomeschooling.com*. You'll be able to start homeschooling immediately with the weekly lessons, hands-on activities, weekly challenges, unit studies, and virtual field trips provided on this educational website. In addition, you can print helpful forms on educational philosophies and goals, weekly planner sheets, reading logs, attendance records, report cards, transcripts, and more, all available on the "Homeschool Forms" section of the website.

CHAPTER 4

Approaches to Homeschooling

You can choose the unschooling method for your child's education, or you can use an online virtual school. You could select a prepackaged curriculum, or you can create your own curriculum. You might prefer faith-based homeschooling, or a secular approach. Whichever method you choose, it should complement your child's learning style, as well as support your family's educational goals and values. If the method you use doesn't produce the results you expect, you can always try one of the approaches described here.

Structured Homeschool Methods

Beginning homeschool families sometimes choose the "structured learning" approach to homeschooling. It might be the method they're most familiar with, as it has similarities to the daily schedule of traditional schools. With this approach, a curriculum is most likely followed, with time periods scheduled throughout the day for focusing on specific lessons. For instance, history lessons are conducted between 9:00 A.M. and 9:45 A.M., math lessons between 10:00 A.M. and 11:00 A.M., science from 11:00 A.M. until 12:00 P.M., then literature after lunch, followed by arts and music.

This type of homeschooling can provide structure and stability to the day, which many families feel they need. If you choose this type of format, you'll want to be wary of turning your homeschool into "school at home." Remember that you can have structure in your days without each day mimicking a traditional school day.

ALERT

With structured learning, the danger lies in the possibility of monotony, too much reliance on textbooks, and too little spontaneous, creative, or engaged learning. This could become disappointing for the child and frustrating for parents, due to the child's lack of interest. Sadly, when this happens, families mistakenly believe that homeschooling didn't work for them.

If you find that the structured approach to homeschooling isn't working for your family, don't give up! Shift the schedule around a bit, loosen up the timeslots, and allow more flexibility in the schedule. If science experiments take three hours one day, instead of one hour, don't stress over it. You can make up the "missed lessons" another day. Or you could try a different method, such as an eclectic style of learning.

Eclectic Homeschooling

Families who prefer an eclectic homeschool approach may use parts of a packaged curriculum along with activity books from the local school supply store, educational games on the Internet, and unit studies. They may pick and choose from a variety of courses, use library books for literature, hands-on experiments for science, history and geography games for social studies, and textbooks and Cuisenaire rods for math.

Eclectic homeschooling combines a good mix of stimulating activities with quiet learning activities. You can offset quiet time spent on an English workbook or online history course with active time spent on chemistry sets, 3D logic puzzles, and robotic construction sets. You can spend family time together reading interesting books from the library, playing a few rounds of challenging board games, and engaging in recreational games outdoors for your physical education class.

Unit Studies or Thematic Units

Unit studies, or thematic units, focus on a specific theme or topic while incorporating the core subject areas into the study. The topic or theme is usually one that interests a child at a certain time in her life—for instance, animals, dinosaurs, vehicles, sports, popular book series, or holidays. There are no limits to the topics, themes, and areas of interest a unit study can cover.

A unit study can last as little as one week or as long as a semester. A unit study focusing on Thanksgiving may only last for a week prior to the holiday. It could run longer or shorter, but after Thanksgiving has passed, interest in the holiday tends to wane. A unit study revolving around animals, sports, or comic books could last for several weeks.

ESSENTIAL

Unit studies are a wonderful way to cover core subjects in an interesting and relevant manner. The theme will create understandable connections between language arts, history, math, and science in a way that makes sense to your child, rather than viewing them as separate subject areas.

Heart of Wisdom (*http://heartofwisdom.com/blog*) offers Bible-based unit studies focusing on history and science. These units can run the length of a typical school year, with five to seven lessons covered in one week.

With these units, you'll want to add math and language arts to complete the curriculum.

Amanda Bennett's unit study series (*www.unitstudy.com*) has weekly learning objectives and daily lesson plans and activities. The units are adaptable to elementary students and middle- to upper-level students. These unit studies are available for downloading to your computer. Or you might prefer to create your own unit studies.

Unschooling and Deschooling

Unschooling and deschooling are sometimes misunderstood. They are more of a natural way of learning, harmonizing with our daily interests and activities. As we live, so do we learn; the experiences encountered each day contribute to one's education. Unschooling usually follows the child's interests and learning style. When children (or adults!) are interested in a topic, they'll learn. And they'll retain what they learn for a longer period of time.

Deschooling is a part of the decompression period when a child leaves a traditional school environment and adjusts to the homeschool or unschooling environment. Parents help to deschool the child—separating him from a rigid school structure—by allowing him the freedom to simply sit and think, to read books for pleasure, to function within his day without the sound of bells or moving through lines, and to spend time playing outdoors. During this time, the child can unwind and decompress, as he moves further away from the confines of a school environment.

Preschoolers

Depending on the age of the child, their self-directed education can encompass a wide range of activities. Preschoolers love to explore everything in their world, play make-believe, and imitate those around them. Through this play and imitation of siblings or grownups, they naturally learn, grow, and fine-tune their skills.

Elementary-Aged Children

By the time they are elementary-aged, most children are eager to "play school." Again, their learning comes through play. By allowing them to play school, you are allowing them to learn. Sometimes, they want to be the student in their play schools, and sometimes they want to be the teacher. As teachers, these new, young students can teach you a lot! You need only sit back and watch in order to be amazed by their fresh knowledge and abilities.

Teenagers

Teens have so many interests, thoughts, and ideas they want to pursue, there is hardly enough time to embrace them all. When they are allowed to follow their interests and self-direct their learning, they are better able to experience—and learn from—the many elements of life that have captivated and inspired them.

Secular Homeschools

With this style of homeschooling, you have many options available to you. You can purchase materials from various publishers or suppliers. For instance, you may choose to use math books from a publisher who specializes in math materials, grammar books from a publisher specializing in language arts books, and so on. You can use a curriculum, or decide the order in which topics are studied, or skip parts of the curriculum that do not meet your family's educational goals.

Secular Materials

Many public school systems offer textbooks and educational materials to homeschool families, so check with your local school district. Local teacher- or school-supply stores also carry a wide variety of resource books, activity books, workbooks, software, and educational games, covering most subject areas.

You can find a wide variety of educational books, materials, and manipulatives online, such as Cuisenaire rods, geoboards, pattern blocks, Backyard Scientist series, and Adventure in Science kits. Usborne offers history-themed, cut-out models of medieval castles, historic forts, or ancient villages. Also popular are the Smart Cubes word games, Learning Language Arts Through Literature series, and many other secular books and games.

Most of these items are available through consignment sites or used homeschool supply stores.

If your child enjoys reading textbooks and answering the questions at the end of the chapters, you might want to invest in a few good textbooks. These can be found at book sales; through online bookstores; or through used homeschool suppliers, such as The Back Pack (*www.thebackpack.com*) or Laurelwood Books (*www.laurelwoodbooks.com*).

Secular Curriculum Providers

If you find that trying to choose among the variety of materials is too confusing, secular curriculum suppliers—such as Oak Meadow (*www .oakmeadow.com*), Core Curriculum of America (*www.core-curriculum.com*) or Curriculum Services (*www.curriculumservices.com*)—might be the way to go. These types of services can provide a complete curriculum for an entire year, or you can create a curriculum specifically tailored to your child's interests and needs.

ESSENTIAL

You can view curricula or educational materials through your local homeschool support group. They often dedicate one or two meetings a year to displaying and discussing the curriculum or resources they use with their families. They welcome families to attend and learn about the many types of curricula available.

Before making a decision, always try to talk with other homeschool families about the materials or services they use. They can provide wonderful insight into the products, format, scope and sequence, and the way the curriculum or materials suit their children's learning styles.

Faith-Based Homeschools

Many families believe that a spiritual foundation is key to a moral education. If this describes your family's philosophy, a multitude of curricula and materials are available for your faith-based homeschool. You may use a traditional curriculum similar to the one taught in public schools, such as the suggestions previously noted, and add a study unit based on your family's religious beliefs. Or you may prefer that each subject area of the curriculum incorporates your family's spiritual beliefs.

A science curriculum, for example, may be secular and focus more on an evolutionary theory, while a faith-based science curriculum may incorporate a creationist point of view. These can be important points for families to consider when purchasing curriculum and supplemental books.

Homeschool curricula and books are available for nearly every religious belief and culture. From Catholic to Islamic, Jewish, Latter-Day Saints, or Native American, you'll be able to find resources to suit your family's homeschool style.

Christian Homeschool Choices

If you plan to incorporate Christian doctrines into your homeschool, you'll have a multitude of curricula and materials to choose from. Many of the Christian correspondence schools and curriculum companies offer testing services, evaluations, grading, record keeping, and diplomas. You often have the choice of teacher assistance to help guide you through the school year, or you can be in charge of the program yourself, allowing for more flexibility.

A Beka (*www.abeka.org*) provides a curriculum package with or without teacher assistance, as well as educational programs available via video or DVD and numerous textbooks to choose from. The A.C.E. program (*www.aceministries.com*) provides a packaged curriculum, or you may enroll your child in their Lighthouse Christian Academy. With Alpha Omega (*www.aop.com*), you can choose the LIFEPAC curriculum, the Switched-On Schoolhouse curriculum on a CD, or the Monarch curriculum online (*www.aophomeschooling.com*).

Bob Jones University Press (*www.bjup.com*) offers a complete curriculum, or you can choose from textbooks, videos, satellite programs, and other resources. The Christian Liberty Academy School System, called CLASS (*www.homeschools.org*), provides a curriculum based upon each child's needs and abilities, plus a full-service plan or a family-service plan, which allows you to control the workload.

Catholic Homeschool Choices

Catholic Homeschool Support (*www.catholichomeschool.org*) provides information and support for Catholic homeschoolers. Seton Home Study School (*www.setonhome.org*) and Kolbe Academy (*www.kolbe.org*) both offer a full curriculum for kindergarten through the twelfth grade. Catholic books, games, and other supplemental materials are available through Heritage Catholic Curricula (*www.chcweb.com*).

More Faith-Based Homeschool Choices

Islamic and Muslim homeschoolers can look to Yemen Links for lesson plan materials and support, as well as Arabic and Yemen resources (*www.yemenlinks.com*). The Muslim Home Education Network provides information and support at *www.muslimhomeschool.net*.

Jewish families can find homeschool supplies at Behrman House (*www.behrmanhouse.com*) and Torah Aura Productions (*www.torahaura.com*).

Latter-Day Saints can contact the LDS Homeschooling Organization at *www.lds-nha.org* or the Latter-Day Saints Home Educators Association at *www.ldshea.org* for homeschooling information, curriculum, and books.

Additional homeschool organizations and groups can be found on *www.hslda.org*. Whatever your spiritual beliefs, there are resources, books, and curricula designed just for you and your family.

Umbrella and Satellite Schools

You might prefer to establish your homeschool under an umbrella or satellite school. These schools are set up to provide cover, or an umbrella, for families who are unable to homeschool on their own or who would rather not go it alone. The umbrella schools are often private or alternative schools.

ALERT

Umbrella schools are not solely faith-based. Some can be, but many are not. Don't be afraid to ask when contacting the school. Better yet, speak with families who are enrolled with the schools, and always ask the school to send their complete information packet to you.

The umbrella or satellite schools can provide curriculum guidance, materials, testing services, record keeping, high-school transcripts, accredited diplomas, and other areas of assistance. Yet the education still takes place in the home; it isn't necessary to travel to a specific school or facility each day. A fee is charged for the services that umbrella or satellite schools provide, depending on what they offer.

To find these schools in your area, contact your local school district and ask if they keep a list of such schools. Your homeschool support group is another good source of information on umbrella schools in your area. If you're unable to locate a school through these resources, try calling local private schools or church-based schools to see if they offer home-education programs through their facilities.

Charter Schools and Cooperatives

Initially, charter schools were set up by a group of interested parents and teachers who drew up a "charter," or written document, outlining the purpose and goals for their school. These schools were usually funded by private individuals or institutions. Today, many charter schools and voucher systems have become projects of the state, and the schools may be publicly funded at the state or local levels. Additionally, when conventional public schools receive failing grades within a certain time frame, students can choose to leave that school and use vouchers to enroll in private schools or other schools of choice.

Recently, many charter schools, as well as virtual schools run by public schools, have adopted the Common Core State Standards (CCSS). These standards were developed to cover students in traditional public schools. Before enrolling in a charter school or virtual school, you'll want to determine their current state standards.

In some states, a charter school may still be funded by private institutions or grants. School boards are formed; members invest in the school; and parents, teachers, and staff operate the school. Even though the charter school may be similar to a traditional school, the teachers and staff have more input regarding the curriculum and teaching methods than they would have in a public school.

Cooperatives as Alternatives

When parents wish to create a place where homeschoolers can come together for learning activities, it's usually called a cooperative, rather than a charter school. If your group is interested in forming a homeschool co-op, spend time discussing your reasons and establish a format that is agreeable to all. If possible, talk with others who have had experience in setting up a homeschool co-op.

You might want to elect a few people or a committee to be in charge of overseeing the activities, to set up meetings or arrange field trips, and to schedule volunteers. Each parent whose child participates in the co-op should be willing to volunteer services or assistance when his or her time comes around.

Teaching in a Cooperative

Parents who have stronger skills in a certain subject area will often be in charge of teaching or guiding that topic. If several parents are interested in the same subject area—for instance, arts and crafts or science experiments—they can contribute on a rotating basis: this parent this week, that parent next week, and so on. If no one is stepping forward with an interest in math or history, perhaps a couple of parents could work together to create projects in those areas.

ESSENTIAL

Co-ops might require fees to help offset the cost of materials, craft supplies, or books. Some may charge a small monthly fee, while others may ask participating families to chip in when planning a specific project, based on the number of children taking part and the cost of materials.

If no one in your cooperative possesses mathematical or scientific skills, don't worry. Contact your local college or association of retired business professionals and see if they know of anyone who might be interested in guiding the children. The same is true if your group appears to have no one with artistic or musical talents. Your community's parks and recreation department often offers art and music classes, so contact them about your co-op's needs. The fee to bring in an outsider might be more than your co-op had planned for, but the dividends could pay off quite well in your children's education and hands-on experiences.

Hosting a Cooperative

In some cooperatives, parents take turns hosting the classes in their homes—perhaps in a family room or basement. In other co-ops, one or two families offer to host the classes, understanding that some families simply don't have the extra space or that their schedules don't allow for hosting regular classes. Some co-ops have found that they can meet at a local church, and, for some projects and climates, they find that using the shelter in a nearby park works well.

Independent Study Programs

Independent study programs, such as Clonlara School (*www.clonlara.org*) or American School (*www.americanschoolofcorr.com*), are a form of correspondence or distance-learning schools. The concept is that a student is sent a curriculum package via mail. He then studies, completes the lessons, and returns the lessons to the school to be assessed and graded. Tests are sometimes administered, graded, and returned to the student, or evaluations of the student's capabilities may be conducted.

Most of these schools take care of the record-keeping process (and can provide verification of such to your school district, if need be), and they take care of the lesson planning, both of which free up a parent's time. As a result, you will have more time to spend with your children, providing the interaction and one-on-one guidance that is important in a homeschool setting.

Not every child is suited to the independent study procedure, though. In many cases, families supplement the program with additional hands-on activities, field trips and learning excursions, and more participation in community events to help add variety to the program. In fact, most distance-learning programs encourage students to become involved in the community and in a variety of extracurricular classes and projects.

Many of these schools are well respected and accredited, keeping transcripts of your child's high-school years and granting diplomas upon graduation. Some even go to the next level, holding formal graduation ceremonies and encouraging all graduating seniors to attend. They may even hold yearbook signings and proms for students who live nearby or who are able to travel the distance to attend.

Enrolling in an Independent Study Program

Before contacting a school, have a list of questions ready, and obtain as much information as possible over the phone. When you receive an information packet, be sure it answers all your questions. If not, call the school for further information.

FACT

Some independent study programs offer a choice of textbook-based studies, video-based studies, online courses, or lessons on DVD. Some may offer umbrella or satellite programs in lieu of the traditional correspondence programs. Be sure to ask which formats the program offers when requesting its informational packet.

Before enrolling your child in an independent study program, you will want to consider several points:

1. Be cognizant of your child's learning style and study habits. If your child is not one who can learn well while sitting still or who requires more physical activity while learning (a kinesthetic-tactile learner), some independent study programs may not be for her.
2. Discuss with your child her ability to study on her own and to stay on a task with limited reminders from others, as well as her ability to be fairly responsible for her studies.
3. Determine how much structure, or flexibility, your child seems to need in her studies.
4. Request the school's information packet and samples of its typical lessons or assignments, then go over these with your child.

5. Talk with other families enrolled in the program and have them share their experiences with you and your child.
6. Find out from the school exactly how much busywork, reading, worksheets, or homework is required, so that you and your child will know what is required from the beginning.
7. Ask the school if they accept artwork, construction projects, hands-on activities, or extracurricular classes to meet some of the requirements for the program.
8. Determine exactly what each fee covers, and find out if the school offers a refund policy if you decide to cancel within a specific time frame.

Costs of Study Programs

Tuition fees can range from $500 to $2,500 per school year, perhaps more, depending on the grade level and the school. Fees at some schools are all inclusive, while others may have extra fees for additional services. In some cases, costs may be broken down by enrollment or registration fee, tuition fee, and materials or supplies fees. Keep in mind that a kindergarten or first-grade curriculum is usually priced lower than a fourth-grade or sixth-grade curriculum. The costs for high-school programs are often based on a per-course fee. Most schools have installment payment plans available.

ALERT

If your teenager is interested in a high-school independent study program, check to be sure it's fully accredited. The Distance Education Accrediting Commission (DEAC) keeps track of accredited high schools, colleges, and business and training schools that provide correspondence studies. Visit its website at *www.deac.org* to view a list of accredited schools.

You can check with the following distance-learning schools for information on their services.

- American School: *www.americanschoolofcorr.com*
- Chrysalis School: *www.chrysalis-school.com*
- Citizens' High School: *www.citizenshighschool.com*

- Clonlara School: *www.clonlara.org*
- CompuHigh Online: *www.compuhigh.com*
- Heritage Home School Academy: *www.heritagehomeschool.com*
- Keystone School: *www.keystoneschoolonline.com*
- Laurel Springs School: *www.laurelsprings.com*
- Oak Meadow: *www.oakmeadow.com*

Virtual Schools and Online Learning

A virtual school is not necessarily a virtual charter school. Many school systems offer courses via the Internet, based on the public school curriculum. Other forms of virtual learning could include the independent study programs described earlier, or individual courses available online. In many of these programs, students can study online, complete assignments online, and correspond with instructors and classmates via e-mail, thus reducing the turnaround time of lessons, grades, and feedback.

On the downside, online courses can eventually become as tedious as workbook pages. Supplementing a virtual learning program with hands-on learning will enliven the child's environment, helping to keep learning fun and challenging. By monitoring the coursework and topics being studied, you and your child can develop experiments, activities, and field trips that can complement and reinforce the online courses.

You might be interested in checking out these virtual schools:

- E-Tutor: *www.e-tutor.com*
- K^{12} Inc.: *www.k12.com*
- Obridge Academy: *www.obridgeacademy.com*
- Wilostar 3D: *www.wilostar3d.com*

Year-Round Homeschooling

Your state may require that you homeschool 180 days a year, but they may place no restrictions on when those days fall. You might want to homeschool from September through May, so that your children are off in the summer when the neighbor kids are on their summer break. Or, instead of homeschooling five days a week, four weeks a month, which is twenty days per month, your homeschool days could include each day of the month, covering approximately thirty days per month and reaching the 180-day quota in just six months, rather than nine months. Therefore, you might homeschool from the first of January until the end of June.

Following a structured schedule for thirty days in a row, month after month, can become stressful, though, even if you do get done three months early! For some families, following a structured schedule for twenty days each month can also be a bit much. That's why some like the concept of year-round homeschooling. You can cover the same amount of ground, but you get to take breaks more frequently.

A Flexible Schedule

With year-round schooling, you may choose to start in September, then take a week off each month. Your schedule will then include fifteen home-schooled days each month (five days a week, three weeks a month). Following this schedule, you'll reach the 180-day quota within twelve months, resulting in year-round schooling, but with a week off each month.

ESSENTIAL

Before purchasing a curriculum or enrolling in a school, try to visit curriculum fairs and homeschool conventions so that you can personally look over the products or services. Have a list of questions ready to ask the representatives at the conventions. Also, talk with homeschool families about the types of educational format they've chosen to use in their homes.

Another option is to follow the traditional twenty-day month, but take a month off between Thanksgiving and Christmas, a month off in the spring, and a month off in the summer, rather than taking the entire summer off. You'll still end up with twelve weeks off.

Sometimes grandparents or friends may plan to spend a month with your family. You'll want to juggle the homeschool year to accommodate their visits and not be tied to a specific schedule while they are in town. Or your family might be expecting a new arrival, and you'd like to set aside three months in a row to welcome the new bundle of joy into your family. You can always reschedule the homeschool year accordingly.

Benefits and Drawbacks

Other benefits of year-round schooling include spending less time on review at the beginning of the school year and less time getting the children back into a more formal schedule. When lessons and learning are spread throughout the year, the skills and the schedule come more easily.

If more breaks occur regularly throughout the year, children and parents are better able to disconnect from the schedule and recharge their batteries more often. Less frequent, but longer breaks can make it difficult for both parents and children to get back into the school habit when the free days of summer come to an end.

One of the most common drawbacks of year-round schooling is that children feel cheated out of their summer break, which they feel all the other kids have. A good way to handle this is to allow your children to take off the first week or two that corresponds with the public school's first weeks of summer vacation. After a couple weeks of being with their friends again on a daily basis, summer boredom can begin to set in. Then you can start drawing your children back into the homeschool by following a less structured summer-school format, with more activities, field trips, and explorations, and fewer workbooks and assignment sheets. By inviting some of the neighbor kids to participate, too, everyone may spend more time at your house, enjoying the fun and novelty of summer homeschool.

Resources for Eclectic Learning

For more on eclectic homeschooling, visit the Eclectic Homeschool Online at *www.eclectichomeschool.org*. The Family Unschoolers Network at *www.unschooling.org* provides support and resources for those interested in unschooling or self-directed learning.

Helpful books on unschooling include any of John Holt's books, such as *How Children Learn* and *What Do I Do Monday?*

CHAPTER 5

Socialization and Social Skills

At one time, the "socialization issue" was a prime topic of discussion regarding homeschooled children. Today, it's not an issue at all. Time has proven that children educated at home are just as socially adept and well-adjusted as their traditionally schooled peers. In many cases, homeschooled children have even more opportunities to socialize with people of varying ages and often display a higher level of maturity than their peers.

Social Skills and Self-Esteem

It's important to note that there is a difference between *socialization*, which means to participate in a social group setting, and *social skills*, which are closely related to good, old-fashioned manners. It's not necessary to attend a formal school in order to learn proper manners or sound social skills.

Social Skills

Concerns over the socialization of homeschooled children tended to center on how they would learn to interact with, or get along with, others. The ability to socialize well with others is based upon learning and implementing proper social skills. Social skills include taking turns, sharing, praising and thanking others, treating others with respect and kindness, listening to others, conversing with others, showing interest in others, following directions, exercising patience and tolerance, resolving conflicts, and resisting negative peer pressure.

A child can achieve these social skills in the home by learning basic manners and proper conduct, interacting with family members, developing quality friendships, engaging in conversations with others, and through role-playing to further hone social skills for a variety of situations he or she may encounter in life. When a child has practiced and achieved good social skills and proper manners, and understands right from wrong, these qualities will see him through nearly any social gathering.

FACT

Children with higher self-esteem and self-worth usually perform better academically than those with low self-esteem. In a study conducted by Dr. John W. Taylor of Andrews University, homeschooled children were found to have a higher degree of self-concept and self-esteem than their conventionally schooled counterparts.

Family Ties

It's no surprise that the early years of a child's life between birth and age five are important for developing familial bonds and emotional ties. Many child development experts believe that children build their social skills upon these close family ties. By age five, most children have learned basic concepts of right and wrong. For instance, it's okay to play in the yard, but it's not okay to play in the street. It's okay to hit a ball with a bat, but it's not okay to hit a car with a bat. If they step out of the bounds of right and wrong, they risk damaging something (themselves in the street, the car with a bat). They also risk losing the pride and trust of their parents. The disappointment reflected in their parent's eyes or demeanor, because of their misbehavior, can be crushing.

As children continue to mature, learn more complex rules of right and wrong, and develop stronger bonds with their families, the desire to jeopardize their parent's respect and trust further diminishes. This closely describes the relationship homeschooled children have with the family unit. They are less likely to be left to the care of strangers each day, interacting with others outside the family unit. Rather, homeschooled children continue to develop close relationships with the very ones who love them and care about their well-being.

Parental Involvement

According to Child and Adolescent Health and Development (CAHD), a department of the World Health Organization (WHO), the importance of parental involvement in the *overall development* of children is critical. CAHD refers to child development as "maturity in terms of physical, cognitive, language, social-emotional, temperament, or fine and gross motor skills development."

The U.S. Department of Education has found that parental involvement in the education of their children has positive influences on the overall success of their children as youths and adults. Recent studies have found that "parental involvement in education is associated with higher grades and test scores, better attendance, more homework completion, more positive attitudes and behaviors, and higher graduation and college attendance rates." They've determined that successful student outcomes are based on parents serving as good role models and on "involving the entire family" in the child's education.

It's not surprising that homeschooled children—whose families are closely involved in all areas of their education—are achieving high levels of success academically and socially.

Socialization Opportunities

It's one thing to practice social skills at home while role-playing, and it's another to put them to use at social gatherings. Having started your child on good manners and social skills when she was young, she naturally employs them when she's socializing with others. This could be with family members and relatives during the holidays or reunions or when she's with friends during birthday parties and sleepovers. The homeschooled child may not attend a traditional school for her education, but she still participates in get-togethers with others, just as conventionally schooled children do. In fact, she sometimes has more opportunities to socialize with a wider range of people than conventionally schooled children, who must remain in the classroom for the majority of each day.

Homeschooled children have ample opportunities to run errands with parents and interact with a variety of people, young and old, from varying backgrounds. Your child may be able to go to work with you, become involved in community activities, take part in church and youth groups, or join scouting groups and clubs like 4-H or the YMCA. They can participate in activities such as music, art, gymnastics, or sports. And, of course, there are neighbor children and their friends, who they'll want to spend time with.

Teen and preteen children have time during the day to volunteer in libraries, nursing homes, hospitals, businesses, nature centers, museums, and other community centers. In fact, homeschoolers usually have more time available for community involvement than do traditionally schooled children. By volunteering and taking part in community classes or events, homeschoolers can interact with various age groups in different situations, allowing plenty of opportunities to exercise their social skills in their daily lives.

Extracurricular Activities

If you fear that your child will have limited opportunities to interact with others, rest assured that it's nearly impossible to *not* have social activities available to you and your child. Nearly every city or town, no matter how large or small, has parks and a recreation department, which may offer numerous classes and activities. Here are some activities generally offered by parks and recreation departments:

- Tumbling, dancing, ballet, and gymnastics
- Martial arts and swimming lessons
- Tennis lessons and golf lessons
- Drawing, painting, or cartooning classes
- Ceramics and jewelry-making
- Woodworking and scrapbooking
- Foreign language classes
- Babysitting courses
- Rent-a-teen programs
- Summer-break programs
- Preschool programs focusing on social skills, listening skills, motor skills, creative play, and kindergarten-readiness skills

School-Sponsored Events

Some school districts may allow homeschoolers to take part in the school band or drama club. However, school sports are often governed by the state's athletic association, and certain regulations apply. This doesn't rule out the possibility of your child playing on a baseball, football, or basketball team, though. Many communities have Little League teams or Pop Warner football teams that your child can join.

Community-Sponsored Events

Check with your parks and recreation department or YMCA about basketball teams, soccer, hockey, and motocross. Your church may have sports teams, too. Or there may be community bowling leagues, tennis teams, swim teams, or golf matches for youngsters to participate in.

Many areas also have community bands, drama clubs, or choirs that are open to anyone, regardless of age. They hold concerts or put on performances throughout the year, to which the public is invited.

Homeschool-Sponsored Events

If there are no sports teams in your area for kids to join, start a team in conjunction with your local homeschool group. Your group's team could play teams from other homeschool groups. Or if there's only one group in your area, your team could divide up and play each other.

ESSENTIAL

There are no limits to the number of social events, fun events, sporting events, field trips, and community involvement projects for home-schoolers. In fact, some families find that they have to cut back on social outings and get-togethers.

In addition to sports, homeschool groups often arrange art or music classes, nature study classes, science fairs, and physical education classes. There may be spelling bees, quilting bees, reading and writing groups, or singing groups. Many go on educational field trips or engage in activities such as horseback riding, swimming, skating, or bowling. And they often get to do these things during weekdays when the facilities are not overrun by large weekend crowds.

Homeschool groups may also host special-event nights. These can include theatrical performances, musical performances, talent shows, magic shows, or cultural events highlighting a certain culture or region of the world. They may hold dances throughout the year, graduation ceremonies, yearbook signings, and may arrange for class rings.

Socializing in the Real World

Much controversy has revolved around what the real world is or isn't. Some believe that a school building contains the real world, and to experience the real world, one must go to the school building each day. Others feel that living and learning at home is the real world, or at least a good training ground for preparing for the real world.

Homeschooled children are more likely to experience actual events or situations that occur in the practical world, as opposed to the academic world. They can spend time at work with Mom or Dad, help Grandfather in the woodshop, or cook alongside Grandmother. They can help with the grocery shopping, bill paying, plumbing repairs, or car repairs.

FACT

The *real world* is defined as "the practical world as opposed to the academic world" or "drawing on actual events or situations." When homeschooled children are exploring the real world each day, rather than confined to a school building, they have opportunities that are not always afforded to their school-bound mates.

Homeschoolers can go along when the dog is taken to the veterinarian, groomer's, or obedience class. They can take advantage of spur-of-the-moment tours at the vet, groomer's, bank, bakery, or copy shop, especially if it's a slow day. While participating in these activities, they often have the opportunity to meet new people, hold conversations with friends on the street or business professionals in offices, and interact with people of all ages and backgrounds.

Socializing Only with Peers

When children are able to move away from socializing only with peers each day, they gain a better understanding of society and its citizens. When a thirteen-year-old spends the majority of his time walking the school halls with other thirteen-year-olds, eating lunch with other thirteen-year-olds, working on projects with thirteen-year-olds, walking to and from school with thirteen-year-olds, talking on the phone with them each evening, and hanging out at their homes on weekends, he begins to lose touch with other aspects of society. And it becomes more difficult to break the pattern and spoil the fun of his lifestyle by going grocery shopping with Mom, helping Dad around the house, or spending time with Grandmother or Aunt Mabel.

Interacting with Young and Old Alike

But when a child has had more opportunities to interact with various ages, old and young, in homeschool gatherings, classes and workshops, running errands, and through community events, he is more sociable and adaptable. He is well-accustomed to spending time with a wider age group, helping in the community and at home, and encountering new situations on a more regular basis. So, when it's time to help out around the house, or go to Grandmother's house, or to visit with Aunt Mabel, it's more likely to be a natural part of his life. Rather than viewing the visit as taking him away from his ²⁴/₇ friends and spoiling his fun, he accepts it as part of everyday living.

There's certainly nothing wrong with children having friends their own age or with their getting together from time to time to have fun and be kids. But exclusive companionship with one's peers, while shutting out all others, is not healthy and can lead to dangerous situations.

Maturity Levels of Homeschooled Children

"What a nice young man!" the clerk commented to a shopper's son. "I bet you're homeschooled, aren't you?"

The mother was amazed. How could the clerk have guessed that her son was homeschooled after less than twenty minutes around him? Perhaps it was a lucky guess, or perhaps the clerk could simply tell. More and more homeschool families are being surprised by others' observations of them. Maybe it's because homeschooling is more common today, and people have had more interaction with homeschooled children. Maybe it's the social skills of the homeschooled children that give them away, or their level of maturity.

FACT

Professor Roland Meighan studied homeschoolers while writing an article, "Home-Based Education Effectiveness Research and Some of Its Implications," for *Educational Review*. He found that research "demonstrates that children are usually superior to their school-attending peers in social skills, social maturity, emotional stability, academic achievement, personal confidence, communication skills, and other aspects."

Kids tend to mimic those with whom they spend the most time. When kids are homeschooled, they naturally spend more time with their parents.

Consequently, the parent becomes a major role model in their lives. Children listen to and learn from their parents, when they observe their parents talking to neighbors, handling situations in stores and restaurants, banks and post offices, and generally interacting with others in society on a day-to-day basis. Children absorb this information, learn from their parents' actions, and reflect their parents' behavior.

Socialization Studies

A study conducted by Dr. Gary Knowles, then an assistant professor of education at the University of Michigan, centered on adults who had previously been homeschooled. His study showed that homeschooled children do not suffer from a lack of social interactions. Of those interviewed, 94 percent believed that homeschooling had prepared them to function as healthy, independent adults, and 79 percent said that their homeschool experiences led to interactions with others from different levels of society.

Dr. Thomas Smedley conducted a study using the Vineyard Adaptive Behavior Scales test to determine the maturity levels and well-adapted behaviors of public-schooled children and homeschooled children. He found that homeschoolers ranked in the eighty-fourth percentile, while the public-schooled children ranked lower, in the twenty-seventh percentile. He concluded: "In the public school system, children are socialized horizontally, and temporarily, into conformity with their immediate peers. Home educators seek to socialize their children vertically, toward responsibility, service, and adulthood, with an eye on eternity."

The ERIC Clearinghouse on Disabilities and Gifted Education notes that several studies have concluded that homeschooling is helpful to a child's social skills and maturity. They cite the research of Dr. Linda Montgomery, which found that "Homeschooled students tend to have a broader age-range of friends than their schooled peers, which may encourage maturity and leadership skills." They further cite studies by Dr. Larry Shyers and Dr. John W. Taylor, indicating that homeschooled children are "likely to be socially and psychologically healthy," based on studies of the homeschoolers' social adjustment and self-esteem.

Family Values, Morals, and Manners

Most families worry about the messages being sent to children today via television, video games, and the media. When children pick up immoral messages, carry them to school settings, and share them among classmates, it becomes a grave concern. At home, you can discuss moral behavior and immoral behavior in ways that are appropriate to your child's age and understanding.

ESSENTIAL

Family values and morals are not easily learned at school or in textbooks. Rather, they are a part of life that must be witnessed, felt, and practiced in the real world. You can include your children in discussions about the values that are important to you, your family, and society.

Child psychologist Robert Coles stresses the importance of modeling moral behavior in front of your children. He insists that parents and all adults should ". . . live out what we presumably want taught to our children. Our children are taking constant notice, and they're measuring us not by what we say, but what we do." As homeschool parents, you have the excellent opportunity to guide your children in developing moral behavior that will be an asset to them and to society.

Proper Etiquette and Manners

Proper etiquette and good manners go hand in hand with the sound social skills you teach your child. Proper etiquette is an important key to a child's social success, and it's the parent's responsibility to teach good manners early on. These manners, as well as the family's values and moral principles, must be exercised within the home on a daily basis in order to instill them in children. In this way, they become healthy, everyday habits.

Character Education

Clearly, there's a need for parents to focus on teaching good manners and proper etiquette, social skills, family values, moral behavior, and overall character education. In many homeschools across the nation, these principles are as important in the children's education as the core subjects laid out by curriculum guidelines. Many popular homeschool curricula or correspondence schools include character education as part of the overall package. If they do not, families can find other ways to incorporate character education into their days with unit studies, discussions, and role-playing that accentuate citizenship, responsibility, respect, caring and kindness for others, fairness, trustworthiness, honesty, good sportsmanship, and other important factors of good and civil behavior.

Stephen Carter, author of *Civility: Manners, Morals, and the Etiquette of Democracy*, advises parents to closely observe their children's activities so they can determine where conflicting messages regarding moral and civil behavior come from. He names school, peers, television, music, and the Internet as areas that can compete with a parent's teachings on values, morals, and civil behavior.

Preparing for the Future

Homeschool families want their children's learning experiences to be enjoyable and fruitful and to lead to a lifelong love of learning. If this means that they need to more closely observe their child's social interactions, then they accept it as part of the duties of responsible parenting. If socialization is a determining factor in their child's happiness and success in life, then they'll ensure that their child has plenty of opportunities to socialize in ways that are positive and uplifting for the child.

Families who choose to homeschool feel that they are more aware of their children's friends and the type of peer pressure their children may be subjected to. In addition, they feel that the character education they incorporate into their homeschools, along with strong family values and morals, help their children make good decisions when associating with friends.

Resources for the Socialization Question

Many homeschool families wonder how to respond to those who ask the dreaded "S" question: "But what about socialization?"

A simple answer, such as, "We prefer that our child meets and makes friends with people we know rather than with strangers," or "We'd rather guide our children in the social arts than have them pick up bad habits from questionable sources."

And as for other adolescent socialization issues, you can mention that homeschoolers hold their own dances, proms, graduations, etc. Nearly every community has at least one homeschool group, and these groups sponsor the dances, proms, parties, graduation ceremonies, and various other events throughout the year. And of course, homeschoolers can also date traditionally schooled teens.

CHAPTER 6

Understanding Unschooling and Unit Studies

Children are born with a natural curiosity. When their curiosity is suppressed, their learning is diminished. When their curiosity is encouraged with nurturing guidance, their learning accelerates. Unschooling focuses on interest-driven activities and nurturing guidance that can help enhance your child's curiosity, creativeness, and education.

Curiosity and Unschooling

Research has shown that curiosity increases activity in certain parts of the brain, helping people to absorb and retain information longer. When you are interested and curious about a topic, your brain becomes more inclined to learn about it. Children are naturally curious about everything, and because curiosity helps them to learn, it's a trait that should never be discouraged. From their first "Why?" questions as toddlers to their "But *why* can't we have the car keys?", your children can't help but ask "why" of their surroundings and their lives. It's the way of children; it's an innate part of the way they learn. Children must be encouraged to ask why, and they must be able to find answers to the reasons why.

Unschooling is one of the most natural ways for children to seek the answers to their why questions, and one of the most natural ways for children to acquire knowledge. You'll want to keep their curiosity alive and encourage them to follow their interests as they learn about the world.

FACT

Children who are allowed to ask questions, and to remain curious about the world around them, remain eager to learn. "The whole art of teaching is only the art of awakening the natural curiosity of the young mind," observed French author Anatole France.

Children gain a huge amount of knowledge and skills between birth and age five, without formal schooling. They learn by experimenting, doing, trying and failing, then trying again. Rarely are they deterred, and rarely do they give up. Young children love to experiment—they enjoy trying one way, and if it doesn't work, trying another. Just as curiosity is an innate quality in children, so is the desire to learn new things.

Typical Unschooled Days

A typical unschooled day for Micah, Mark, and Megan, ages 9, 11, and 14, might not resemble a conventional homeschooled day. Their mother, Katy, believes in the children's ability to learn through their own interests, which can encompass a large and varied amount of knowledge.

Fourteen-year-old Megan loves reading, writing, art, and crafts. She has incorporated these interests into her many scrapbook projects. Currently, she is focusing on vintage techniques, as well as Victorian-era styles to her artwork and scrapbook pages. In doing so, Megan is not only honing her artistic skills, but her interest in the Victorian era is taking her in new directions. She's developed a love of reading Victorian-era authors, such as Charlotte and Emily Brontë, Jane Austen, and Charles Dickens. Inspired by these authors, she's studied their backgrounds and homes, and she's now writing her own stories in a similar vein.

Her brothers, Mark and Micah, ages 11 and 9, are more interested in exploring a variety of historic periods, as well as inventing and building futuristic gadgets for tomorrow. After reading and watching *The Time Machine* by H.G. Wells, the boys decided to design and construct their own "time machine." Through a series of prototypes and experimentations, they created one that works perfectly for their toy action figures. Now when they transport their figures to different historical periods, they research the period together so they "get it right." They also record the time-travel sequences digitally and turn them into "mini-film productions" on their home computer.

These are just a couple examples of how Katy's children are learning on their own, through projects that interest them. They are being creative, inventive, using reasoning and thinking skills, mathematical and hands-on skills, artistic and designing skills, and learning about history, literature, authors, writing, and film production—all as a result of something that initially piqued their interest.

Trying the Unschooling Method

If you're not sure about this method, great times to observe unschooling in your children is during weekends, vacations, and summertime. Watch them play, and you'll see them learn. Encourage their curiosity, and guide them in finding answers and resources. Follow their interests, and you'll learn alongside them. You'll certainly be amazed at how adept they are at learning through the myriad topics that interest them.

Unschooling Activities

Children are often eager to play, and, consequently, learn. Sometimes, though, they might feel that they've forgotten how to play, or can't think of anything to do. Spend time brainstorming ideas together. Ask your children what they'd like to do if they had all the time in the world to do whatever they liked. Then explore those ideas to the best of your abilities.

Revisit fun activities from the past, which they might've forgotten about, but which could interest them in a new or different way now. These could include:

- Building simple models or 3D structures
- Performing plays based on books or movies
- Creating new types of board games to play
- Designing video games for handheld devices
- Learning to play new instruments and composing music
- Writing and creating comic books or cartoon strips
- Performing and making videos of scientific experiments
- Using LEGO sets or electronic kits to create new gadgets
- Cooking or baking new concoctions for the family

Taking Activities Further

When your children are engrossed in activities, you can encourage them to branch out or explore the topic further. If your suggestions don't interest them, that's okay. But your ideas could possibly pique their interests in other areas or spark more ideas. Here are some activities that could complement or branch off from a child's interest in a project, such as a dollhouse, birdhouse, or robot:

- Build a birdhouse, dollhouse, robot, radio, model plane, or model city.
- Research the history of dollhouses, robots, radios, planes, or cities.
- Research the scientific background of birdhouses, robots, radios, or planes.
- Encourage the questioning of how these work, why they work, how they could be improved.

- Write a short book about a dollhouse, robot, or model city that comes to life.
- Create artwork for the book, draw diagrams of the project, and take pictures for the book.
- Design the book, type it on the computer, print and bind the book, and distribute it to friends.
- Branch off from current interests and activities to explore new projects and ideas.

When it comes to unschooling topics, there is no limit to the ideas and activities that can extend outward from an area of interest. One thing often leads to another, and then to another, until you're amazed at the significant amount of information your child is exploring and absorbing, all on her own.

Deschooling Each Day

Rather than learning for the purpose of passing a test or achieving a specific grade, deschooling encourages learning for the purpose of gaining knowledge, learning how to think on one's own, and learning how to learn. Ivan Illich shared his thoughts on deschooling in his book, *Deschooling Society*. Like many who believed that conventional schools lacked the ability to teach to each child's needs, he felt that schools taught children only what they needed to know to pass tests and to meet the school's grading system. Meanwhile, children weren't learning how to think or how to further their own education.

A curriculum can take on the same qualities of a school—uniformity instead of individuality, mass production instead of singular creativity. Thus, a *deschooled curriculum*—in other words, an individualized and customized education—should be the goal in the unschooled homeschool. The educational format should be geared toward your child's learning style and your child's areas of interest. It should be flexible and stimulating enough to be fun, yet challenging.

For your family, deschooling and unschooling could mean using no formal curriculum. Or it could mean using a curriculum as a guideline, but doing hands-on activities and taking educational field trips rather than hammering out worksheets. You may prefer to design your own lessons based on your children's interests to help them grasp concepts. Or, you may prefer to let your children learn through following, researching, and exploring their interests on their own. Your child may prefer to learn through reading voraciously or by spending hours conducting experiments. Whatever her individual learning style, she can actively pursue knowledge in a way that makes real connections with her life and with her world, in a style that makes the most sense to her.

Children as Teachers

Children of all ages love to share information with others. Young children love to play school, and they enjoy taking on the role of a teacher in their make-believe schools. But the learning that occurs is not make-believe as they slip into their teaching roles. The learning is quite real. Regardless of age, children enjoy playing teacher. A child who can convey new ideas, concepts, or knowledge to an adult is acting in the role of teacher and learning at the same time.

When children of any age have the opportunity to teach by sharing information and knowledge with others, they automatically and indelibly inscribe that information upon their minds. By listening to your children and showing your appreciation and respect for their abilities and ideas, you encourage them to continue in their pursuit of new information and knowledge. They can see that someone cares enough to listen to them. They realize that someone truly values their opinions and even learns from them. They realize that not only are they able to teach themselves, but they are able to teach others—one of the most rewarding and satisfying achievements in life.

Discussing Ideas

Allow children plenty of opportunities to share their findings with you. Listen attentively to their ideas and opinions, and avoid the urge to say you've "heard that before" or to correct their views. When a young child plays school and shows you how to print the alphabet, you wouldn't walk away, saying you already know how to do that. You would show interest and take part in the fun activity. Similarly, you would want your older child to feel free to share thoughts, ideas, and information with you, because through sharing, doing, and discussing together, you both will learn.

Finding Answers

When youngsters have ideas, questions often follow. When they have the time to pursue those ideas, they can often formulate their own hypotheses based on the information they've gathered. They have the time to analyze their questions and the time to seek answers. By allowing them to come up with their own ideas, you set the stage for them to think, question, seek, and learn, all on their own. You're not getting in the way of that natural process by insisting that they read a specific passage to find the answer, or that they complete a lesson to arrive at what *you* feel is the correct answer. The investigation was *their* idea, and it should be through *their* method of analysis that they come up with the answers they are seeking.

ALERT

Children don't necessarily want quick answers to their questions. Rather, they want to stretch their mind, broaden their conceptual-thinking abilities, and consider the what-ifs and how-tos of a thought or idea. Refrain from giving quick answers to their questions; instead, help them find resources that will assist them in exploring their questions and ideas.

If, however, youngsters *want* your help and guidance, if they're unsure of how to pursue a thought or idea, or if they don't know where to look for possible answers, by all means offer your assistance. When voicing their thoughts and ideas, children need to know that there is someone who will seriously listen to them without dismissing their notions as inconsequential. They need to know that there is someone who has the time and the patience to provide feedback, suggestions, and discussions on their ideas.

Unit Studies Year-Round

Unit studies are a grand way to cover a lot of subject areas while focusing on a special area of interest. For the family that is not as comfortable following an unschooled style of home education, the unit study may be the next best thing. For families who would like their children to keep learning all year long, the unit study is a fairly painless way to attain this goal. Indeed, a summer unit study can capture the interest of the neighborhood children, as well as your own.

Introducing a Unit Study

Perhaps you're considering a unit study on railroads. Try to visit a real train station and ride the train, or at least take a tour of the engine and train cars. This is a perfect way to begin a unit study because the actual experience makes the topic real and exciting from the outset. Many towns and communities have railroad museums that often include miniature trains and villages, or electric trains weaving through a town set up to look like yours. Virtual train museums and virtual train rides can be found online through several websites, too.

QUESTION

What are some good unit study topics?
Insects, animals, dinosaurs, marine life, weather, seasons, holidays, sports, artists, musicians, famous people, explorers, presidents, inventions, transportation, travel, your state, the rainforest, environment, ancient civilizations, cultures and traditions, the solar system, space travel, favorite books, and favorite hobbies are some good unit study topics, just to name a few.

Science and Math Lessons

Science topics for your railroad unit study could focus on the force required to blast through mountains for train tunnels, or replicating bridges that could support the weight of simulated train cars. You could experiment with steam-powered motors or gadgets to see firsthand how steam engines worked, or create your own simple, electric trains.

Math lessons could include problems dealing with train speeds, traveling distances, stopping distances, weight, and velocity. Or working out the time and manpower for laying the rails, the number of workers required to nail the spikes, or the miles of rail laid over a period of weeks.

History and Humanity Lessons

The development of railroads and steam engines is, of course, steeped in history. Tracing the roots of this form of transportation will take you back to the Industrial Revolution and to the expansion of our country. The railroad played a huge role in the growth of towns across the nation, from east to west, following the railway lines—a topic that provides wonderful geography lessons.

From the earliest days of the railroad to the high-speed trains of today, your unit study could cover the lives of pioneers and presidents, of politicians and immigrant workers, of scientists and wars. It could include the popular Boxcar Children series of books or even the Underground Railroad. Although not a railroad, the Underground Railroad connected human beings across the country and brought change and progress to our nation. It could easily become a unit study all its own, as an interesting jumping-off place from your railroad unit study.

Art and Music

Throughout your unit study, include art-related projects, music from the era, the songs the workers sang as they worked all day on the railroad. Listen to your children's ideas as they create, cut out, and construct trains and the various train cars, or run their own electric train around the tracks. Read and discuss the topics together, keep the unit study fun and hands-on, and the knowledge they gain will be profound and lasting.

Thematic Studies

When integrating ideas into a theme or unit study, children will use and enhance their knowledge of core subject areas—reading, writing, history, geography, science, and math, as well as art, music, and physical education—all interwoven with a topic that interests them at a certain point in their lives. Each area of the curriculum connects in a cohesive manner, helping children to understand the reason that different skills are important and how they relate to a single purpose. Besides putting their reading, writing, and math skills to use, they can hone their research, thinking, and problem-solving skills in a way that is fun and almost effortless. And because the subject matter is one that especially interests them at this time in their life, the chances of growing bored and resisting the lessons are quite diminished.

ESSENTIAL

To make your unit study preparations even easier, use the Internet to get ideas. Some homeschooling and educational websites include outlines and ideas for theme studies that you can put right to use. Libraries, bookstores, educational supply stores, and hobby shops are other great resources for pulling together a unit study.

It's helpful to plan unit or theme studies in advance, so that you can help guide children when they have questions, need to acquire special supplies for projects, or seek additional research methods. If you know, for instance, that you'll be doing a unit study on gardening, you'll want to have gardening tools on hand, vegetable and flower seeds, and a good idea of where you'd like the garden to be planted—before the children head into the yard with shovels and hoes. You may want to make notes or create an outline of what you plan to accomplish in each phase of the unit study, and you'll want to have an idea of how long you expect each phase to last.

Eclectic Homeschool Methods

The eclectic method of homeschooling draws upon an assortment of elements from various educational resources. It can also incorporate elements from different styles of homeschooling. If you would like to try unschooling, but you are hesitant about drifting too far from your current curriculum, use a combination of ideas presented in this chapter as you test the waters.

Exploring Interests

You can begin by allowing more free learning time and encouraging children to explore their own areas of interest. This could be so foreign to them that they may not even know how to begin. They might think that nothing interests them if their opportunities for exploration and free thinking have been shut down for too long. It could take some family brainstorming sessions to get your children in touch with things that truly interest them, or discussions of hobbies or topics that they might want to pursue and explore.

Using Unit Studies

Introduce a couple of short unit studies, and help your child become comfortable with that educational experience, which can be quite different from a traditional curriculum. Start with a new interest she recently discovered, and create the unit study around that topic. When she realizes that schooling can revolve around her own interests, it will open up a whole new view for her.

Adding Unschooling Days

Let her take the unit study or theme-centered learning style even farther by allowing for some unschooling days. On those days, she's free to work on the unit study, work on her original curriculum, or simply be involved in some project, whether it's reading, writing, cooking, sewing, painting, playing music, or working on a totally new idea that interests her.

The Result

Within a few weeks of experiencing this new, eclectic style of homeschooling, composed of a variety of styles—her original curriculum, unit studies, unschooling, and exploring new interests—your child will no doubt surprise you with her enthusiasm; her creative, innovative side; and her ability to demonstrate how much she is learning—and is teaching to you!

Resources for Unschooling and Unit Studies

To try some unschooling ideas today, visit *www.everythinghomeschooling .com* and click the "Unschooling" section. Or try our "Unit Studies" for thematic units covering seasons, holidays, presidents, weather, gardening, movies, and more.

CHAPTER 7

Fun Learning Activities

When learning is fun, children will naturally learn more. But even better, they will remember and retain more of what they learn. Here you'll see how to thread fun through all the subjects that make up a homeschool curriculum. Be imaginative, flexible, creative, and joyous, then let the fun begin!

Language Arts Activities

Language arts encompasses English, reading, writing, spelling, vocabulary, grammar, composition, literature, drama, poetry, listening and speaking, and related written or oral activities.

Reading Activities

Reading need not be dull. Famous or popular movies are made from books and stories! If your children are not especially interested in reading, try reading movie scripts together, such as Disney movie scripts or family movie scripts featured on *www.SimplyScripts.com*. Use the scripts to act out the movie, and compare scripts to the book version of the story.

Turn your visits to your local public library into field trips or scavenger hunts. Have children find books that will take them to another land, another planet, or an imaginary world. See if they can locate books by particular authors or stories that focus on a particular time period. Make it fun! If they're having no luck finding such books, see if you can help. Pull out a few selections from the shelves and point out the colorful pictures or delightful illustrations. Then wonder aloud what might be occurring in the story. Begin reading a few of the pages aloud, and soon their interest will be piqued.

ESSENTIAL

Reading lists and book suggestions are available at *www.KidsReading Circle.com* and *www.bookspot.com/booksforchildren.htm*. The Book-Spot site also includes online books to read with your children, such as *The Call of the Wild*, *The Jungle Book*, *The Secret Garden*, *The Swiss Family Robinson*, and many more.

Breathe life into the stories you read together. In addition to discussing the characters and events in the stories, create your own plays or dramatic performances based upon the stories. Or simply take turns reading the lines of the different characters in the voices that seem to reflect their personalities. This often results in fits of giggles and reading fun!

Read to them, share written stories with them, read newspapers aloud, and read information aloud, even if it's the cereal boxes at breakfast or a sign in the dentist's waiting room. The key to encouraging children to read is to read, read, read!

Parts of Speech

Use illustrated books or even comic books to help children become more familiar with nouns, verbs, adjectives, adverbs, pronouns, prepositions, conjunctions, and interjections. After reading the stories, pick out the different parts of speech together. When done on a regular basis with stories children enjoy, you'll be surprised how quickly they'll learn the different parts of speech and how long they'll retain this knowledge.

Here's a fun activity many children enjoy. They can assign colors to the different parts of speech. Then, with colored construction paper at their fingertips, they can jot down the nouns they find in a story on red construction paper, for instance. They cut up those nouns on red paper and drop them into a jar or box. Then they jot down the verbs from the story on blue construction paper, cut up the verbs, and drop them into the jar or box. They can continue with yellow adjectives, green adverbs, etc., cutting up the words and dropping them into the container.

Later, they can shake up the container and select a red noun, blue verb, yellow adjective, green adverb, and create their own fun or silly sentences. Over time, as they continue to add colorful words to the container, they'll have quite a collection of nouns, verbs, adjectives, adverbs, all color coded and clicking in their mind. And they'll become much better at spotting the different parts of speech in sentences as they read.

Writing Activities

Brainstorm new story prompts or creative writing ideas together each day. For instance: What if time ran backward? What if you could read everyone else's thoughts? What if you had webbed feet and a beak? Describe what your day would be like, or write a story based on your what-if ideas. Keep a daily writing journal full of your creative thoughts and stories.

As a family, think about a story you'd like to write. Decide on the characters, setting, plot, and storyline. Then have each family member write his or her own version of the story. Read your stories aloud and see how similar or different the stories are.

In today's digital world of texting, instant messaging, and e-mail, letter-writing is still an important skill. Children can hone those skills by writing letters on a regular basis to friends and families. Remind them to write thank-you notes for gifts or favors, as well. They can also write letters and thank-you notes to famous folks. What might they write to Dr. Seuss? What would they thank him for? What would they write to Pocahontas, or to Lewis and Clark, or to Mark Twain? They can write letters to other favorite authors, actors or actresses, or local heroes.

Spelling and Vocabulary Fun

Use Scrabble game tiles, magnetic letters, or other types of letter tiles for spelling practice. See who can spell the words the quickest. See who can create the silliest word. Spell out words on each other's backs with your fingers, and see who is the most ticklish!

FACT

Spelling lists are available for grades 1 through 12 at *www.KidsSpell.com*. Click on the Select a Spelling List link and choose the appropriate list. Use words from these lists for your spelling games or spelling practice.

Use word scrambles, word searches, crossword puzzles, and other word games for spelling practice, as well as vocabulary enhancements. For online spelling and vocabulary fun, browse word games at *www.FunBrain.com*.

Math and Reasoning Activities

Mathematical learning opportunities surround your child every day. From telling time to food preparations, measurements, temperature variations, counting, adding, money matters, time requirements, sports scores, game strategies, construction toys, craft creations, algebra and building projects, distances and speeds, fractions and percents, fascinating Fibonacci numbers—your child can practice math in real life every day!

Daily Math Fun

From shape-sorting games to determining the perimeter and area of each of the shapes, you can apply that exercise to nearly any object. Take that idea further by determining the perimeter and area of the room you're in, as well as each room in your home. Step outside and determine the overall perimeter of your entire house or complex, then calculate total square footage. Which room is the largest in your home? Which room is the smallest? Why are the rooms and homes designed in the size and shape that they are?

In this way, a simple shape-sorting game has grown into a real-life learning experience, making connections between basic shapes, living spaces, and home design. This is an important lesson: Take fun, simple games or daily lessons and *make connections* to the things that are *real* in life, the things that are a part of *everyday life*. This is when education and knowledge clicks, and learning makes sense and solidifies in a child's mind.

With math opportunities all around us, it's easy to practice mathematical skills each day. Simply discuss math concepts as you play together, do household chores together, cook and bake together. When you run errands or take your daily walks together, determine distances traveled, the speed you're traveling, and the time it takes to travel those distances. The more your children practice real-life math exercises, the better they'll become.

Math Games

Board games and card games are great ways of developing and sharpening math skills, as well as reasoning and strategy skills. Bring out the board games each evening, on weekends, or anytime during the homeschool day! Play old favorites, such as Risk, Monopoly or Monopoly Junior, PayDay, or chess. Try games such as Math Bingo, Equate math game, fractions games, and similar math games.

As a family, play "store" and see what it's like to open and run your own shop. Use play money or real money, "sell" retail items or consignment items, and keep a running inventory in your pretend store. Record expenses and sales in homemade ledger books, and determine the daily and weekly income—or income potential—of your shop.

Another way of running a business is trying the online game of Lemonade Stand at *www.coolmath-games.com/0-lemonade-stand*. Kids will gain experience in nearly every aspect of a business: pricing, sales, inventory control, and handling the ups and downs of the economy over a period of several days. Make a pitcher of lemonade and head over to the computer and open your lemonade stand!

Science Projects and Experiments

You won't need a chemistry lab for your children to perform science experiments. Your kitchen makes a wonderful science lab, and entire days can be spent on experiments and science projects. The act of performing experiments includes the use of mathematical skills, reasoning and analytical skills, research, asking questions, recording data, reporting conclusions— all key steps in the scientific method of conducting experiments. These steps not only incorporate science and math skills, but reading and writing skills, and historical discoveries, too.

Hands-On Projects

Try some of the following experiments in your kitchen science lab. For instructions on these, visit *www.JulianTrubin.com* and click the Experiments link.

- Experiment with colors, compounds and substances, density, ice, liquids, mixtures, oxygen, gasses, and properties.
- Grow algae, fungi, and molds; try photosynthesis, seed germination, plant growth, acid rain, greenhouse effects, biodegradation, and water experiments.

- Replicate earthquakes, magnetic fields, erosion, tornadoes, tsunamis, volcanoes, and the water cycle.
- Make hot air balloons, boomerangs, kites, paper airplanes, parachutes, model rockets, water rockets, wind tunnels, and more.
- Create lemon batteries, electric motors, magnetic levitation, loudspeakers, static electricity, lightning, and telegraphs.

For more science experiments, check out *The Everything® Kids' Science Experiments Book* by Tom Robinson, *Science in Seconds for Kids* by Jean Potter, and *365 Simple Science Experiments with Everyday Materials* by E. Richard Churchill.

Interesting Experiments

In the kitchen lab, you can conduct all types of experiments on water mixtures, freezing and thawing, heat and conduction, acids and bases. As with all experiments, always provide close supervision.

Determine what happens, and why, when you mix oil and water. In a small water bottle, add a few drops of food coloring to the water. Next add a couple of spoonfuls of cooking oil. Place the cap on the bottle and shake the water bottle vigorously. Have your child observe what happens after shaking the bottle. Research oil and water mixtures to understand the results of the experiment, and encourage your child to describe the experiment in his science journal.

Or make gak in your kitchen lab. Similar to slime, but not as messy, kids love making and playing with this substance, using borax powder and Elmer's white glue. Pour an eight-ounce bottle of Elmer's glue into a mixing bowl. Then fill the empty glue bottle with warm water and shake. Pour this water into the Elmer's glue in the bowl and mix well. Add a few drops of food coloring, if desired. Measure a half-cup of warm water in a measuring cup, then add a teaspoon of borax to the water and stir. Slowly add the borax-water mixture to the Elmer's glue in the mixing bowl and stir gently. As the molecules begin linking together into strands, use your hands to mix, mold, pull, and play. Continue experimenting with the substance by adding more of the borax-water mixture. Have fun!

Experiment with convection and heat. Help your child cut a spiral shape out of aluminum foil or construction paper. Have him hold the cut-out, dangling spiral above a lamp with the light bulb turned off. Turn on the lamp for him and watch as the light bulb warms up. As the bulb gets hotter, what happens to the dangling spiral? Ask your child to hypothesize what occurs and have him research the principles of convection.

Record the many experiments your child performs with photographs, digital photos, or smartphone videos. Keep these in your child's portfolio, science journal, or a science folder on your family's computer. Encourage children to write about their experiences in their science journals, too.

History, Geography, and Social Studies

To know where you're going, you need to know where you've been. Children need a sense of their place in the world, starting with their place in the family, their home in the neighborhood, their community's businesses and stores, the boundaries of their town and their state, and where the neighboring towns, cities, states, and countries lie.

They'll be interested in knowing who started their town and why. Who were the earliest pioneers in their state, and when did their state establish its statehood? Who were the statesmen who worked hard to create the great state that children know as their home state? Who helped establish the United States of America, and where did America's forefathers come from? Why did the earliest explorers to America leave their countries to travel to a land that was foreign to them? What was life like in the countries that those explorers left?

As you can see, geography, history, and different cultures and lifestyles all revolve around one another. And they all help to establish a child's place in this world. You can start with the simplest maps of your child's neighborhood and broaden into state maps, world maps, and globes to help him see where he is in this world. You can use storytelling as a way to describe not only his history and his family's history, but also the history of his town, state, country, and world.

Mapmaking Fun

Children can draw maps, as large as they want, of their backyard, play areas, or the parks they visit. They can label the different spaces and use symbols for trees and paths, playground equipment, picnic tables, buildings, and playhouses. Then mark the routes they often follow, such as the path between the house and play areas, or the trek between the playground and parking lot at your local park.

Broaden their mapmaking skills as your children's sense of community grows. Have them draw a map of your neighborhood or town, showing your house, the park, the nearby grocery store, gasoline station, the bank, post office, hospital, library, churches, schools, fire and police stations, and other pertinent locations. Encourage them to decorate and label the maps in creative and colorful ways, then display them on a bulletin board. As they learn about new or different areas in their towns, have them add those locations to their maps.

Use nicely illustrated books about your state to help children learn all it has to offer. Create a basic map of your state and have children mark their town or community on the map. Next, have them locate and label the city that is nearest to their home. Then locate and label the capital of your state.

Now, using interesting books on your state, allow children to select points of interest or places they would like to visit someday, such as a state park, a cave, lake, waterfall, ocean, amusement park, ski resort, raceway, zoo, aquarium, museum, pioneer village, covered bridge, tower, or skyscraper. Have children locate and label those places on your state map.

Visit those areas of interest as time and circumstances allow. When children explore the places they have learned about, their world becomes much more real to them. Do the same with maps of the United States and the world. Although you may not be able to visit all the areas you would like, beautiful travel videos or DVDs can bring distant places right into your home.

Living History

History should not wither away within dry pages of dull textbooks. History was, and is, made by living people, real people, people of the past, and people we may know today. Choose a famous person from the past and be that person. Research him or her; learn what that person was like, what he wore or how she spoke, where the person lived, what life was like when that person was alive, and how the culture or lifestyles differed from others. Create that person's style of clothing from paper or cloth. For instance, if it's Abraham Lincoln you're emulating, replicate his stovepipe hat, black jacket, pants, and famous beard. If it's Sacagawea, make a copy of her costume and papoose. Find pictures of famous people by using the Google Images search engine or checking illustrated library books.

What are some good biographies to read on historical figures?
The Who Was Biographies, DK Biographies, and Sterling Biographies cover a wide range of historical figures, such as Davy Crockett, Joan of Arc, Frederick Douglass, Marie Curie, Henry Ford, Albert Einstein, Amelia Earhart, Neil Armstrong, Steve Jobs, and more. Use biographies to learn more about each era's events and lifestyles.

Crafting History

Bring out the craft box, construction paper, craft sticks, glue, markers, pipe cleaners, and begin crafting history. Help children construct medieval castles, Viking boats, the *Mayflower*, teepees and longhouses, western frontier buildings and wagons, or the White House. Use library books on castles, boats, the Wild West, or the White House as guides for replicating the objects and for learning more about each creation.

Make pipe-cleaner people to inhabit the places your children create, then let the stories from long ago unfold. Hands-on activities always serve to raise a child's level of awareness and help to embed the learning experiences in his mind for years to come. Whenever possible, incorporate hands-on activities into your daily lessons.

Arts, Music, and Crafts

Fun automatically revolves around art, music, and crafts! Turn up the music and start dancing and singing. Or, turn down the volume, play peaceful classical music, and literally draw upon the inspiration it conveys. Put pencil to paper and draw the emotions the music imparts. Listen to arias or Broadway hits while crafting a stage or performance hall within a diorama. Place tiny, handcrafted ballerinas or actors on the stage, and let the show begin.

Artistic Creations

Finger-paints, tempera paints, or food coloring dissolved in water provide color-mixing fun for children. Let them experiment with the colors and see how red and yellow mixtures produce orange, or blue and red produce purple. Make foamy whipped cream paints by mixing food coloring with whipping cream. Create 3D textured paintings by using thick impasto paint, made by mixing shredded toilet tissue, white glue, and tempera paints.

Enjoy *plein-air* painting. Take trips to the countryside, seaside, or parks in your town, and encourage children to paint or sketch landscapes, gardens, or meadow views. Take trips to the city or the historic section of town, and capture the architectural details of buildings and homes. Remember to have children paint or draw their own homestead, too!

ESSENTIAL

Hundreds of artistic ideas for all ages and in all mediums are available at *www.KinderArt.com*. Whether it's painting, drawing, sculpting, printmaking, art history, multicultural art, or seasonal crafts, you'll find enough ideas to keep your children creatively busy all year long!

Learn art history through cave drawings, ancient pottery, tapestries, and murals. Use art books from the library to view the artwork of the Byzantines, Renaissance artists, Impressionists, and others. Have children try their hand on famous paintings that will stay in their minds long after the paint has dried.

Musical Moments

Make musical instruments and start a band! To see how to make guitars, banjos, drums, maracas, bells, tambourines, and more, visit *www.ArtistsHelpingChildren.com* and select the Music theme page from the Crafts by Theme link. The instructions for crafting your own instruments range from easy to more complex, for preschoolers to teens. Or check books at your library on how to make musical instruments. Listen to favorite music, then try creating your own style of music with your handmade instruments.

Take advantage of music lessons given by retired music teachers in your area. Not only will your children learn to read music and play an instrument (a skill that will stay with them for a lifetime), they'll brighten a music teacher's day. Those who teach music, love music, and they enjoy passing that love on to others. A happy music student, who enjoys playing an instrument, is every music teacher's dream.

Have fun learning about the symphony at *www.DSOKids.com*. Play the online games, create your own music, and learn about musical notes at *www.ClassicsForKids.com*. Engage in visual and auditory learning of classical music, composers, and instruments at *www.SphinxKids.org*. Become more familiar with the classical composers, such as Bach, Beethoven, Chopin, and Mozart, by playing the Composers Card Game, available in most book or toy stores.

Technology and Computer Skills

Chances are, your children are already computer savvy or know their way around a smartphone screen. Technology continues to advance at a rapid pace, and children are rarely intimidated by the latest innovations. In many cases, *they* can teach *us*. If you don't have a computer at home, with supervision children can use those available at local public libraries or community learning centers. Allow them the opportunity to explore digital learning in conjunction with their more-traditional styles of learning.

Basic Computer Skills

Children can learn, or improve, their keyboarding skills simply by typing stories, letters, or writing assignments on your family's home computer. To learn touch typing, a great online program for kids is available at *www.TypingClub.com*. The helpful steps, tips, progression of lessons, and the ability to type and follow along are wonderful.

ALERT

If websites charge a fee, you'll want to check the site carefully and determine if the fee is reasonable for what they offer. Similarly, if the site wants you to set up an account, it might just need a first name and password, rather than personal information. *Always* supervise your children when they're using the computer, Internet, or smartphone.

Games or websites, such as *www.FunToType.com*, also provide fun ways to practice typing skills. Many computer games, tutorials, and lessons are free on the Internet. However, some sites might switch to charging a fee or requiring you to set up an account. Read their "About" pages and look over the website to determine how beneficial it could be for you and your children.

Advanced Computer Skills

Your child might want to create 3D animations or design video games. She might want to learn graphic design or fashion design, or create websites and mobile apps. She can learn Java programming or HTML coding. A course for nearly every digital- or technology-based application is available online. Simply do a search on the ones that interest her.

These more advanced programs are usually not free. However, *www.w3schools.com* still currently offers a load of free tutorials on coding and programming, including HTML, JavaScript, CSS, SQL, PHP, and more. Here, a child could quickly teach herself the basics of creating a website or application. Code.org is another site where children can learn free coding and programming skills.

In-depth, comprehensive lessons are also available on these topics, but often at a higher price. For instance, *www.YouthDigital.com* offers programming and graphic design lessons in the $200 price range, while *www.Tynker.com* currently offers courses in the $50 price range. Check the websites, the lessons, and the testimonials to help you decide which courses are best for your children and their current computer skill levels.

Creativity and the Computer Age

Some fear that the computer age has impaired creativity in children. They point to the smartphone or handheld devices that seem to be permanently attached to the hands of children and teens in restaurants, malls, at sporting events on the weekends, in the family room of their homes at night. Often seen right beside them, are adults who are also looking at their smartphones, checking their e-mail, sending a text message, uploading a picture to Instagram. It's a part of today's stay-connected world.

Some think that children no longer build forts in the woods, fabricate soapbox derby race cars, construct a life-sized robot that may or may not walk, or chase after fireflies in the dark and marvel at their magical glow. But children do. And children will. As long as there are parents to suggest a variety of ideas for fun projects and intriguing activities, children will use their creativeness and inventive minds to build, construct, explore.

With creative parents as role models, children will be creative, too. The key, as with most anything in life, is "moderation in all things." Include a good balance of computer skills, creative thinking, inventive designing, hands-on experimentations, project building, family games, educational games, physical activities, nature walks. And wait until another day to upload the pictures of your family's fun, creative projects!

Life Skills and Social Skills

One of the main reasons many families choose to homeschool is to ensure that their children develop proper social skills and learn important life skills. They want their children to understand etiquette, practice their manners, show respect and kindness to others, care about their communities, and become good citizens. They also want their children to learn how to make intelligent choices, learn a variety of skills, live happy and healthy lives, and pursue areas of interest that may lead to their lives' work.

Decision-Making Skills

We all want our children to become mature, independent adults who are capable of making decisions, running their lives, and finding happiness in the choices they make. It takes a lot of training to reach that point, which is why it's never too early to allow even the youngest child to make simple decisions or to be a good little helper around the home. Give children some choices each day, so that they become accustomed to considering possibilities and exercising some control in their lives.

Play what-if games with your children, such as: "What if you could choose between living in the country or living in the city? Which would you choose?" Then discuss the pros and cons of both options, and why one might work out better than the other. Try to play these types of games each day, to help hone the decision-making skills. When children are given ample opportunities to make choices in the safety of your home, they'll have you, the parent, helping them weigh the consequences of their decisions. As your children grow, their choices will become more critical. But with practice, they'll be accustomed to considering all possible outcomes before they jump into any situation too quickly.

Social Skills

Children naturally imitate their parents. When parents exhibit kindness, consideration, respect, politeness, and manners, children will imitate the examples they set. Homeschooled children often accompany parents on errands to the bank, post office, and other public places, where they observe their parents interacting with others in the community. Be aware of the examples you set, how you treat others with kindness, and display proper etiquette in various social settings. Your children will follow your examples.

ESSENTIAL

For helpful books on social skills, check out *365 Manners Children Should Know* by Sheryl Eberly, *Ready-to-Use Social Skills Lessons & Activities* by Ruth Weltmann, or *Social Skills Picture Book for High School and Beyond* by Jed Baker.

To prepare children for new or different experiences, try role-playing activities in the home. Perhaps your family will be attending a special social event, or dining in a sophisticated restaurant, or your child will be a guest in another's home. Role-play these situations to help children fine-tune their manners and display proper behavior in each scenario.

Life's Work

Whether your life's work is finding a cure for cancer or keeping a happy home and raising healthy children, it is, by far, the most meaningful work that you have ever done. Your life's work is the catalyst that fires you up in the morning, inspires you to greet each day with joy, keeps you running with enthusiasm all day, and brings intense satisfaction at the end of each day.

Love of work and purpose is what we want our children to know and enjoy, too. As discussed earlier, each child has his own unique learning style. Similarly, each child has his own special interests. Even within the same family, one child might love animals, another might prefer computers, and another might enjoy staying busy outdoors all day long. When allowed to follow their own interests, one child might eventually work in a veterinarian's office, another might become a software developer, and the other might help build grand office buildings. This is the beauty of homeschooling—children have the time, space, flexibility, and encouragement to follow their dreams.

In the home environment, children will also learn how to keep a home, care for others, and share responsibilities—not only in the evenings or on the weekends, but throughout each day and night. They will learn the life skills needed to prepare meals, shop for food and clothing, and keep shelves and closets stocked with necessities. They'll participate in home maintenance, lawn maintenance, and car maintenance, plus see how to make home repairs and car repairs. They'll sometimes learn the family business, or at least help to monitor family income and expenses, follow a budget, help make buying decisions, and balance the checkbook. They'll learn the difference between wants and needs and when to fix something in the home or when to replace it.

All of these exercises are simply a part of living within the family unit each day. They aren't skills that are necessarily taught in school. But even if they are taught in school, they'd lose their real meaning. In school, they would be one more thing to learn. At home, the family's daily life—and eventually our children's lives—will depend on knowing and understanding these life skills. At home, these life skills are a part of loving and caring for one another, and that makes all the difference.

Resources for Weekly Lessons

For weekly lessons and homeschool activities in all subject areas—language arts, math, science, social studies, arts, and life skills—visit *www.EverythingHomeschooling.com*. Fun, interesting lessons and activities that children enjoy and remember are added daily, weekly, and monthly.

CHAPTER 8

Frugal Homeschooling

Homeschooling can cost as little or as much as you'd like. It depends on your family's budget and your current needs. In many cases, homeschooling can be almost free! Your local public library includes a world of education and knowledge for you and your children. From math to reading, science to social studies, art to music, here are money-saving ideas to keep your homeschool affordable, and keep your children learning and loving it.

Libraries for Learning

Textbooks are not necessary when library books are available. But, you may wonder, how will your child learn about history, the ancient Greeks, the Mayflower Compact, the Western Movement, or the World Wars without textbooks? It's easy. Your library has books on all these topics, plus thousands more. And it costs you nothing but a trip to the library and time spent with your children.

You can save even more time by going to your library's website and placing holds on the books you'd like to use for the next few weeks in your homeschool. Simply do searches by title or subject matter, such as ancient Greeks, then use your library card to place your hold on the books.

QUESTION

If I don't have textbooks, how will I know what topics my child should study?
Determine what topics you want to study by viewing the "Typical Course of Study" for all grade levels, found in the Family section at *www.WorldBook.com*. The main curriculum requirements for preschool through grade 12 are listed for your convenience.

Library Services

Your local public library usually has information on homeschool groups and homeschool events in your area. They offer story time, craft time, current reading lists, book discussion clubs, and magazines and newspapers for kids and teens. You'll find educational DVDs, instructional videos, CDs, and music. Do you want to learn French or German? Do you need to see how algebra or calculus works? No problem; your library will usually have the DVDs on hand to help you learn, or they can get them for you.

Many libraries offer art or drawing workshops, photography workshops, board games, chess clubs, puzzles, films, computer access, educational software programs, and computer research assistance. In addition, seasonal activities, hands-on science programs, nutritional programs, tech labs, and math or trivia challenges are usually offered at many libraries. If not, talk with the librarian to see what would be necessary to establish more educational programs for children.

Book Activities

Here are some activities you can do with books you check out from your library. Create a colorful chart with areas for listing the book title and author, describing the characters, plot, setting, main events, conclusion, and feelings about the story. Be creative with the chart, decorate it, add stickers, and draw cartoon-like caricatures of the people in the story.

ESSENTIAL

For hundreds of fun book report ideas, see the Web English Teacher site at *www.WebEnglishTeacher.com/bookreports.html.* You'll find 150 interesting alternatives to standard book reports, 20 different ways of looking at a book, 90 ways to respond to literature, and over 300 book activities, book report forms, and more.

Or, have children rewrite the story with a slightly different plot or different ending. Publish the story on the computer or on paper, design and make a colorful cover for the book, and bind it with thread. Display the book on one of your family's bookshelves, and be sure to read it often, too. It will inspire children to write and publish more of their own books in the weeks and months ahead.

Free Books and Educational DVDs

Thousands of books are now available online, free of charge. Some are available for free downloads to handheld electronic readers, such as the Kindle, Nook, or smartphone. Search for classics or children's books online, or visit some of the sites listed here, where you can search by title or author. The majority of the books are available as Adobe PDFs or in standard HTML format.

- Archive's Children's Library: *www.archive.org/details/iacl*
- Bartleby: *www.bartleby.com*
- Bibliomania: *www.Bibliomania.com*
- Classic Bookshelf: *www.ClassicBookshelf.com*
- Project Gutenberg: *www.Gutenberg.org*
- University of Pennsylvania Library: *http://onlinebooks.library.upenn.edu*

Educational DVDs can be found in your public library or shared through local homeschool groups. If your homeschool group has several members, each might like to contribute a couple dollars per month toward the purchase of special DVDs to share within the group. The educational DVD company LeaningFromDVDs.com offers instructional DVDs on every topic imaginable at *www.LearningFromDVDs.com*. Rock'n Learn provides musical DVDs that capture the interest of children for science, social studies, math, phonics, reading, writing, test-taking strategies, and more at *www.rocknlearn.com*.

For a fairly affordable alternative, try a free monthly trial from Netflix.com. They feature over sixty pages of "Educational and Guidance" DVDs in their Children's category on topics such as animals, book characters, fine arts, language, health, math, phonics, poetry, reading, science, social skills, sports, and much more!

Learning Through TV and Movies

According to Science Daily, only one in eight educational television shows for children are high-quality programs. The report notes that most commercial television broadcasters are failing to deliver a minimum of three hours of children's educational programming per week, as required by law. With a bit of research, though, parents can still find informative programs on stations like Animal Planet, Discovery Channel, History Channel, Learning Channel, NASA, and PBS. Recommended educational programs include *Sesame Street*, *Reading Rainbow*, *Schoolhouse Rock!*, *Beakman's World*, *Super Why!*, *Cyberchase*, *WordGirl*, and *Teen Kids News*, among others.

Visit the websites of educational TV stations, and select shows that would be age-appropriate for your children, such as *Weird, True, and Freaky*; *Whale Wars*; or *Wild Kingdom* on Animal Planet. See what will be showing next on *Planet Earth*, *Nextworld*, *How It's Made*, *Time Warp*, *Prototype This*, and similar shows on the Discovery Channel. But don't just watch the shows together. Discuss them, research the subject matters further, design and create gadgets or inventions similar to those seen on the shows, create collages of animals and animal facts inspired by shows on the Animal Planet, or build a miniature replica of a battlefield seen on the History Channel. Ask your children for ideas on similar projects. You'll find that their ideas will come faster than you can write them down!

Movie Unit Studies

You can create unit studies based on classic children's movies or favorite movies today, and use the movies as learning opportunities. Through movie unit studies, your children can gain knowledge on geography, history, vocabulary, writing, arts, and life lessons. And you'll enjoy watching the movies together, too!

Field Trips and Expeditions

Most homeschool support groups work diligently to arrange educational field trips for families to enjoy together on a monthly basis. The cost is minimal, and the learning that results from visiting museums, zoos, aquariums, and other attractions pays off greatly. It's also a wonderful way for children to socialize, not only with other homeschoolers but with the many people they meet on the trip.

As you go about errands in your town, make a mental note of places your homeschool group—or your family—could visit on their next educational excursion. Don't forget short field trips to the beach, lake, park, orchard, antique shop, or sporting events, where you'll nearly always have new or interesting experiences. Children can take photographs of places they visit, then write captions or summaries of their trips to add to their writing journals or scrapbooks.

Here are some field trip ideas you may want to consider in your community:

- Bakeries, pizzerias, and fast-food restaurants
- Publishing companies and printing presses
- Soda-bottling and manufacturing companies
- Car-racing tracks, horse-racing tracks
- Pioneer villages, log cabins, and antique shops
- Farms, ranches, orchards, and gardens
- Museums, zoos, airports, and shipyards
- Television and radio stations
- Post offices, courier services, and banks
- Fire stations, police departments, and city hall
- Performing arts halls, concert halls, and sports stadiums
- Traveling exhibits (dinosaur exhibits, Vietnam Moving Wall)
- Your place of business or a friend's place of business

If you're unable to take field trips locally, you can take virtual field trips on the Internet. Though not as exciting as the real experience, children might enjoy the novelty of such a trip. Try the online field trips and accompanying educational activities at *www.FieldTripZoom.com* or *www.EverythingHomeschooling.com*.

Science Lab Equipment

Sometimes it's difficult to ignore the desire to see and use an astronomer-quality telescope or scientific lab equipment. That's what field trips are for. Visit the children's science museum often, and make use of all the hands-on equipment. Locate the specialized museums, such as the planetarium, imaginarium, laboratorium, aquarium, holographic museum, and even the wax museum. Nearly all these facilities offer the opportunity to partake in some hands-on experimentation.

Group Science Labs

Families in your homeschool group might be interested in sharing or renting out lab equipment they already own. Or families could chip in to purchase equipment for the homeschool cooperative. This could be a nice investment not only for your group's children, but also for all the homeschool children yet to join your group.

Affordable telescopes, microscopes, chemistry sets, test tubes, beakers, petri dishes, Bunsen burners, litmus paper, chemistry sets, and similar lab equipment can be found on Amazon.com. Edmund Scientifics Online offers hundreds of science products and parts for all types of science projects, along with unusual or hard-to-find items, at *www.scientificsonline.com*.

Online Science Labs

Use this digital microscope at *www.open2.net/science/microscope/frames.html* to view plant leaves, roots, and stems; animal blood vessels, muscle, skin, bone; and microbes, bacteria, and more, all at adjustable magnifications.

Experiment with online chemistry labs, such as the Virtual Chemistry Laboratory at *www.chem.ox.ac.uk/vrchemistry*. Click the virtual experiments and select chemicals to mix, then observe the bubbling reactions! Study metal ions in solutions and watch the animated experiments in progress. Help children read about and describe the experiments in their own words.

Online Lessons and Learning

Children today are well accustomed to the online world. Reading and writing e-mail messages is more natural than writing letters (although letter-writing skills are still important). Reading the newspaper online is often quicker than reading the traditional newspaper. When answers are needed quickly for research or for those sudden questions that come to mind, the Internet is the place students turn to most often, rather than opening a reference book.

Whether it's for the best or not, the online world is the world of today, and there will be no turning back. The child who is familiar with using the Internet and learning through the Internet will have an easier time in today's world and in the world of the future.

Homeschool Lessons Online

The Everything Homeschooling website provides numerous lessons and activities for your family. The easy-to-use site, at *www.EverythingHomeschooling.com*, provides weekly lessons for all grade levels in all subject areas: language arts, social studies, math, science, life skills, computer skills, health and fitness, arts, crafts, and music. The weekly lessons are fun, interesting, and challenging for children from kindergarten through twelfth grade.

QUESTION

What are the benefits of online learning?
Through educational online sites, children can learn anytime, anywhere. The content provided on educational sites is usually current or continuously updated to stay on top of changing events and technology. The Internet offers nonstop learning possibilities, with the world literally, and constantly, at your fingertips.

In addition, the site provides special sections full of hands-on activities, science experiments, daily learning activities, creative writing prompts, unit studies, virtual field trips, weekly challenges, and unschooling activities. For families with younger children or older teens, there's a section for preschoolers and a section just for teens, each containing age-appropriate learning activities. Weekly planner pages, homeschool forms, attendance records, report cards, high school transcripts, and worksheets can be printed from the site, too.

Art Lessons Online

The free art lessons at *www.KinderArt.com* are available for preschoolers through high school. The lessons include architecture, art appreciation, art history, artistic styles, drawing portraits, painting techniques, and more.

Music Lessons Online

Learn to play the piano with the Piano Nanny at *www.PianoNanny.com*. This site offers beginning piano lessons, intermediate studies, and advanced piano lessons. The instructor is a professional studio musician and composer.

Take guitar lessons online at *www.FreeGuitarVideos.com*, and learn to play classical guitar, blues, country, jazz, rock, or other favorite types of music. Learn tablature and watch videos of the lessons at the same time.

These educational sites are simple, but wonderful ways for children to become more familiar with today's digital age and the online world. They will see, firsthand, how fun it can be to learn subjects through an online medium that offers mostly free lessons or activities.

Learning Every Day

Learning opportunities often present themselves when we least expect it. A fleet of excavation equipment suddenly appears in the lot across the street, and a new construction project begins. A pair of owls decides to raise their young in a tree in your backyard, and weeks of observations enthrall you. The garbage disposal becomes clogged, and you all gather on the floor beneath the kitchen sink and learn how to dismantle and unclog the disposal. Your family is feeling out of sorts one day, so you decide to get away and spend the day in the local state park, hiking, canoeing, and exploring.

These are just a few of the surprise events that can occur in the course of a homeschool week. In these examples, the lessons that result include learning about the excavation process, the heavy equipment that is used, and the architectural design and construction processes. As the building across the street takes shape and goes up, have children design and create a building of their own. Then build it with LEGO bricks or other construction sets, or with cardboard and glue.

The owls and their young in the backyard will have children racing to the computer to view owl pictures online. They'll want to determine if their owls are barn owls, screech owls, barred owls, snowy owls, great horned owls, or another type. Children will want to know how many babies owls will have, how long the youngsters will stay with the parents, how the young will learn to fly, what the owls eat, how the parents feed their young, and other owl facts. They'll want to take pictures of the owls, draw sketches of the owl family, and tell friends about the special family living in their backyard.

Hands-On Learning

The clogged garbage disposal is a wonderful hands-on learning opportunity. Everyone should know how to take apart the drain pipes under sinks, clean them out thoroughly, and reassemble them with no leaks. Taking apart the garbage disposal is an added bonus. Now children can look inside the previously mysterious contraption, see the blades and mechanisms, observe how to carefully clean out the disposal, and learn how to reassemble it properly. Repairs such as this are exceptional opportunities, as they not only help children see how things work, but they prepare children for the times ahead when they'll be responsible for their own home repairs.

Getaway Days

The getaway day to a state park is a wonderful reward for a homeschool family. They normally spend their weekdays and weekends together, living and learning in their home. But this unexpected break in the routine breathes a breath of fresh air into their daily lives, taking everyone away to a completely different environment. But, does the learning cease? On the contrary!

Living and learning is what homeschooling is all about. Deep in the forests, surrounded by wildlife and plants, waterfalls and lakes, rocks and hills, lookout towers and nature centers, the learning is just beginning. As children hike through the forest, climb over rocks, canoe around the lake, and observe the wildlife, their knowledge of nature grows by leaps and bounds.

Resources Around the Home

So far, you've seen how to create learning opportunities based on free services, free or inexpensive materials, and everyday events. But don't overlook materials you already have in your home that can be incorporated into your homeschool lessons. With your children beside you, explore each room, closet, and cabinet in your house, and consider how the objects and items can become learning tools. Children have such wonderful imaginations, and they often see the possibilities that adults might miss.

Go on scavenger hunts throughout the home for materials you can use, such as those listed here. Then consult craft or activity books on ways to use the learning materials you have on-hand. Helpful books include *Look What You Can Make with Dozens of Household Items* by Kathy Ross and *365 Simple Science Experiments with Everyday Materials* by E. Richard Churchill.

Kitchen Learning Materials

Your kitchen can easily be converted into your science lab. It also offers the following items. Be creative in using these for math, art, and science projects all year long:

- Beans, dry macaroni and spaghetti shapes, marshmallows, and cinnamon sticks
- Food coloring, vinegar, baking soda, and play dough ingredients

- Aluminum foil, wax paper, plastic wrap, paper plates, and grocery sacks
- Straws, toothpicks, coffee filters, plastic containers, scissors, and tape
- Egg cartons, milk cartons, plastic bottles, empty boxes, and Styrofoam
- Mixing bowls, measuring cups and spoons, thermometers, scales, and rulers
- Water, corks, ice, heat, candles, balloons, funnels, and pots and pans
- Cooking utensils, baking supplies, foods and oils, cookbooks, and recipes
- Calendars, clocks, timers, magnifying glasses, and binoculars
- Cameras, flashlights, batteries, paperclips, and junk-drawer items

As you scan through the list, ideas for using the materials will come to mind. The beans and macaroni shapes can be used for dimensional artwork or macaroni people. Vinegar and baking soda can erupt in a volcano. Straws, plastic bottles, and empty boxes can be turned into musical instruments. Corks float, balloons fill with pressure, magnifying glasses can observe insects up close. Gather some of the items together, set them on the table, and see what types of projects or experiments your children can create.

Crafty Fun

Make your own learning materials, such as counting beads, fraction circles, tangram shapes, geoboards, and other hands-on math manipulatives. For craft projects, use any items stashed away in your kitchen, sewing room, drawers, or closets.

- Paper of all types, paints, brushes, glitter, glue, and paste
- Scrapbooks, photo albums, binders, and notebooks
- Cardboard, construction paper, index cards, brads, and rubber bands
- Crayons, colored pencils, markers, dry-erase board, and chalk and chalkboard
- Cloth materials, felt pieces, sewing notions, cotton stuffing, and bubble wrap
- Beads, buttons, sequins, string, thread, yarn, twist ties, and pipe cleaners

Garage or Workshop Projects

Encourage inventiveness and inspire creativity while guiding children in the use of tools. Make small wooden toys, build shelves or birdhouses, create objects d'art, or construct unique sculptures with miscellaneous materials such as these:

- Wood, plastic, metal, cardboard, and paper
- Spools, dowels, wheels, ball bearings, and casters
- Nails, screws, nuts, bolts, washers, rivets, clamps, ties, and glue
- Pipes, wires, hoses, boxes, bags, fabrics, and ropes
- Tape measure, squares, levels, lasers, and templates
- Motors, engines, shafts, gears, pulleys, belts, and brackets
- Appliances, lamps, fans, clocks, and electronics
- Hand tools and power tools with instruction and supervision

Miscellaneous Resources

You will already have many of these items in or around your home. Just remember to use them in fun, educational ways.

- Board games, trivia games, card games, dice, spinners, and homemade games
- Musical instruments, rhythm instruments, radios, and CDs
- Magazines, newspapers, periodicals, and books, of course
- Reference books, atlases, maps, charts, globes, dictionary, thesaurus
- Diaries, journals, and notebooks for writing and sketching
- Outdoor materials, nature items, plants, seeds, leaves, flowers, insects, animals, rocks, and shells
- Rain gauges, outdoor thermometers, anemometers, and weather station
- Toys, model sets, puzzles, construction sets, play money, and costumes or clothing for dress-up and drama
- Sandbox, swing sets, climbing bars, trees to climb, tree houses, playhouse, lawn games, sports games, and water games

As always, ask your children for their ideas on using the items in and around your home. They often have unique or different perspectives that can result in new, fun learning activities.

CHAPTER 9

Choosing a Curriculum

A curriculum encompasses the lessons, activities, and projects that your child will use to meet certain educational goals or standards. It focuses on the knowledge, skills, and abilities your child should achieve in order to meet those goals. Your curriculum options range from a full, packaged curriculum, complete with pencils and paper, to a curriculum you design yourself. You might have a few hundred dollars to spend for a year's curriculum, and you might prefer a less-expensive option. Whatever your desires or budget, you'll be able to find a homeschool curriculum that will fit your family's needs.

Curriculum Guidelines

Whether you decide to use a packaged curriculum in your homeschool or to go the unschooling route, the day may come when you wonder if your child is on track or is covering everything he would cover in a traditional school. One way to do this is to review the "Typical Course of Study" from World Book, Inc. They put together their guidelines based on several national curriculum guides and courses of study.

Even if you're not overly concerned about the point where your children are in their education, you might pick up some homeschool ideas from the guidelines. Visit World Book at *www.WorldBook.com* and select the "Typical Course of Study" from the Family category. The general curriculum guidelines for preschool through grade 12 are listed for your convenience.

Packaged Curricula

A wide variety of curriculum providers, programs, and packaged curricula are available for homeschoolers. You can choose from secular curriculum suppliers, biblically based curriculum providers, and specific faith-based programs, such as Christian, Catholic, Islamic, and Jewish. Review the sources mentioned earlier in our chapter on "Approaches to Homeschooling" under "Secular Homeschools" and "Faith-Based Homeschools."

With many of the curriculum packages, you have the option of purchasing a standardized curriculum for the entire school year, or you can have a curriculum tailored more closely to your child's interests and needs. The companies can provide testing services, evaluations, grading, and record keeping, or you can choose to handle these yourself, saving yourself the additional fee that most require for the service.

A packaged curriculum can be beneficial when you are new to homeschooling, if you have a career and a family to keep up with, if you are uncertain about creating your own lesson plans, or if you're not sold on unschooling. If your children especially enjoy reading textbooks, doing worksheets, and following a regular daily schedule similar to that of a traditional school, a packaged curriculum may be just the thing for your family.

Structure and Method

Packaged curricula often follow the scope-and-sequence teaching method of public schools. This means that the curriculum has a specific outline of topics to cover in a predetermined amount of time (scope), and children will need to master the lessons in the order they are presented so they can move on to the next level (sequence). This method may be suited to your child's learning style, or it may be too constrictive. Check with the curriculum provider to see if their materials follow the scope-and-sequence method, or if their programs allow for flexibility, and, if so, how much.

ALERT

With any homeschool method, you'll want to add variety to the daily schedule. Otherwise, homeschooling will quickly grow stale. The kids won't be as enthusiastic as they once were, and their learning will suffer. Spice up the curriculum with activities, explorations, and games. Let the kids contribute their own learning ideas, too.

Cost Considerations

Price is also a consideration when purchasing a curriculum package. Curriculum packages can range from $400 to $1,000 for one grade level. The lower grades are less expensive, while the middle- to upper-grade curricula run more. Prices usually include the basic package, which includes nearly everything you need. In some cases, it may even include pencils, papers, rulers, and compasses. If you'd like to have additional products, such as certain readers or math books, there can be an extra charge for those.

Design Your Own Curriculum

You'll want to consider your children's wishes and input for the homeschool curriculum during the decision-making process. Children will often surprise you with the wonderful ideas and learning suggestions they come up with! Together, you and your children can create a curriculum that is fun, interesting, and challenging to ensure a well-rounded education, year after year.

QUESTION

Components of a Curriculum

A curriculum is based upon your educational philosophies, educational aims or ambitions for your child, and the learning goals or objectives necessary to achieve those aims. These are explained more fully here:

- **Educational philosophies** center on what you feel your children should learn in order to achieve happiness and success in their lives. This can include morals and values, respect and responsibility, manners and kindness toward others, faith and spirituality, a love for learning, and a love for life.

- **Educational aims or ambitions** for your children could include solid life skills and self-reliance, critical thinking and reasoning skills, creative thinking abilities, the ability to work well with others, to enjoy one's work and career, to show love and respect for one's family, to be a responsible and upstanding citizen, and/or to contribute to the community.

- **Learning goals and objectives** should support your educational philosophies and aims for your child. For instance, learning self-discipline and self-control is critical to a happy family life and career. Proper manners, social skills, and speaking skills are important when working with others or when contributing to the community. Good reading, math, and science skills are imperative to all areas of one's life, from daily living to getting ahead in one's career. Artistic and creative skills can add joy and meaning to one's life. Learning and maintaining healthy habits can contribute to a long, productive life.

Writing a Curriculum

Once you've determined your family's philosophies, your aims and ambitions for your child's education, and the goals or objectives to support those aims, you can begin designing the curriculum. But don't forget to consider your children's interests and learning styles! (You may want to review the different learning styles mentioned earlier to determine what method works best for each child.)

To write your curriculum, you'll want to record your educational philosophies, aims, and objectives, and keep them in a special folder, entitled "Curriculum." On those days when you forget where you are headed with your child's education, reviewing your goals and objectives will be a great reminder.

Your curriculum outline for grade 5 social studies could center on:

- United States history
- Discovery of America and early settlements
- Colonial and pioneer life in America
- American Revolution and independence
- Westward movement
- Geography of United States
- Industrial Revolution
- Natural resources
- Cultural resources and relationships

The lessons and activities you do with your children will be based on the topics noted on your curriculum outline.

When you've determined the subject areas your child will study (math, science, social studies, language arts, fine arts, health, and life skills), you'll want to slant them toward the goals and aims that you have for your child's education. For instance, a goal for your child might be to have a healthy, productive life. In studying the human body in science, you might want to emphasize the lessons on health and nutrition. Therefore, the objectives of the science lessons could focus on the way the body functions, how the bones and muscles work in tandem, how blood carries nutrients and oxygen to all parts of the body, how the respiratory and digestive systems work, and how proper nutrition, exercise, and healthful habits help the body function as it was designed to function.

As you can see, once you have your aims and goals established for your child (for example, a healthy, productive individual), you'll be able to focus on the objectives that you want the lessons to convey (in this case, how to achieve and maintain a healthy, productive body).

Children master skills at varying rates. One child may grasp the relation between decimals and fractions at age eight, while another may not grasp the concept until age ten. One child might write well in cursive at age nine; another may not display attractive penmanship until age twelve. Consider your child's unique skills and abilities when setting educational goals and objectives.

Following a Less Formal Curriculum

Designing your own curriculum might seem like a lot of work. Yet, most parents already have an idea of the educational goals for their children, even if they haven't written it down in a formal outline. Many parents are already in tune with their children's interests and learning styles, so it may not be necessary to document the objectives of each lesson or the manner in which the studies will complement the child's interests and the parent's goals.

In an unschooling environment, the curriculum tends to accommodate the children's curiosity and their interest-led activities. If you need to present evidence of the curriculum you use for your unschooled homeschool, illustrate how your children's interests and activities (such as their hobbies, games, experiments, talents, research, discussions, educational travels, creative projects, or books read) accomplish the goals and philosophies your family believes in.

Create Your Own Lesson Plans

Lesson plans are the activities or studies that complement and carry out the intent of the curriculum and educational goals for your children. For instance, one of your goals may be for your child to play an active part in your community as a caring and responsible individual. Therefore, you may want to create a lesson plan for social studies that has the objective of interacting with others for the good of the community.

For this particular objective, lesson plans could include researching the history of volunteerism in communities (with examples including Benjamin Franklin, who helped to establish the first volunteer fire department, or Clara Barton, who founded the American Red Cross through volunteering her services). Your child could read a book on ways to volunteer in the community, then write or share his thoughts on how he could help others in the community.

Other aspects of the lesson plan could include drawing posters of volunteers, visiting the headquarters of local volunteer associations, and taking an active part in community volunteer programs, such as canned food drives, clothing or toy collections, animal shelter assistance, or visiting with the elderly in nursing homes.

Lesson Plan Basics

Lesson plans help convey information about a subject and make connections. Creating them is not difficult. Presenting the lesson plans in an informative, stimulating way that connects with your child is more important than using worksheets from activity books or generic lesson plans.

Formal, written lesson plans usually cover the following points:

- **Subject:** The subject area the lesson relates to.
- **Grade level:** The grade or age level the lesson is suited for.
- **Description:** A brief overview of the lesson and its intent.
- **Objective:** What you want the child to learn from the lesson.
- **Procedures or plan:** The details of how you'll present or handle the lesson.
- **Materials:** The books, artwork, and/or supplies you'll need to carry out the lesson.
- **Evaluation or assessment:** A determination of what the child learned from the lesson.

It's not necessary to write elaborate lesson plans, unless you like the idea of doing so. But you might want to keep these points in mind when creating your lessons.

FACT

Building upon previous knowledge and skills is the sequential or cumulative way of presenting and mastering lessons. Some feel that testing is one way to determine the child's mastery of knowledge. Others believe that observing the child's overall capabilities is a better way of judging the child's knowledge and skills.

Sample Lesson Plans

Some lesson plans are geared more toward active participation, while others may encourage writing, speaking, calculating, evaluating, or artistic skills. Most are expected to build upon previous skills. For instance, no one would be expected to read Tolstoy's *War and Peace* until he had mastered the ability to read a short story. Similarly, a child isn't expected to add or subtract decimals and fractions until he has grasped the concept of parts and wholes.

When children are allowed to learn at their own pace, the family can spend the time that is necessary to help the children comprehend and eventually master skills and subject areas. As you monitor your child's comprehension, acquisition of knowledge, and maturation of skills and abilities, you'll know what topics he is ready for as he sequentially builds upon his knowledge base and interests.

To view some sample lesson plans or obtain ideas for creating your own plans, visit these lesson plan websites on the Internet.

- Discovery Education: *www.DiscoveryEducation.com*
- Lesson Plan Search: *www.LessonPlanSearch.com*
- Lesson Plans Page: *www.LessonPlansPage.com*
- LessonPlanz: *www.LessonPlanz.com*
- Teachers Corner: *www.TheTeachersCorner.net*
- Teachers.net: *www.Teachers.net*

Free Educational Resources

A homeschool education can be free or nearly free. Some may argue that you have to at least purchase pencils and paper, yet rare is the home that does not already contain a pencil and some paper. Most homes with children at least have crayons and paper of some sort for coloring or drawing. For books, many families use the public library almost exclusively for their homeschool needs.

Learning on the Internet

If you have Internet access, a world of information is literally at your fingertips. You can find free curriculum guidelines, free lesson plans, free educational games, and free worksheets. You can visit virtual museums and participate in virtual experiments and virtual classrooms. To find these resources, you need only type a relevant word or phrase into a search engine such as Bing, Google, Yahoo!, or Ask.com, then share the virtual learning experiences with your children.

Free Educational Games

The Internet offers some learning games that kids can play for free. Remember: Always monitor your children's activities when they are on the Internet. Here are just a few of the many resources available:

- Education for Kids: *www.Edu4Kids.com*
- Education Place: *www.EduPlace.com/edugames.html*
- FunBrain: *www.FunBrain.com*
- Owl and Mouse: *www.YourChildLearns.com/owlmouse.htm*

Free Worksheets

These websites offer worksheets, most of which are free and printable.

- ABCteach: *www.ABCTeach.com*
- Learning Page: *www.LearningPage.com*
- SchoolExpress: *www.SchoolExpress.com*
- Tampa Reads: *www.TampaReads.com*
- TeAch-nology: *www.Teach-nology.com*
- TlsBooks: *www.TLSBooks.com*

Sometimes a free website might begin charging a small fee or subscription price for educational games or activities. You'll want to view the site and all it offers to determine if you would want to pay the fee or subscribe as a member. That should be a personal choice based on your current educational needs.

Your Child's Input and Ideas

Always keep your children involved in your educational plans. When you sit down to create lesson plans and activities for your children, ask for ideas on what they'd like to learn. They may currently have an intense interest in snakes, castles, basket making, or a movie that's popular at the theater this year. Let them talk about their hobbies and interests, and encourage them to come up with ideas related to those. For instance, an interest in snakes could branch off to lizards, frogs, and other reptiles. Your son might mention that he'd like to know where the poison dart frog or Komodo dragon lives, and to learn more about them and their predators. This is something you could incorporate into your lesson plans for the science curriculum.

Your daughter might wonder what materials basket weavers used centuries ago when making baskets that were necessary for hauling firewood, gathering berries, perhaps even carrying water from a stream. Was there a way to make the basket waterproof, or did families need to mold pottery from clay in order to transport water? This is a lesson plan idea for history.

Have children brainstorm ideas, too. They may have grown tired of a hobby and now have no new interests on the horizon. Look through age-appropriate magazines, read about others' hobbies, browse through course catalogs and even toy catalogs, and see what sparks their interest.

If they were able to do anything they wanted, ask them what that might be. You may get answers like travel to Mars, fly to Hawaii and go surfing, or visit the Arctic Circle. These thoughts and interests can be worked into lesson plans on space travel for science or geographical travels for social studies. Never take your children's ideas lightly; rather, put them to good use in your lesson plans.

Handling Advanced Subjects

The first years of homeschooling your elementary-aged child might be a breeze. But when she expresses an interest in learning French, learning to play the violin, or learning computer programming or calculus, you might be at a loss. Never fear; your child's ambitions won't need to be nipped in the bud.

Local libraries usually have CDs or DVDs on conversational French and other foreign languages. There might be accomplished violinists in your area who are eager to teach the violin to your child; contact local music stores or nearby colleges for recommendations of instructors. If your child is eager to learn computer programming, once more you can turn to your local college. They may have programming students who could start your son or daughter on the road to writing code.

ESSENTIAL

Retired professionals, especially retired teachers, are often interested in tutoring or being a mentor to a child. Contact your local association of retired professionals, and arrange a meeting between interested parties and your family.

When subjects become too difficult for you to confidently handle, then a tutor or mentor may be the answer. Tutors can be found online or in the Yellow Pages. If your searches are not fruitful, call your local school district—they often keep lists of tutors—or contact the public library or college.

Resources for Creating a Curriculum

To design your own curriculum, read *How to Write a Low-Cost, No-Cost Curriculum* by Borg Hendrickson or *Home Learning Year by Year* by Rebecca Rupp. Or use the "Typical Course of Study" from WorldBook.com as a guideline for subjects to include in your homeschool curriculum.

CHAPTER 10

Common Core State Standards

The Common Core is a set of academic standards that was created to make sure all students obtain the skills and knowledge they need to succeed in school, college, the workforce, and in life. In order to boost the academic progress of all American students, the standards established consistent learning goals across states. However, the standards have stirred controversy in communities around the nation, including their impact on homeschooling families. Many homeschool families are opposed to the Common Core State Standards, due to unproven outcomes from the standards, as well as unhappiness with government involvement in families' educational goals, values, and personal standards. As with any educational guideline or mission, though, it can be helpful to have an understanding of the standards and their impact on education today. This chapter explains the standards and how they may influence your homeschooler, so you can make informed choices for your child's education.

Purpose of Common Core Standards

The Common Core State Standards (CCSS), established in 2009, were developed by state education chiefs and governors of forty-eight states. Approximately forty-five states adopted the Common Core Standards, but some states have since opted out of the program. The original intent of these standards was to "ensure that all students graduate from high school with the skills and knowledge necessary to succeed in college, career, and life," according to the Common Core State Standards Initiative.

Concern had mounted over the uniformity of educational standards in public schools, which could vary from one state to the next. Many colleges and universities found that they were spending more time on remedial education, especially in mathematics, as students entered their institutions. With a more consistent set of standards for states to follow, educators and college admissions officers are hoping that students' level of knowledge and skills will be more uniform upon graduation from high school.

The Common Core Standards were built upon previous state standards. The developmental team used input from teachers, state commissioners of education, and education researchers to upgrade the previous state standards and create the current standards. They focused on the skills and knowledge that students would need to be "globally competitive."

Timeline of the Standards

In 2008, an advisory group was formed to discuss and research the creation of a new set of standards. The advisory group consisted of state governors, education chiefs, and researchers. They set about developing the new standards and drafting outlines of the standards for review. In 2009, the majority of states had agreed to participate in the process of reviewing and providing feedback on the new Common Core Standards.

By June 2010, a final, revised version of the standards was released. In 2011 and 2012, individual states went through the process of reviewing and adopting the standards, with forty-five states adopting the standards in 2013. By 2014, a few states had opted out of the standards, with more states intending to reevaluate the impact of the standards over the next two to three years.

Examples of Core State Standards

Explanations and examples of the Common Core Standards for English Language Arts (ELA) and for Mathematics can be found on the Common Core website at *www.corestandards.org*. On the website, select the "Read the Standards" page, then choose the "English Language Arts/Literacy Standards" or the "Mathematics Standards" from the menu.

The "English Language Arts Standards" are provided on the right of the ELA page, where you can select any grade level between kindergarten and grade twelve. The "Mathematics Standards" are listed on the right of the Mathematics page for kindergarten through grade eight. The high school math standards are listed by topic, such as high school algebra, geometry, and statistics and probability.

English Language Arts Example

The following is an explanation and example of using standard English from the Common Core website for English Language Arts for Grade 5:

- Demonstrate command of the conventions of standard English grammar and usage when writing or speaking.
- Explain the function of conjunctions, prepositions, and interjections in general and their function in particular sentences.
- Form and use the perfect (e.g., *I had walked; I have walked; I will have walked*) verb tenses.
- Use verb tense to convey various times, sequences, states, and conditions.
- Recognize and correct inappropriate shifts in verb tense.
- Use correlative conjunctions (e.g., *either/or, neither/nor*).

Mathematics Example

Here is an explanation of writing and interpreting numerical expressions from the Common Core website for Mathematics for Grade 5:

- Use parentheses, brackets, or braces in numerical expressions, and evaluate expressions with these symbols.
- Write simple expressions that record calculations with numbers, and interpret numerical expressions without evaluating them. *For example,*

express the calculation "add 8 and 7, then multiply by 2" as 2 × (8 + 7). Recognize that 3 × (18932 + 921) is three times as large as 18932 + 921, without having to calculate the indicated sum or product.

As a homeschool family, you're not required to follow the Common Core State Standards. However, it's possible to use the standards as a guideline, if desired, in helping to select educational activities or topics for language arts or math. That should be a personal choice made by your family, based on your goals and standards.

Impact of Standards on Curriculum

Although the Common Core Standards Initiative states that the Common Core is not a curriculum, there is still a concern that it will evolve into a national curriculum. The standards are seen by some as an intent to mold a curriculum, resulting in a *national standard*, rather than a *state standard*. With the majority of states adopting the Common Core Standards, the possibility of a *national curriculum* becomes more real.

A national curriculum is concerning because it could lead to pressuring homeschoolers to adopt a curriculum not of their choosing. One of the main reasons you choose to educate your child at home is to follow an educational path that best serves your child's unique learning style and your family's goals and values.

Education cannot be forced upon anyone, and learning cannot be forced upon your child. However, when your child enjoys the curriculum, activities, and lessons you use, his learning, skills, and knowledge will continue to grow. If his education is not progressing as hoped, you have the freedom to change your curriculum or your homeschooling method. However, if a national curriculum were to be implemented and homeschoolers were pressured to use it, your freedom to choose or change your curriculum could be impacted.

Effect on Educational and Test Materials

Educational materials, such as textbooks and workbooks, are sometimes used by homeschoolers. Some of those materials have been revised to reflect the

Common Core Standards—or marked as Common Core compatible—and the prices attached to such materials are often high. The problem is that rather than developing new textbooks, many textbook publishers have simply added labels or seals to indicate that the texts align with the Common Core Standards.

Even when textbooks indicate that they align with the standards, teachers and educators have found concepts outlined by the Common Core Standards Initiative missing from the texts, or the concepts might be included in a textbook for a different grade level. This results in problems with the Common Core standardized testing required of students. Without true Common Core textbooks, it's up to the teacher to provide the missing links or to "teach to the test" in order to prepare students for the standardized tests.

Tests and Homeschooling

In homeschool families, the main educational goal is not "teaching to the test." Rather, the goal is to provide an expansive, well-rounded education and encourage children to think creatively, imaginatively, inventively, and logically from many different angles and perspectives.

As an assessment tool, some states have allowed homeschooled children to take part in standardized tests if desired. For families who might have chosen this path, the idea of the Common Core-aligned tests is not a welcome choice. A few states could require the test as part of their state's homeschool laws. In most cases, it is possible to opt out of the standardized tests, but you'll want to check with your state's requirements ahead of time to be sure.

College Admissions and the Standards

Some colleges are changing their readiness standards based on the Common Core Standards and are working in conjunction with public high schools to prepare students for their particular institution. This would be discriminatory toward the private school or homeschooled student. Similar to state standardized tests, some college admissions tests are being rewritten to accommodate the Core Standards.

Homeschooled students often score higher on standardized tests. For some families, it's not the test or the scores that's an issue. It's the standardization of education, the control of education, and thus, the standardization and control of people, as a whole, which becomes the bigger issue.

One of the problems with Common Core today is not knowing the outcome of the standards or the impact upon students' learning, test results, graduation, and college preparedness. It will still be several years before the successes or failures of the standards can be assessed and evaluated. This can place public school students in an uncertain situation until further results are observed.

Privacy Issues and Data Tracking

Student-data tracking in public schools is another area of concern for parents. With the development of state longitudinal data systems, the adoption of a national student database containing personal student information becomes more real. Some believe there is a connection between data tracking and the Common Core Standards Initiative. However, the CCSI states that there are no data requirements of states using the standards.

Whether there is or isn't a connection to Common Core, many school systems do collect and keep student information. In the past, this included school records, courses studied, grades, and transcripts. Today, the data can include a student's health and fitness levels, student activities, test results, attitude and behavior issues, social issues, disciplinary matters, and drug or alcohol use. The information can be compiled and maintained in databases permanently. Databases can be hacked and personal information leaked or accessed at any time in the years to come.

Seen as an invasion of privacy, parents are understandably opposed to student data-tracking and to state and federal encroachment into their lives. This is just one more reason that parents turn to educating their children in the safety and security of their own homes.

Opposition to the Standards

Homeschool families choose homeschooling for a variety of reasons. Most feel that the one-on-one attention they can give to their child exceeds the attention a child can receive in the classroom. Many feel that the home environment is a safer, more natural environment for learning to occur. Many found that the public schools were not succeeding—whether that was last year, or five years ago, or ten or twenty years ago.

Initially, the Common Core Standards were developed for public schools. However, homeschool families are concerned that state and federal involvement could affect virtual charter schools, many of which are run through public schools.

Charter Schools and Common Core

Public-school-based charter schools also adhere to the Common Core Standards if their state has committed to the standards. So although you might be homeschooling your child through a virtual charter school, you could be committed to the Common Core Standards, as well.

Melissa and Todd had enrolled their daughter in a well-known and highly recommended virtual school. At first, everyone was happy with the arrangement. Their daughter could learn at home, rather than spending nearly an hour on the bus to and from school, in addition to six hours at the school.

But it wasn't long before Melissa and Todd heard their daughter complain that the lessons were "just like school" or similar to homework assignments. She—and they—had expected more from her homeschooling experience. They soon joined a local homeschool group and were surprised to hear from other families that the virtual charter school was basically public school online. In addition, the curriculum followed the Common Core Standards, which they hadn't been a fan of from the beginning.

They changed to a more flexible learning style, embracing more variety and creativity in their days. Melissa noticed an immediate improvement in their daughter's outlook. "Now, she's eager to homeschool," said Melissa, "and she looks forward to delving into all sorts of projects. It makes me happy to see her happy and learning. She's also moving ahead quicker in all her lessons. I can see that she's retaining what she's learning more thoroughly, too."

Unproven Outcomes

As parents teach and guide their children each day, they can closely monitor what their child is grasping or not grasping, how quickly their child is advancing, or where their child is stumbling. At that point, parents can make adjustments or take the time that is necessary to get their child on-track, to help their child comprehend and understand, to learn and advance, in a way that works and succeeds for that particular child.

With new, unproven State Standards, which rely upon revised, standardized tests, the results or outcome of the Common Core Standards might not be known for years. The homeschool parent, however, can see results or outcomes in their child every day, and they can address those results accordingly.

Educational Standards as Guidelines

As a homeschool family, you're already accustomed to setting your own educational standards for your children, following those standards, and ensuring that your children are making progress in accordance with those standards. Educational standards have been created and implemented for public schools for decades. These standards change and evolve over time. For some families, a set of standards can be helpful as a guideline to follow or for additional learning activities, should you run out of your own educational ideas.

ESSENTIAL

Don't confuse educational standards with a curriculum. Standards are a statement of goals and expectations you have for your child's education. A curriculum is made up of lessons, activities, and projects that your child can use to achieve your educational standards and goals.

You might want to compare your standards and your curriculum goals with those outlined in the Common Core Standards, and make choices based upon your own child's current skills and abilities. This can be particularly helpful if you plan to enroll your child in a public school within the next few years. In this case, it would be wise to stay up to date on your state's standards and keep your curriculum in line with your state's educational standards.

For most homeschool families, though, the beauty of homeschooling is the ability to create your own standards and adapt your curriculum, learning activities, and lessons to best serve your children's educational needs now and for the future.

CHAPTER 11

Homeschool Schedules

Organizing your homeschool day might seem impossible at times. Your daily schedule could be similar to a conventional school day, or it might revolve around free-flowing "unschooled" days. Whichever style of homeschooling you've chosen, this chapter will help you develop a schedule or format that will work well for your family.

Create a Plan

The type of schedule your family follows will largely depend upon the type of homeschool your children are involved with. If they are enrolled in a correspondence school, their schedule may need to accommodate the school's time requirements for completing assignments and courses. If they are enrolled in a self-paced independent study program, they're encouraged to complete certain portions of the program within a suggested time frame. If you're using unit studies, you may allot one week or several months for a unit, and you'll have topics you'll want to cover within a period of days or weeks. If your family is following an unschooled or eclectic style, your schedule may be somewhat more relaxed than others.

Getting Off to a Good Start

When you first begin homeschooling, ease into it gently. If homeschooling has been a way of life at your house since your first child was born, the transition into homeschooling comes naturally. If, however, you decide it's time for school when your child turns five or six, or you've just removed your eight-, twelve-, or fifteen-year-old from a traditional school, the transition requires some tender handling.

For the child removed from school, allow for the much-needed decompression time before implementing a homeschool schedule. She will need time to unwind from the hectic schedule she's been following. She will also need to learn how to move through her day without the prompting of bells. She'll need to get in tune with the natural ebb and flow of daily life in her own home.

For the five- or six-year-old who is ready for school, ease into a homeschool schedule that fits her abilities, skills, attention span, and level of maturity. Some kindergarten-aged children can sit still for thirty minutes at a time, while others simply can't. Some have well-developed fine motor skills, enabling them to handle crayons and pencils well. Others still have difficulty getting the pencil to move exactly where they'd like. For these children, spending thirty minutes printing A-B-Cs is nearly torturous, sometimes leading to painful cramping in the fingers and hand. Other children, however, might enjoy printing their A-B-Cs and writing letters or stories for an hour at a time. Know your child, her learning style, and her abilities before implementing a homeschool style.

ESSENTIAL

Flexibility is the key to a smooth-running homeschool, and it is also a stress-reliever. When you expect too much of yourself—or too much of your children—you'll burden yourself with a schedule that's difficult to keep. And you'll set your family up for a less-than-enjoyable homeschool experience.

Avoid the temptation to structure homeschool days based on your memories of school schedules. School schedules were developed to handle hundreds of students each day and move them through the system as quickly and efficiently as possible. Since you won't have nearly as many children in your home, a school-based schedule is neither appropriate nor necessary.

Easing into a Schedule

Schedules shouldn't be too binding or restrictive. Basically, schedules provide structure to our days, and structure helps to delineate our daily lives. For children, structure can provide feelings of security and stability. It helps to establish a foundation with everyday routines and a way of life that children can depend on and feel comfortable with.

As you create a schedule for your homeschool day, stick close to the routines your children are already familiar with. If your children are accustomed to waking at 7:30 A.M. and having breakfast at 8:00 A.M., there's no need to change that schedule when you begin homeschooling. After breakfast, the children can help clean up the kitchen, make their beds, and get ready for their day. You can plan to have lunch and dinner at your usual times, playtime and bedtime as before, and weave the educational activities into the daily routine.

Start gently, perhaps by reading aloud from a favorite book in the mornings and doing artwork or crafts before lunch. Following lunch, the children can play quietly with puzzles or games, then go outside or into the garage for recreation time or take a walk to the park. Upon returning to the house, you may want to do a lesson that focuses on history or science. The next day, perhaps you'll want to include a math lesson or a spelling game. Most important, avoid trying to do too much in one day, especially as you are starting out.

Flexible Schedules

Once you're able to look back on a few weeks and see how much your child has learned on his own, you'll understand that adhering to a strict schedule is not a requirement in the homeschool. Children will learn; you need not worry about that. As long as you set a good example, show interest in reading and learning new things, show interest in your children and in their interests, provide some guidance and be available to help answer their questions, children will learn.

Now, they may not always learn exactly what you want them to learn at the exact time you want them to learn it, but that's the beauty of built-in flexibility. If they don't learn algebra this year, they can learn it next year. If they can't grasp genetic engineering this year, they can try again next year.

As you've found, not every child walks, or talks or learns to tie his shoes or ride a bike, at the same age. Similarly, not every child can grasp algebra at age fourteen or genetic engineering at age fifteen.

The Unschool Schedule

The schedule an unschooler follows may not include English class from 9:00 to 9:30, math from 9:30 until 10:00, and so on. However, the unschooler usually finds himself reading and writing each day, mainly because he enjoys it. And, as a result, his English and composition skills improve through practicing something that he enjoys. The unschooler often uses math skills, logical thinking skills, and computational skills as he designs, measures, and builds a birdhouse or helps reconcile the family's checkbook and learns how to live within a budget.

ESSENTIAL

Although an unschooler's day may not be as cut and dried as a more stringent homeschool day, you can still keep daily records. Write down the activities your child is involved with each day. Document the books read, the progress of projects, research conducted, and experiments performed, or have your child write them in a journal.

The unschooler understands that part of his responsibility as a youngster in his household is to get a good education. He has usually been encouraged to read anything that interests him, to pursue any hobbies that interest him, and to research any subjects that interest him. As a result, the unschooler naturally establishes a routine of sorts that works for him and his areas of interest. Although it may not be the type of homeschool schedule some families follow, it's a familiar direction that his days take, one that he's comfortable with.

Trusting Natural Learning

Since many children have never experienced unschooling or natural learning, they could feel confused by the concept of it. To see how they respond, try opening up your homeschool schedule by allowing more free time between studies for pursuing things that interest your child. For instance, if you have English from 9:00 to 9:30, let your child work on a hobby between 9:30 and 10:00, then go on to a math lesson for half an hour, then allow a couple hours for scientific explorations that interest him.

After lunch, you could read a biography or history book together, then encourage him to learn something more about the era you just read about. Maybe he'd want to research the type of games kids played in that era, or the toys they had, or how people survived without electricity and technology. Then, rather than writing a report about what he learns, encourage him to reproduce a toy similar to what kids had in those days, and the two of you can play a game with it. Or suggest that he create an invention that could have made life easier for folks during that period of history.

FACT

Some children learn better with a traditional school-like schedule. If you've given your child ample opportunities to try a less-structured schedule and he just doesn't take to it, then he's helped you to better understand his preferred learning style. Rather than trying to change your child to one style or another, let him show you how he learns best.

By suggesting alternatives to doing worksheets and writing reports, you help him open his mind to other ways of learning. Over time, you may find that he learns more—and retains more—when he actively pursues areas that relate to his lessons. He has more control over what he studies and what he learns, he therefore has more interest in it, and, consequently, it has more meaning for him.

Scheduling Suggestions

Here are the average times generally required to cover reading, math, language arts, social studies, and science each day:

- **Preschool and kindergarten:** 30 to 60 minutes
- **Elementary ages:** 60 to 90 minutes
- **Middle-school ages:** 1½ to 3 hours
- **High-school ages:** 2 to 4 hours

In a conventional school, a six-hour day is consumed by attendance taking, quieting the class, handling disruptive students, helping other students, lunch, recesses, physical education, showers, school assemblies, pep rallies, numerous minutes wasted between each class, and oodles of paperwork. In your homeschool, you won't need to schedule many of these events into your day. Plus, you won't be handling twenty-five or thirty children in your homeschool each day.

ESSENTIAL

Rather than a six-hour school day, or even a four-hour school day, you can generally cover the required subjects within one to three hours, depending on your child's age. Maybe you'll focus on lessons for a couple hours in the morning, then spend an hour on lessons later in the afternoon. The schedule should blend smoothly with your family's daily routines.

Remember that your child is unique. Your kindergartner may only need thirty minutes of formal studies each day, or she may enjoy sixty minutes.

Your thirteen-year-old may cover her lessons in two hours, or she may spend four hours on her lessons. Take time to observe your child, her interest in her studies, her attention span, the way she tires, or the way she seems to get a second wind later in the day. When you work with her capabilities, rather than trying to force someone else's schedule upon her, the homeschool day will proceed more smoothly.

Covering the Core Subjects

Even though math, language arts, social studies, and science are important subjects to be covered, you can build flexibility into your schedule. If it generally takes two or three hours to cover these subjects for a middle-grader, it doesn't mean they all have to fit into those daily two- or three-hour slots. Here's a summary of one way that could be used to cover lessons for a middle-schooler:

- **Monday:** In science, spent three hours reading about convection and conduction, performed several experiments under supervision with steam and heat vapors, and wrote a summary of what was learned.
- **Tuesday:** In social studies, spent two and a half hours reading about the Battle of Shiloh, learned more about General Grant's and General Johnston's roles, drew a map of the battlefield, and began working on a model of the battlefield.
- **Wednesday:** In language arts, spent four hours reading a story, rewrote it in a screenplay format, assigned characters to the parts, designed props, and made plans to perform the play.
- **Thursday:** In math, spent three hours working on a lesson in the geometry textbook, did logical reasoning puzzles in a software program, used foam models to draw accurate representation of cones and cubes, and used geometry concepts to help design and create model of Shiloh battlefield.
- **Friday:** Worked on battlefield model more, began reading book by Gary Paulsen about the Civil War, got together with friends for games and experiments, began writing a story about a boy during the Civil War.

Although this schedule may not be a conventional schedule, this middle-schooler spent about the same amount of time on each subject area over the course of one week as a child following a more typical school schedule. More important, he had special interest in each topic he participated in, had time to expand upon the topics or to put new knowledge into practice, and consequently retained the information longer, due to his interest and involvement.

Adding Variety Each Day

In addition to the time spent on required subject areas, such as math and English, you can keep a wellspring of ideas for other educational opportunities for each day. Before or after the required subjects have been covered, children can focus on their special areas of interest, try a new hobby or craft, work on an ongoing project, or research new ideas.

One family cut up dozens of strips of plain paper, then began jotting down things they enjoyed doing, or things they'd like to do, on the strips of paper. They then folded the strips and dropped them into a plastic jar. On days when the kids couldn't think of anything to occupy themselves with, or they were simply bored, they would reach into the jar and pull out a strip of paper with an idea on it. If that idea didn't strike their fancy at that particular moment, they could always drop the paper back into the jar and select another slip of paper. Soon, the kids were immersed in motivating activities that they had forgotten about, that they enjoyed doing, and that helped to supplement their education.

Time Management Tips

When you have a family to take care of daily—perhaps a baby, a toddler, and a couple of older youngsters—and a house to keep tidy and errands to run, it may seem as though the day is gone before you've even had a moment to think about it. How will you incorporate homeschooling into such a busy schedule that already consumes the majority of your day? As often as we've heard it, it's still true: We *do* make time for the things we want to do in our lives. It just depends on how badly we want it. If homeschooling the kids is important enough to you, chances are you can find the time to do it.

ALERT

Remember: Homeschooling is not a school at home. Don't confuse yourself or your children, thinking that it should be. You'll only make it harder on yourself. A *school* is an institution or a facility. A *home* is where you live with your family. *Homeschooling* is a way of living. It includes training and guidance in the home—a warm, comfortable, safe environment within the family unit.

As you've previously seen, you don't need to follow a school-at-home schedule. Simply allow your kids to learn, have an idea of what they should be learning, provide some guidance and ideas for them each week, and be there to help answer their questions, to provide direction, and to be a sounding board for ideas to bounce off of for input and feedback.

Setting Weekly Goals

Goal-setting is the key to time management. Each weekend, decide the five most important things you want to accomplish in your homeschool during the upcoming week, and write them down. You have five days ahead of you to accomplish those five goals. Cross one off each day, or cross two off one day and one off the next. However you want to handle it, try to accomplish and cross off your five goals at some point during that week. Do this each week, and you'll be surprised at how much you are capable of accomplishing.

Try to focus on the most important goal, then move on to the next. The goals may vary from week to week. For instance, this upcoming week, your most important goal may be to cover three lessons in the math book. The least important goal this week may be to read about the Industrial Revolution.

When focusing on the math goal, determine the period of time during the day when your child is most alert and receptive to math lessons. This could be first thing in the morning, or it could be at 4:00 in the afternoon. If the math lessons need your undivided attention, and you have babies or toddlers in the home, try to time those lessons with the younger children's naptime. If that's not possible, perhaps an older child can entertain the younger ones while you help your child with math lessons.

Simplify Daily Tasks

Each person living in the home has duties to fulfill within the family. A list of responsibilities for each person, children included, can be posted in plain view, so that no questions or squabbles arise. Each child can certainly be responsible for his or her room, bed making, linen changing, closet cleaning, polishing of furniture, vacuuming of floors (if capable), or general tidying up. In the rest of the house, everyone can take turns vacuuming, polishing furniture, and cleaning bathrooms. You may do it one week, the next week your daughter may handle it, the following week your son may be responsible for it, and so on. Or, you can all jump in together one afternoon and complete the housecleaning in an hour or two.

Here are some ways to streamline the chores:

- Prepare and cook several dishes, soups, or casseroles on Saturday or Sunday afternoon, then freeze them for the upcoming week.
- Enlist the help of children in daily meal preparations; mixing muffins, setting the table, clearing the table, scraping off dishes, putting away leftovers, and so on.
- Assign each child certain responsibilities in the home, or let them select, switch, or share chores with each other.
- Give each child a box or basket and send them through the house to pick up any items that are out of place.
- Play classical or pop music to make the cleanup time more enjoyable for all. Sing and discuss the music as you clean house, and you've just covered your music lesson for the day.
- Have children help on laundry day as they sort colors, remove clothes from the dryer, match socks, fold and hang clothing—all while you're discussing a history lesson.
- Combine errands, when possible, to save on driving time.

Timesaving Tips from Homeschool Parents

Here are timesaving tips that homeschool parents have shared. Try them in your homeschool:

- Keep all homeschooling books, supplies, records, and logs in one closet so they are easy to locate.
- Jot down weekly goals and lesson plans while having your morning coffee, watching the evening news, or nestling a baby in your lap.
- Have older children keep their own daily logs of books read, assignments done, and projects completed.
- Encourage older children to help younger ones with lessons and to record some of the younger children's activities in the daily log.
- Use colorful, stimulating books from the library to cover subjects that children tend to drag over.
- Incorporate as many skills as possible into a lesson plan, such as reading and writing skills, experimentation skills, estimation or calculation skills, and analytic skills.
- Include several periods of free time during the day, providing a break for the children and time for you to accomplish other activities.

Read to children and discuss as many topics as possible, rather than assigning chapters in textbooks. This reduces time spent dawdling over dry material and answering chapter questions. You also won't have to spend time grading papers when you engage in discussions. Plus, children retain more from lively discussions than from textbooks.

Time to Unwind

Now it's time for some much-deserved rest and relaxation! Both are necessary components for a stress-free day, so be sure to allow time for them in your homeschool schedule. Each day should have a pleasant balance of active time and quiet time. The experiments, construction projects, nature walks, sports, and other physical activities should be interspersed with reading time, quiet playtime, and rest time.

If you find that a half-hour of rest each day isn't enough, try an hour of rest and relaxation. If that still isn't enough to refresh you, or you feel stressed every day, it could be time for some extended rest and relaxation—in other words, vacation time! And that's one of the benefits of homeschooling—you can take a break or vacation whenever you need it. And when you return to your homeschool schedule, you'll have the energy to see you through until it's time to take another well-deserved break!

Resources for Organizing Your Homeschool

To keep track of lessons and activities, use the charts and forms on the "Homeschool Forms" page at *www.EverythingHomeschooling.com*. Or read *Homeschooling at the Speed of Life* by Marilyn Rockett on organizing and de-stressing your homeschool days.

CHAPTER 12

Homeschool Record Keeping

Your state could require you to keep homeschool records of some sort. These could include "attendance" records, immunization records, or daily or weekly logs of educational activities. Even if it's not mandatory in your state, homeschool records are still valuable tools. They'll help you keep track of lessons, monitor and assess your child's progress, provide verification of your child's education, and document the educational background of your child for college officials.

A Curriculum Outline

Your state department of education could require an outline of your planned curriculum or course of study. Even if it's not required, a curriculum outline makes it easier to plan and record your lessons for the upcoming weeks or months. Earlier, you determined the educational goals and aims for your child. You can use that outline to plan your homeschool year, and to break down your goals into monthly and weekly lesson plans.

Educational Objectives

Your family's educational objectives may include the following:

- Reading quality literature and classics
- Improving speaking and writing skills
- Improving mathematical and scientific abilities
- Understanding world and national history
- Enhancing musical and artistic skills
- Functioning responsibly and respectfully as a citizen

From these objectives, and others you may have, you can decide what subjects to study during the upcoming year to help achieve the goals for your family. You can select literary books to read, English and math textbooks you'd like to use, science and history activity books, music and art courses, and a character education program.

Keep a list of the books or materials you may want to use for your homeschool. Research them, or check with other families who have used those materials, to determine if they'd be compatible with your educational aims.

Topics to Cover

If you're using a curriculum guideline, such as the "Typical Course of Study" from World Book, Inc., or a guideline from a curriculum provider, you'll have a good idea of the subjects you plan to cover during the homeschool year. Another way to determine what you'd like to cover during the upcoming year is to check the table of contents in used textbooks for your child's grade level.

For example, a third-grade science book might list the following chapters in the table of contents: Animal Life Cycles; Plant Life Cycles; Environment and Habitats; Adaptation; Matter; Energy; Machines, Force, and Motion; Sun, Moon, and Planets; and Natural Resources. You'll see topics or areas to study listed under each chapter. Under Natural Resources, you may see topics such as air quality, air pressure, atmospheric gases, climatic changes, the water cycle, water sources, drinking water, pollution, and so on.

FACT

Midsummer is the prime time for ordering homeschool materials for many families. If you plan to start homeschooling in the middle of August, you'll want your materials on hand a few weeks prior to your start date. Therefore, you'd want to place your order in July. This means that June would be a good time to establish a plan for your upcoming homeschool year.

By reading the table of contents in textbooks, you'll gain a better understanding of the topics to cover during the year, and you'll be able to formulate more succinct ideas for lesson plans. With your ideas in hand, research the local library or Internet for books or materials to help present the lessons and activities. Make a list of books and items you plan to use, and keep the list in your plan book.

If you homeschooled the previous year and did not cover everything you had planned, you can work these areas into summer activities or carry them over to the upcoming year. Be sure to list them in your plan book. Keep notes on areas that may need extra attention, too. Take these areas into account when planning lessons for the upcoming year.

Your Lesson Plan Book

In your lesson plan book, record descriptions of lesson plans for each day of the week. Write plans and activities to cover four weeks in a row, and you'll have your homeschool agenda planned for an entire month. This record of daily lesson plans serves as a timesaving map that will keep your family pointed in the right direction all year long so that you can, indeed, reach your goals.

It's not necessary to purchase a formal teacher's plan book. You can create your own with notebook paper or copy paper. Or you might prefer to keep track of lessons in a spreadsheet or computer program. Divide the sheets of paper into columns, headed with the days of the week. Two pages provide adequate room for listing schooldays from Monday through Friday. Along the side of one sheet, list the subjects, such as math, language arts, social studies, science, and so on. Allow space for notes on special activities, goals, or field trips you may have planned for the week.

QUESTION

I'm running out of lesson plan ideas. What do I do?
For quick lesson plan ideas, look through homeschool supply catalogs and homeschool magazines, check lesson plan sites on the Internet, or browse the shelves of a nearby teacher supply store. For weekly lesson plans throughout the homeschool year, visit *www.EverythingHomeschooling.com.*

Make several copies of your lesson plan templates, and simply fill in the blanks for each day of the week. If there's a format that works better for your homeschool style, feel free to use it. Then place your lesson plan sheets into a three-ring binder or folder, and you have your lesson plan book.

Creating Lesson Plans

Saturday or Sunday afternoons are often a favorite time to create lesson plans for the upcoming week. Most of the week's work has been completed, and the kids are usually playing contentedly in the bedroom or backyard, or spending time with Dad or with friends. You can relax in the living room or at the dining table and spread out your notebooks and your thoughts as you contemplate the week ahead.

You've already established your goals for the year, and you've created your short-term goals regarding the subjects you plan to cover. Consequently, you know what topics you'll want to cover in the upcoming week. You consult your stack of library books or look over the "Typical Course of Study" guidelines, and begin jotting brief descriptions of lesson plans for each subject in your lesson plan book.

Depending on how much preparation has gone into your homeschool goals and how organized you are, writing up a week's lesson plans can take an hour or two. Therefore, writing up lesson plans for an entire month may require a few extra hours out of your afternoon. This may sound like a lot, but many homeschool parents find it an enjoyable and inspiring way to spend an afternoon.

Keeping a Daily Logbook

Some states require homeschool families to keep a logbook or other types of records. To check your state's homeschool laws, consult the coordinator of your school district's homeschool department or contact your state department of education. Even if you're not required to keep such records, it's helpful to have documentation of your child's homeschool years, subjects studied, lessons covered, and other proof of educational activities. So, rather than feeling relieved that you're not required to keep records, consider the benefits of doing so and enjoy the process.

Creating a Logbook

The lesson plan book mentioned in the previous section helps to map out your curriculum week by week. It can also double as your homeschool logbook. If yours is a more freestyle unschooling format, you may not create actual lesson plans for each day. Therefore, the logbook is ideal for jotting down activities your child participated in during the day. A lesson plan book is generally prepared in advance of each day's lessons. The logbook is updated after the day's events have occurred.

You can purchase a weekly logbook for homeschoolers, or you can create your own. In many ways, it's like keeping a diary or journal. Once again, you can use notebook paper, copy paper, or the computer. Put the day's date on the paper, and write brief descriptions of what your children did that day in each subject area. Then place the paper in your three-ring binder or folder. You could also use a pocket calendar or an inexpensive day planner with plenty of writing space to describe what your child accomplished that day.

Recording Materials Used

In addition to the daily or weekly logbook, some states want to see a list of books, resources, or other materials used in your homeschool. On the back of your weekly log sheets, you can add a section for recording the titles of books or educational DVDs, as well as space for notes or activities related to lessons. This makes it easy to keep everything together, week by week, in one binder. When the homeschool evaluator looks over the material, she could flip through the binder and quickly see what books, resources, and activities accompanied the weekly lessons.

You can create a similar chart on the back of your daily log sheets. Block off space for the title of the book or resource, the author or publisher, and the date. You may even want to note how the resource was used. For instance:

Title of Book: *The Young Naturalist*
Author/Publisher: Usborne Books/EDC Publishing
Date Read: 9/7/2015 – 9/14/2015

Notes: Used in science for identifying insects in a freshly dug patch of soil; identifying fungi on tree bark; creating a bottle garden; and dissecting the parts of a flower and identifying under the microscope.

You can also list any educational videos or DVDs your children watched or books they read for pleasure. This provides the homeschool evaluator more insight into your children's interests, or simply helps you keep track of books your children have read. If the books relate to lessons in any way, you can note that as well.

Your Child's Learning Log

If your children are old enough, they can keep their own learning logs. When they write about the projects and topics they learned each day, it helps to imprint that knowledge in their minds, and they will retain the information longer.

Keeping their own learning logs will accomplish three things. It will: 1. Save you time recording their activities, 2. Provide daily writing practice for language arts, and 3. Establish the habit of writing down notes, which will be helpful to your children's education in the years ahead.

Maintaining a Homeschool Portfolio

If you're required to keep a homeschool portfolio, some states want it available for inspection monthly or quarterly; others may request to see the portfolio annually or upon request, usually with a thirty-day advance notice.

The portfolio is fairly easy to maintain and it's often an important part of the annual evaluation process. Plus, it makes good sense to have documentation of what your child is doing and achieving month by month, regardless of how formal or informal your homeschool is.

ALERT

Your child's portfolio can be helpful when it's time to apply to college. You may not need to keep *every* worksheet, assignment, drawing, or project for the portfolio, but maintain a good variety for each subject area. A well-rounded portfolio helps college officials gain a clearer picture of your child's homeschool years.

Your child's homeschool portfolio can include the lesson plan book or weekly learning log, books used and read, attendance records, daily worksheets, creative writing assignments, book reports, and written evaluations or test results. You can also include examples of typical days, artwork, scrapbooks of hobby projects, inventions or projects built, and descriptions or photos of projects, experiments, special activities, or field trips. Another good way to document your child's abilities is to video-record speeches, performances, concerts, sport competitions, trips, and other events.

Reviewing the Portfolio

Check with your local homeschool officials in advance and see how much they expect you to bring when it's time to present your child's portfolio. Other items you may want to keep with the portfolio are copies of your child's immunization records, verification of your child's homeschool registration with your school district, or paperwork certifying that your child is enrolled with a private school or distance-learning program.

Keeping Attendance Records

Some states could require you to keep attendance records. This may seem somewhat silly, considering the fact that your child is obviously in attendance in the home each day. But your state might require that the child is homeschooled a specific number of days or hours each year, and they want to see proof of it. Check with the homeschool division of your local school district or with your state department of education to determine their exact requirements for homeschool attendance keeping.

Some homeschool officials consider the weekly learning log, which documents the activities and studies conducted each day, as an adequate attendance record. It shows the weekly dates, the number of days your child was involved in educational activities, and the hours your child was engaged in educational activities each day. Or, you may be able to keep a simple calendar with your weekly learning log, and jot down the number of hours spent on home education each day.

ESSENTIAL

Forms such as attendance records, learning log pages, lesson plan sheets, grade records, evaluation forms, and high school transcripts are available on the Internet or in many homeschooling books. These are usually available for downloading, printing, or photocopying.

Other officials may prefer to see a traditional style of attendance record, documenting your child's name, grade level, the year, and the week, with each day of the week listed at the top of the page. Under each day of the week, from September 21 to September 25, for example, you would mark the number of hours spent on educational activities each day. If the time spent studying core subjects was three hours, and the time your child spent reading or pursuing other educational activities that day was three hours, you would record six hours for the day.

Assessment Alternatives

You'll need to have a way to determine what your children are learning and retaining each week. In conventional schools, tests or essay papers are a common method for assessing children's knowledge. In the home, you may prefer to assess your children's abilities based upon your close observations of them.

When you determine what your children already know, or where their weaknesses lie, you can supplement the curriculum accordingly. There's no need to focus repeatedly on the Civil War if your child already has a good understanding of it. Through your observations, you may find that he doesn't have a good grasp of the voting process or the branches of the government. Therefore, instead of studying the Civil War again this year, you can spend more time on the processes of the government or perhaps create a unit study on it.

Evaluating Progress

Talk with your children daily about what they're studying and learning. Engage them in family conversations about topics they've read, researched, or been involved with. From general conversations and your child's responses to questions, you can easily determine what your child is learning. After a lesson, you could have your child explain what he gleaned from the lesson and have him elaborate upon it, perhaps even making a video recording of his presentation.

Your child could write a short paper about what he learned, or draw and label the parts of a plant cell and an animal cell, for instance, or match proper definitions with new science vocabulary words. He could do a project based on the lesson, such as create a model of a plant cell and an animal cell from clay. You could also give him quizzes based on the information he just read or discussed, and have him write down his answers.

Reporting Progress

From observing, listening, grading, or assessing your child's knowledge and abilities, you can compare them against your educational goals for your child. You'll be able to determine how he's progressing, and you can make improvements where needed before too many days or weeks have passed by. At the end of each semester, you'll have an ongoing progress report to keep with your child's portfolio. You can refer to this report from year to year to refresh your memory of his progress, plus it will be helpful to homeschool officials who may want to assess your child's abilities.

Recording Grades and Credits Earned

It can be beneficial to keep a record of your child's grades or credits earned per subject, particularly as he enters high school. You can purchase a traditional grade book like the ones that teachers use. This could be a timesaver if you're keeping track of grades for several children. Or, you can simply create your own grade book in a notebook or on the computer.

ALERT

Although grades can be an indicator of your child's comprehension of material, they are also a measure of the teacher's ability to convey information and guide the learning process. If your child is having difficulty grasping subjects, re-evaluate the teaching and learning styles within the homeschool, then try a new approach.

If you grade your children's papers (answer sheets are included in most workbooks and teacher edition textbooks), you can record their grades under each subject heading. To calculate grades, you can use a handheld cardboard grader, such as the E-Z Grader, to determine scores and letter grades on tests and worksheets. These sliding charts are inexpensive and are available at most teacher supply stores.

At the end of each six- or eight-week period, you can average out your children's grades. By acknowledging their grades *and* closely observing their daily performance or struggles with certain topics, you can help them improve on any weak areas.

Credits Earned

For high school graduation, a child usually needs about twenty-four credits in most states. Check with your state to determine their exact requirements. You can keep track of credits earned by entering credits on a high school transcript.

A credit is generally based upon 130 to 140 hours of study in a particular subject. If a child spends 45 minutes on English for the 180-day school year, he'll have spent 8,100 minutes, or 135 hours, which equals one credit.

In most cases, a half credit is earned in a subject in one semester, resulting in a full credit for a year's study in that subject. For instance, one semester of freshman English can equal one-half credit. The second semester gains another half credit. By the end of the child's freshman year, he has earned one full credit in English. At the end of four years, he should have earned four credits in English, as well as two or three credits in each of the other required subjects.

ESSENTIAL

Achievement awards and certificates can provide a sense of accomplishment and pride for your children. Educational supply companies or online sites have certificates available for nearly every situation: reading awards, science awards, honor roll and citizenship awards, high school diplomas, and more. These certificates and awards can serve as tangible signs of progress throughout the homeschool year.

After completing four years in your homeschool high school, your child can acquire twenty-four credits. These could include four credits in English, four in math, three in science, three in social studies, two in a foreign language, two in physical education, and six credits in electives (art, music, computer courses, business courses, or special courses of interest).

High-School Transcripts

Keeping track of credits earned through the high school years may not be mandatory, but if your child is planning to attend college, it's a good idea to keep a transcript. This is something your child can easily do. Create a transcript form by listing the subjects studied in the high school years. List the subjects by starting with the most important: English, literature, math, history, government, economics, science, and so on. List foreign languages and elective courses toward the end of the transcript.

At the end of the semester and the year, have your child record the number of credits earned in each subject or elective. Keep the transcript in a safe place with your child's other homeschool records, in case he should need to present a copy of it when applying for college.

A blank transcript form, and an example of keeping the transcript, is available for downloading and printing from *www.EverythingHomeschooling.com*.

Software programs for recording transcripts and calculating GPAs can be purchased from websites such as *www.FastTranscripts.com* or *www.HomeschoolTranscripts.com*.

Resources for Homeschool Records

You can select and print planner logbooks, attendance records, report cards, high school transcripts, and other forms from *www.EverythingHomeschooling.com*. For certificates, awards, diplomas and diploma covers, graduation announcements, and other high-school accessories, see *www.homeschooldiploma.com*.

CHAPTER 13

Organizing Your Homeschool

An efficient organization system allows your homeschool to run more smoothly. When you declutter your space, you also declutter your mind. This in turn frees up more time for fun, creative activities with your family. Your organization system should work for you and your family's needs, not the other way around. Look at the way you use the space in your home, determine how it could work better for your family, then put these tips to use.

Everything in Its Place

One of the most time-consuming activities is looking for misplaced items. To remedy this problem, create a place for everything and keep everything in its place. Remind your children to always return items to their spaces. Show them how to do a "clean sweep" of the room at the end of the day, to ensure each item is in its proper place and ready for the next day's activities. To declutter your spaces, take inventory of your homeschool supplies at the beginning of the year. Eliminate the nonessentials to make room for the new. Sell, recycle, or give away those books or games you just don't use. If there are items that you haven't touched for over a year and that are not imperative to keep, it may be time to let them go. Once they're gone, you'll have more space available for organizing the necessities.

These items will help solve most storage or display problems in the homeschool:

- Clear plastic containers for holding manipulatives or craft items
- Bins or baskets for textbooks, workbooks, or library books
- Plastic or cardboard containers for folders or projects
- Bookshelves for books, binders, puzzles, and science equipment
- Desks, tables, or trays for pencils, paper, and writing supplies
- Storage cabinets for craft materials and miscellaneous supplies
- File cabinets for important documents or lesson plan ideas
- Dry-erase boards for noting important memos or reminders
- Bulletin boards for displaying artwork or photos of projects

You and your children can make many of these storage or display items. Be creative and imaginative when decorating, labeling, and color-coding your storage containers. Design your own bulletin boards, using cork or foam board, fabric, and ribbons. Make your own memo stations, using chalkboard paint and dry-erase whiteboard material, available from home-improvement stores.

Storage Solutions

Keep all homeschool supplies in one area when possible. Many families devote a hall closet or former linen closet to their homeschool materials.

One shelf holds textbooks, another holds workbooks or folders of worksheets, another holds microscopes and chemistry sets, another holds arts and crafts supplies, and the floor holds boxes containing idea files, portfolios, binders, and other important homeschool documents.

Cardboard boxes can be used for storing binders or books flat, or to accommodate hanging file folders. Storage boxes with lids, drawers, or string-and-button closure systems are available in office supply stores. These usually provide adequate labeling space for noting the contents and the date of the materials.

ESSENTIAL

The day may come when you'll need proof of what your child accomplished during his homeschool years. Store papers, portfolios, and photos of projects by sealing them in plastic containers and labeling with your child's name and school year. Keep them in a well-protected area of the attic or basement, or on the upper shelves of a bedroom closet.

Declutter Your Domain

If there are certain areas in the home where things tend to pile up—for instance, on the dining room table, a side table, or a section of the snack counter—consider ways to declutter those areas. Clear out the bottom of a dining room hutch or kitchen cabinet to hold books or notebooks often left on the dining room table. These cabinets are normally located near the dining room and only require a few steps to transport the clutter from the table to the cabinet.

Organizing Baskets and Bins

For items that stack up on a side table, use an attractive wicker basket that can easily slide under the table, leaving the tabletop clutter-free. If your snack counter bears the brunt of a clutter attack, create areas where family members can tuck things away. A spice rack with drawers can hold rubber bands, paperclips, staples, pushpins, map tacks, and erasers. A letter holder mounted on the inside of a pantry door can contain a pocket calendar, notepaper, pens and pencils, a box of crayons, or a roll of tape. Plastic vertical files (such as those seen on the doors in doctor offices), mounted on the inside of a hall closet door, can hold current lesson plans, file folders, worksheets, or other paper supplies.

Clear plastic bins are excellent for storing anything from library books to workbooks, paint supplies, or math manipulatives. You can easily see through the bin and determine what it contains, further reducing the time spent looking for items. Plastic storage bags with zip-style tops are convenient for storing puzzles and puzzle pieces, games and game pieces, magnets and magnetic wands, packs of flash cards, art supplies, and more. They come in different sizes to accommodate a variety of items, large or small.

A Central Station

A desk or a table with drawers makes a convenient central station for homeschool supplies. Perhaps you have a family computer that can be set up on the table or desk. Place plastic organizers in the desk drawers to hold paper, pens, markers, crayons, paperclips, staplers, scissors, paste, glue sticks, rolls of tape, construction paper, index cards, and other supplies. Keep a spiral-bound notebook in a drawer by the family computer to jot down favorite homeschool websites and ideas for learning projects.

Place stackable letter trays on your desk, table, or bookshelf to accommodate worksheets and assignments. One tray could be for daily assignments that need your attention. One tray could be for artwork or miscellaneous projects the children have completed. Another tray could hold worksheets or project ideas for children to select and do on their own. For multiple children, set aside a stack of red trays for one child, blue trays for another, yellow for another. Each child can then easily find and retrieve his lessons, projects, or artwork.

Storing Magazines and Catalogs

It won't be long before you begin receiving numerous homeschool supply catalogs, flyers, newsletters, and magazines in the mail. Dedicate a box or bottom of a file cabinet or closet to your supply catalogs. You never know when you might want to browse through them—either to order something or to spark fresh educational ideas. As new catalogs arrive to replace the old, remember to toss the out-of-date ones. Store current catalogs and magazines in a bookcase or in cardboard magazine files for quick access.

You'll probably want to keep your homeschool magazines for a while. Most include an index near the end of the year, so that you can easily locate helpful articles or learning ideas that appeared in previous issues.

Create an Idea File

For further organization, create an idea file for each subject area. If you're planning to study oceans this month, browse through reference books or Internet sites for lesson ideas, jot down the ideas, and place them in your science idea file for this month. At the same time, you might come up with geography ideas relating to the study of oceans, or history ideas relating to early explorers who sailed the high seas. Place these ideas in the proper files—science, geography, history—then file those under "Oceans." You'll soon have a unit or theme study compiled for your study of oceans.

ESSENTIAL

Index cards and a recipe box are great for jotting down and storing lesson-plan ideas, websites to visit, or library books to check out. Use the tab dividers in the box to indicate the subject areas, such as math, science, language arts, social studies, as well as subcategories of these topics. Then file your notes and ideas in the corresponding sections. Store the file box alongside your idea file.

As you research lesson-plan ideas for the upcoming month, you'll often come across ideas that will be great for the following months, perhaps on the environment, the solar system, or inventors. Jot down those ideas and place them in your idea files for the future. If you don't have time to record your ideas fully, note the book, page number, or Internet site that contains information on those ideas and slip the reminder sheet into a file entitled "Future Studies." Near the end of each month, review your notes and revisit the resource book or website and delve further into those topics to create lesson plans.

Store your notes in color-coded files. For instance, math ideas could be stored in red file folders, language arts in blue, science in green, social studies in yellow, and so on. Or, if you use plain manila file folders, use different colored markers to label the different files. Color-coding labels, many of which are removable, are available at office supply stores. Soon, you'll see red and think "math," blue and think "language arts," all helping to speed up the lesson planning process.

Activity Centers and Science Labs

You can carve space out of your home for activity centers, reading corners, homework tables, as well as areas to set up lab equipment for conducting experiments. The age of your children and their learning styles will determine how you arrange your educational areas. Spend time observing how they prefer to learn before you create learning spaces. They may decide to read and do projects at the dining room table, or sit at their own desk in their bedrooms, or sprawl across the living room floor. Ask for their input and ideas on activity centers and how they'd like to use them.

Math Learning Centers

When you think of math, you think of manipulatives and hands-on, real-life projects. On a bookshelf or easy-to-reach plastic table, you can set out bins full of pattern blocks, plastic counters, linking cubes, Cuisenaire rods, geoboards, play clocks, play money, fraction pieces, balance scales, rulers, math games, and more.

For extra fun, you and your children can make many of these manipulatives from household items. Dry beans and macaroni are great for sorting, counting, adding, and subtracting practice. Pattern blocks, fraction pieces, play money, and clocks can be cut and created from poster board or empty cereal boxes. Cubes, rods, and even geoboards can be molded from play dough or clay. You can also make your own number charts, multiplication tables, and flash cards.

Keep dry-erase boards or chalkboards in your math center for quickly working out math problems. Another fun idea is to write a new math problem on the board each day. Encourage children to use their manipulatives to work out and solve the math problems. They can jot down how they solve the problems, as well as take photos or videos of their daily math experiences.

Science Lab

Your kitchen is the most logical space for your science lab. Conducting science experiments is one of the high points of homeschooling, so you'll want to spend many hours in your science lab/kitchen. Most homeschool families consider the time spent experimenting and discovering the mysteries of science in the kitchen as some of the most treasured of their homeschool memories. Therefore, don't skimp on science experiments just because you're afraid you can't accommodate them.

To be on the safe side, you might want to protect certain surfaces in your kitchen when setting up lab equipment. Sheets of hard acrylic or self-healing cutting mats can protect countertops. Plastic mats or runners can protect the kitchen floor around the experimentation areas. The floor mats can remain in the kitchen by the sink and range when not used for protection. The sheets of acrylic can slide into a nearby cabinet where they'll be out of sight, yet still handy.

Store the chemistry set inside a kitchen cabinet or hutch (out of the reach of small children), along with a few good books containing science experiments. You can also store the safety goggles, microscope, Bunsen burner, petri dishes, beakers and test tubes, litmus paper, dissecting kit, and magnifying glasses in the cabinet.

It's a good idea to install a fire extinguisher in your kitchen. Even if you don't need it for a chemistry experiment gone wrong, you may become so absorbed in the science activities that you forget about dinner cooking on the stove.

Arts and Crafts Area

Set aside a special area for arts and crafts projects. Consider the crayons, markers, and paints that may bleed through or spill across the table and onto the floor. In light of possible accidents, you might want to invest in an affordable folding table with a plastic or melamine top that is scratch- and water-resistant. Set the table along a wall in the dining room, playroom, or in one of the children's bedrooms. Place bins full of art and craft supplies on shelves adjacent to the table. If the flooring below the table is of concern to you, position a clear plastic mat or runner beneath the table. Now your family has an area for art projects where they won't have to worry about marker stains or paint spills.

Quiet Spaces and Reading Corners

A daily homeschool schedule achieves a good balance when there are periods of recreation and activity, and periods of rest and quiet time. When you step onto the volleyball court or bring out the chemistry set, children gear up for the activity they anticipate, and their level of energy or enthusiasm increases accordingly. Likewise, when you retire to a quiet corner to read or curl up on the couch with a book or writing pad, children will relax and unwind. The stimuli in the environment, whether it is high or low, will have a corresponding effect on children.

A Reading Corner

By establishing a reading corner, you'll create a quiet space that is settling and free from distractions. You can locate this area in a corner of a den or a bedroom. Add a bookcase, books, and a couple of beanbag chairs or sleeping bags, and you've designed a welcoming and comfortable library for your children.

If you have no extra space for a reading corner, mount sturdy shelves in your child's bedroom to hold books. Then add colorful pillows in different shapes and sizes to his bed. He can prop up several pillows against the headboard, grab a book, stretch out his legs, and read to his heart's content.

A Room for Writing

A desk stocked with adequate writing materials in a quiet corner of a room is ideal for crafting stories or journaling. Clear the desktop of any distracting clutter, add a good lamp to properly illuminate the desktop, and provide a comfortable chair for the young writer. Place a dictionary, thesaurus, and reference books on writing and grammar nearby. And, if possible, ensure that there is a door that can be closed for peace and quiet.

Writing requires one to focus mentally on the task at hand. It's not something that can be done well when others are chattering, playing music, or watching television. The mind must formulate ideas, grapple with ideas, process the ideas, and construct them in a manner that can be captured on paper. It can be quite a mental challenge for anyone, young or old. However, it can be an extremely enjoyable activity when the writer has a quiet environment for producing pages of wonderfully written words and stories.

The Library

One of the most-used areas in your home will probably be the library. Yours may not be the library of your dreams, with floor-to-ceiling bookcases lining all four walls of the room. Yet, all of us treasure the collection of fiction and nonfiction books, textbooks and activity books, reference books and picture books, on our own bookshelves, no matter how large or small they may be.

The library in your home—which you might want to incorporate into your reading corner—should contain a few choice books to help your children learn and to encourage their interest in reading. The dictionary and thesaurus are important tools, not only for writers, but for any reader. A set of encyclopedias is also a wonderful asset to the home library. These can be found reasonably priced at garage sales, consignment shops, or used-book stores.

ESSENTIAL

Books for young homeschoolers might include *Ippie Unschooled, Allison's Story: A Book about Homeschooling,* or *Kandoo Kangaroo Hops into Homeschool,* as well as traditional, exciting picture books and first reader books. Books for older readers could include homeschooling books such as *Real Lives: Eleven Teenagers Who Don't Go to School Tell Their Own Stories, The Teenage Liberation Handbook,* and *A Sense of Self: Listening to Homeschooled Adolescent Girls.*

And, of course, any classics, popular books, or nonfiction books that interest your children are always worthwhile investments. These can be found reasonably priced at used-book stores, so visit them often. When you glance into your child's room and see him completely absorbed in another book, knowing that he's developed a true love of reading, it's a rewarding and heartwarming feeling for any parent.

Keeping Home and School Separate

The time may come—generally sooner, rather than later—when the homeschool begins to overtake and overrun your home. If you've applied some of the tips in this chapter, you will hopefully stay fairly well organized. But even the organized areas may begin to infringe upon your family's living space until it seems as if there's no place left to escape the influence of homeschooling. Or, when company comes to visit, you sometimes wish the overflowing, floor-to-ceiling bookcase in the dining room wasn't quite so prominent.

If you're fortunate enough to have a separate schoolroom or playroom, it would, of course, be an ideal location for worktables, bookshelves, and storage closets. Some families can create such a space in an attic or basement. If you're tight on space, though, you can set up an activity center in a corner of your child's room, or use attractive partitions, available from department stores, to separate a portion of the family room.

ALERT

Everyone needs a chance to disassociate themselves from the homeschool environment during evenings and weekends. By dedicating specific areas to the learning theater, you leave other areas of the house free for the daily activities of eating, sleeping, relaxing, playing, or simply conversing with family and friends.

As often noted, homeschooling is a lifestyle and not a school at home. You needn't reproduce a classroom in your family room, a chemistry lab in your kitchen, a cafeteria in your dining room, or a gymnasium in your garage. Your family can easily live and learn in your home, using what is conveniently available to them and coexisting comfortably alongside your homeschooling spaces.

Resources for Organization Help

For more help on organizing your homeschool days and learning spaces, see *www.HomeschoolHelper.com/homeschoolorganization.html*. Or see the tips and suggestions at *www.EverythingHomeschooling.com*.

CHAPTER 14

Typical and Atypical Days

If you're interested in home education or simply curious about how your child's homeschool experience compares to others, you could seek descriptions of "typical homeschool days."

However, with the many different methods of homeschooling available, it can be difficult to describe a typical homeschool day. Therefore, the term typical day might actually be a misnomer. But it's still interesting to read about "typical days" in other families. It's a good way to gain insight and ideas from the fun, exciting life homeschoolers lead!

Typical Homeschool Days

A *typical homeschool day* is the name given to the description of a day in the life of a homeschooled family. As many families can attest, their days are not exactly typical. It's a little like trying to define an average family. What is average? How can average be measured or compared when referring to individuals?

The same is true for the typical day. What may be typical for one family may be impractical for another. When reading or hearing about others' typical days, don't feel that you should pattern your days after theirs. It's fun to hear about others' experiences, and you might even pick up some interesting ideas you hadn't considered before. But your homeschool day reflects your family's lifestyle and the things that work for you and your children. If it's working for you, there's no need to change it!

Recording Typical Days

When homeschoolers are registered with the school district in some states, they may be asked to submit a copy of their typical day. Of course, not every day is going to be the same, nor will it necessarily be typical. Generally, homeschool officials simply like to know that your children are staying active, pursuing areas of study commensurate with their abilities, engaging in learning activities throughout the day, and spending time developing and furthering their skills and knowledge.

A Homeschool Schedule

If you need to submit a typical homeschool day to your district at any point, you might ask them if they have a preferred format. Many are written in basic paragraph style, starting with events that first occur in your homeschool day. Others may follow a more structured timeline, such as the following:

- **8:00–9:30:** We spend this time having breakfast together, discussing what we did yesterday and what we're planning for the day ahead. Our daughter plans to practice her violin lessons after finishing the story she's writing for language arts. Our older son plans to try a couple science experiments from a book he's reading. Our younger son wants to build a Viking ship with his construction set.

- **9:30–10:30:** The two older children did their math assignments on fractions and decimals, and used manipulatives from their math centers to illustrate the math problems. Our younger son used math manipulatives for counting, sorting, adding, and subtracting.
- **10:30–11:30:** For science, our older son conducted the experiments he wanted to try: one on bending water and the other on creating a force field. Everyone gathered around to observe his experiments and discuss their theories and the results of the experiments.
- **11:30–12:30:** We have lunch and do a few basic chores. Then it's time for language arts, reading, and writing activities.

The rest of the typical day is recorded in much the same style, noting the books read, papers written, topics discussed, and so on. Obviously, the timeslots do not need to be as stringent, as some activities will take longer or shorter amounts of time. When you're done recording your day, you'll be able to provide insight into the various subjects your children study and the way in which they study them, which will be beneficial to homeschool officials, should they need this information.

Typical Descriptions

Rather than a timeline like the one shown here, you can write about the things you did that day in paragraph format. Again, check with your homeschool administrator if they have requested to see a "typical day." They may prefer one style over the other. Based on the homeschool day outlined here, a paragraph style may read similar to the following:

We gathered for breakfast around 8:00, and the kids began talking about the things they wanted to do that day. Our daughter plans to practice her violin lessons after finishing the story she's writing. Our older son plans to do a couple science experiments from a book he's reading. Our younger son wants to build a Viking ship with his construction set. As we clear away the breakfast dishes and do our morning chores, we usually sing together.

By midmorning, our chores were done, and the two older children began their math assignments, using manipulatives to work on fractions and decimals. I helped our younger son with adding and subtracting by using the math manipulatives in our math center.

Then our older son began his experiments: one on bending water and the other on creating a force field. Everyone gathered around to observe his experiments and discuss their theories and the results of the experiments. The kids stayed involved with variations of the experiments while I fixed lunch and provided feedback on their activities. Around noon, we had our lunch, then straightened the kitchen and did a few basic chores. Now it's time for reading one of our favorite books, and writing in our journals. After that, our daughter will practice her violin lessons, and our sons will work on the Viking ship they're building.

Be Atypical

It may seem as if your typical days have turned into lifeless, uneventful days. Your family gets up, eats breakfast, does math, science, language arts, and social studies. So, what's there to write about?

FACT

Keep track of homeschool activities by writing about the subjects you cover each day. Remember to describe some of the fun, surprising events that usually occur during a normal day. Not only will you have a record of a typical day, but you'll create an interesting daily log that your children will one day enjoy looking back on.

Sometimes your days can fall into a rut, or you find yourself with a case of the doldrums. That doesn't mean that it has to stay that way. Do something different or daring to jolt the very foundation of your homeschool day. Break away from the same, old humdrum pattern by doing something totally unexpected. You can start by surprising the kids with your new idea.

Dare to Be Different

If you or your kids are bored, shake things up. Reverse the order of your homeschool schedule. Lock away the textbooks for a while. Ask your kids to create the lessons.

Here's an idea that often works. If you've been doing math every morning at 9:00, science at 10:00, social studies at 11:00, and so on, for the last several months, try this: When the kids shuffle into the room to begin the 9:00 math lesson, tell them you don't want to see a math book for the next two weeks. What? They'll think they heard you wrong!

But, yes, you'll tell them they heard you right. Remove those math books from your sight, hide them, bury them if they must. (Just remember where they're hidden! Because you will need them again at some point. Just not for the next two weeks.)

For the next two weeks, your children's challenge will be to create and present math lessons, without the use of their math books. From their memory, knowledge, and comprehension of math skills, they will use math in some way each day to teach math lessons, to illustrate math concepts, or to simply prove that they can, indeed, do math without using a math book. You'll notice the kids eagerly looking forward to math over the next two weeks, and their excitement will lead to deeper learning, too.

ESSENTIAL

Try handing the teaching part of homeschooling over to the children—the lesson planning, the educational activities, field trip suggestions, and reading and writing assignments. See how many creative ideas they can develop for learning. This will add some spark and excitement to the previously uneventful days.

Try an Atypical Homeschool Day

If your typical homeschool day seems okay, but it's become a bit too commonplace, try an *atypical* day. If you normally do lessons at the dining room table, inform the children that all lessons will be done outdoors today. If necessary, carry some chairs and TV trays outdoors, and that's where the day's lessons will take place. You can take advantage of the outdoors by using objects in nature to complement math, science, and more.

Even better, tell the children to pack a picnic lunch, because the day's lessons will be held at the park or the beach. It's not a day off, though, nor a mini-vacation. Not this time. This time, you'll do lessons just as you would at home, except you'll be in the fresh air all day and in new surroundings far removed from the dining table at home. Of course, the children can play once the lessons are finished, providing a perfect ending to an invigorating day. Now the whole family is animated and rejuvenated.

Try to incorporate atypical days into your homeschool schedule as often as possible, and enjoy the change of scenery.

A Well-Rounded Education

When you write down the events of a typical day, you're often surprised to see how many things are accomplished in one day. At the same time, it may become clearer that some things are not receiving as much attention as others. Maybe you don't spend as much time on art, music, character education, physical education, or life skills as you had planned.

Now is a good time to reconsider your daily schedule and determine how to work toward a more well-rounded education for your children. You don't want to overburden your day by adding more than it can hold. Instead, spread subjects over the course of a week or a couple weeks. In this way, you'll open up more time each day to include character education, life skills, or other topics that haven't received as much attention lately.

Remember when you attended middle school or high school? One semester or six-week period was devoted to home economics, one was devoted to shop, one to art, one to music, and so on. Similarly, you can find blocks of time for these and other topics, without having to squeeze everything into each day. At the end of three months or six months, when you look back over the many topics your child has covered, you'll be impressed with the well-rounded education she is receiving.

Examples of Typical Days

Here are some descriptions of typical days. Although "typical days" vary from day to day, most families agree that each day provides wonderful learning adventures.

The Beals' Typical Day

We have a somewhat structured day, starting with math after breakfast and morning chores. Math is our daughter's least-favorite subject, and she prefers to tackle it first thing in the morning. Our son is twelve, two years younger than our daughter, but he's a bit more advanced in math. So he often helps our daughter with math problems. We do use a couple of math books as guidance, and they include the answer keys, which is helpful. We work on real-life math problems, too. That seems to click better with our daughter, so I'm always looking for ways to weave math into everyday activities.

After spending time on math—which can easily take over an hour—we move on to science. We could spend all day on science; there are so many fascinating topics! We try to stick to a particular branch of science, such as earth science or physical science. But, often, we veer off into other areas. One topic can pique our interest in another area, and next thing you know, we're off and running, chasing down answers to new questions.

For us, science can lead into social studies. We like to make connections between subjects when we can. So if we're studying plant and animal cells, for instance, we learn about Robert Hooke, who first discovered cells in the 1660s. We become curious about other historical events in that era, so we jump from science to reading about other inventors in the 1660s, about explorers, the early colonies in America, or other events occurring in a similar timeframe.

After our lunch break, we spend time on language arts, which could be grammar, reading books or classics, or writing reports or descriptive writing. This is when we'll usually go to the computer, for printing out grammar worksheets or typing reports. The kids will also play a few educational games on the computer—word games, spelling games—plus math or strategy games.

Our formal school day tends to wind down at this point, by 2:00 or 3:00 in the afternoon. The rest of the day is for art, music, hobbies, or any other activities that the kids are involved in. We live fairly close to the parks and recreation department and the library. Both places offer a variety of activities, especially during the after-school hours or on weekends. So our kids stay involved and have the chance to spend time with their friends, too.

The Padricks' Atypical Days

We have three daughters, ages seven, eleven, and thirteen, and they keep things interesting around here. They have such different interests, and are at different learning levels, so that it's difficult to have a really structured schedule. We tried a more typical, school-like schedule in the beginning—we've been homeschooling for five years now—but it just didn't work for our family. The girls were frustrated, and I was frustrated. I felt like I was failing them. So we eased up on trying to follow a specific schedule.

Now we still cover the basics, but in a free-flowing, flexible way. All three girls have definite interests: our older daughter loves art and drawing, our middle daughter loves sports, and our youngest daughter loves crafts of all types. So that's how they start their days: doing the things they love the most. That makes them happy, there's no stress, and it sets a fantastic tone for the rest of the day.

After they've spent much of the morning doing art and craft projects, as well as playing outdoors—volleyball, softball, running—they're ready to settle down to lessons. I keep a guideline of our learning goals for each girl each year, and I consult the guidelines each week. I also keep an idea file of possible lessons, so I go over that each week or add new ideas to the file. Then I go over these details with the girls at the beginning of the week. This way, they know what they'll be studying, what will be expected of them that week, and can plan their days to a certain extent.

The two older girls work through their lessons at the dining room table, while I work with our youngest daughter on her reading and writing skills. Sometimes the older girls are doing math at the same time, or one might be working on a math assignment while the other is researching a history assignment. But either way, we're all together at the table, and they can ask questions or bounce ideas off each other as we work. If I'm particularly busy with our youngest daughter, the older girls know not to interrupt. However, they've been asked to jot down any question they might have on an assignment, so we can go over it as soon as I'm free.

We enjoy that time at the dining room table, working on our assignments. It's a good feeling to all be busy and involved in learning at the same time. We have afternoon snacks and a lot of interesting conversations then, too. After a couple hours, the lessons have been addressed, discussed, completed, and reviewed. One girl or the other might need to spend a little extra time on her lessons, while the others are ready to move on to other interests.

This is an example of one of our days. The next day could be similar, or it could be totally different. The girls' morning interests might evolve into studying Picasso one day, or learning about a baseball hero, Jackie Robinson, or studying the art and history of paper-cutting, dating back to sixth-century Chinese dynasties. That's when their learning really seems to take off—when they're eager to learn more about the things that really excite and interest them.

The Robertsons' Unschooling Days

I run a graphic design business from home, I'm a single mom, and I've found that the unschooling method works best for my son and daughter in our situation. Some weeks, I have so many projects to complete for clients that it'd be hard to follow a strict homeschool schedule. Other times, a couple weeks can go by without any jobs coming in. I have to keep my business highly organized, and the kids understand that. So it's nice to not have to organize our lives quite as much.

My son is fifteen, and he loves graphic design as much as I do. In fact, he provides some unique ideas and feedback on many of my projects. He taught himself website design skills, and he continuously improves his abilities. Together, we've found some online courses on web design and computer programming, as well as free tutorials that expand upon what he already knows, so that's really nice. In the next couple years, he plans to start his own design business, which could complement my current business. Meanwhile, a huge portion of his day is spent on programming and designing websites or related applications.

My daughter is almost thirteen, and her interests fluctuate from one thing to another, sometimes almost overnight. Because she's been unschooled, she's had the freedom to explore most of her interests, ranging from drawing ponies, to creating new worlds with LEGO toys, to currently designing new and unusual fashion styles for girls. She loves reading; she read the Harry Potter books when she was younger, then *The Chronicles of Narnia*, and now she's hooked on books by the Brontë sisters, Daphne du Maurier, Victoria Holt, Mary Stewart—books I read when I was her age. A couple years ago, she taught herself to play the flute, and she likes to compose her own music. Her best friend plays the clarinet, so they often play duets together. Both my son and daughter have close friends who like to come over and take part in their hobbies.

FACT

The best learning seems to take place when questions arise. Who invented the Internet? What makes an engine start? Where do frogs go when it's cold? Why hasn't anyone gone back to the moon? How are skyscrapers built to withstand earthquakes? A single question can lead to a day's worth of research, new knowledge, and new activities!

I realize this doesn't sound like a typical school day. Yes, the kids know how to calculate math problems, though we don't do traditional math assignments. When we've needed to work out mathematical problems, we sat down and worked them out. My son taught himself math concepts that were related to computer programming. I can't do trigonometry in any shape or form. But my son can, because he wanted to, or he needed to, and so he figured it out, through online tutorials or from math DVDs from our library. It's the same way he taught himself to program in HTML or Java. In a similar way, my daughter taught herself to read music, play music, and now compose her own music.

Years ago, the kids learned to read by spending time reading together as a family. They learned to sound out words, to recognize words, to learn the meaning of new words, to write words and sentences to create stories of their own. They learned about the American Revolution and the Declaration of Independence when they wondered why fireworks were set off on the Fourth of July. I recall that we spent one summer learning the origins behind every single holiday we could think of. Not only was it a lot of fun, but the history lessons behind the holidays are profound.

To me, to us, unschooling seems more real, more logical, than going to a building somewhere else to be taught things by someone else. Why would that be necessary? I should understand; after all, I went to a traditional school as a kid. But from where I stand today, and from conversations I've had with many other families, I can't for the life of me see the benefit of traditional schooling. Every family is different, though, and what works for one doesn't always work for another. We each have to find the path that works best for our children and our families.

Trust in Learning Each Day

As you've seen, typical days can vary widely. Just as families and individuals have unique lifestyles and personalities, so do their typical homeschool days. Some days go smoothly and much is accomplished. Other days are not as fruitful. But each day can still provide learning opportunities, be enjoyable, and be worthwhile.

When your day doesn't go according to your plans, simply plan to go according to your day! Treasure the time with your kids, let them open your eyes to new ways of learning, and learn together as a family. Trust in your children's abilities to learn and keep faith in your ability to help guide them each day.

Tips from Homeschool Families

Every "typical day" varies in some way, which is good. Variety breaks up an otherwise dull routine. Flexibility allows for unexpected learning opportunities. Here are some tips from veteran homeschool families:

- Add new, creative activities to each day, such as painting, crafts, photography, playing musical instruments, building projects, or special hobbies.
- Ask your children what they'd like to learn about this week or next month, and get their input on how to best learn about those topics.
- Include fun events or unusual ways of learning to make each day more enjoyable and memorable.

- Have the courage to follow your family's own educational goals and beliefs. But also keep an open mind to what works or doesn't work for your family.
- Talk with other homeschool families for inspiration and ideas, and to share your own experiences.
- Plan special family parties or celebrations every few weeks to commemorate certain milestones or lessons learned.
- Don't worry about bad days or bad weeks. Everyone has a bad day occasionally, whether homeschooling or not. Just relax, share your experiences with homeschool friends, then start again when everyone is more rested and ready.

Resources for Typical Homeschool Days

For more examples of typical homeschool days, read the adventures of other homeschool families at *www.HomeschoolFun.com*. For examples of unschooling days, see *www.SandraDodd.com/typical*. Both sites provide a multitude of ideas for your own homeschool days.

CHAPTER 15

Homeschooling One or Several

The decision to homeschool, or not, shouldn't be determined by how many or how few children are in your family. Rather, your reasons for homeschooling should focus on the desire to provide a good, well-rounded education for your child or children in a safe, caring environment. Whether you're the parent of several children, or of an only child, you'll find encouragement, ideas, and homeschool solutions for your particular family.

Homeschooling Your Only Child

An only child is not a lonely child. An only child has not been accustomed to having siblings, so loneliness isn't as concerning to him as it might be to his parents. At one point, parents might have received the mistaken impression that homeschooling an only child wasn't a good idea. This idea probably resulted from the socialization concern, which, as you've already seen, shouldn't be a concern at all. Your only child can have as many opportunities to socialize as any child.

Either situation—homeschooling an only child or several children—can have its benefits and disadvantages, depending on the viewpoint one prefers to take. What it comes down to, though, is the love, respect, and warmth that each family member feels for the other, regardless of how many people make up the family unit.

Socialization for the Only Child

Socialization might still be a concern for some, but your child can have plenty of opportunities to interact with others and build a network of friends. Children can join playgroups and homeschool groups. They can take gymnastics, music, or drama classes given at city parks and recreation departments. They can join clubs, scouting groups, or sports teams.

QUESTION

How can I help my child get over her shyness?
Shyness is not necessarily a negative thing. But if your child's shyness causes her discomfort, strive to improve her self-confidence and self-esteem. Praise her qualities and capabilities and help her feel good about herself. Never push her into situations she feels timid about.

If you live in a rural area far from cities, towns, or neighbors, consider joining the closest church in your area. Country churches have long been meeting places for families, and they provide an opportunity to get together with others every week. Since the country church is somewhat isolated, they sometimes offer more events to bring the community closer together. They may hold country fairs, spaghetti dinners, fried chicken picnics, youth group meetings during the week, and family games or crafts on Saturday nights. They may even be able to introduce you to other homeschool families in your community.

Learning Alongside Your Child

In larger families, siblings often help each other with lessons, projects, and other educational activities. In your family, that's not the case with your only child. From the beginning, you and your child have shared special times together, as well as normal, everyday events in your daily lives. You've listened to each other, and you've helped each other when needed. When there are things to get done, you've often done them together. When there are places you must go, your child usually goes, too. When your child is in a talkative mood, you discuss a multitude of topics. When your child is in a quiet mood, you both share the silence comfortably. This has been your way of life while raising your only child.

Homeschooling your only child is no different. You will continue to be close, or even closer, as you discuss the many topics of interest that come to mind. You'll continue to help your child when he needs help, listen to him when he has questions, and help him find the answers or knowledge he is seeking. You'll learn alongside each other as you delve into the educational projects that are a part of each day.

Homeschooling Several Children

If you're homeschooling four, five, or more, your home is an exciting, lively place of activity. With multiple children in the home, some families find the unschooling method to work best for them. Others prefer to set up specific blocks of time to spend with each child. As a homeschool family, you have the option to try different methods to find the one that works for you. Once again, flexibility is the key to a good homeschool experience.

Your older children can be wonderful role models for your younger children. When younger ones see brothers or sisters working on lessons, reading books, typing stories, building a shelf, baking a dessert, testing a theory—and enjoying it—on a daily basis in the home, the little ones are eager to become involved, too.

Encourage your older children to be patient with the little one's curiosity and natural desire to learn. Help your little ones to be patient, as well, while older brothers and sisters complete lessons or projects, and record the outcomes. Each age group can learn from the other when a bit of patience is exercised.

Younger children can't always be a part of older children's educational endeavors. But by watching the older children, younger ones can observe the level of seriousness that goes into lessons, or the methods of experimenting and skill that their siblings exhibit when working on projects. These are important lessons in themselves.

Spanning Different Grade Levels

Tanya and Rick had five children, ranging in age from three years to fifteen years. The two older children were in their teens, while the three younger children were under the age of eight. Rick and Tanya's three-year-old daughter liked to tag along with her six- and eight-year-old brothers. But the brothers weren't especially thrilled when she took apart a model or carried off pieces of the 3D puzzle they were building.

The two older children, both teenaged girls, were bored by the models, construction projects, experiments, or lessons that their younger brothers were doing. And the boys had little interest in the lessons or activities the teen girls were involved with. As a result, Tanya and Rick initially found it challenging to learn together as a family.

Educational Alternatives

The family's original idea had been to use unit studies, which could focus on a central theme but still allow the studies to be adapted to the different ages and interest levels. However, this turned out to be far more difficult than imagined for their particular family.

Next they tried online courses, one that worked fairly well for the boys, and another that better served the educational needs for their older daughters. But the time required to monitor the lessons, in conjunction with the kids eventually losing interest in the courses, led to seeking other alternatives.

A New Strategy

Eventually, Rick and Tanya realized they needed to trust their children's desires to be creative or inventive, or to follow their own current interests. With that in mind, Tanya tracked down a couple of websites that provided lists of good books for each grade level. With the lists in hand, they made numerous visits to their local library to find books on a wide variety of topics.

Tanya shared her mission with the librarians, who also assisted her in finding books on science experiments or medieval castles for the boys, or math books and science books geared toward teenaged girls, plus books for reading enjoyment, too. At the same time, Tanya's three-year-old daughter was able to enjoy story-time and puppet-time at the library.

The library books provided the basis for the educational topics the children would learn about each week. Rick and Tanya jotted down ideas from the books, then shared the ideas with the kids. At the beginning of each week, they outlined what they expected the kids to learn during the coming week. By using the library books, the computer, and a few, kid-safe Internet sites, the kids could do additional research on the topics, write about what they learned, and try some of the projects, experiments, and math techniques.

Family Time Together

Tanya and Rick found that their kids enjoyed this style of homeschooling better, and they are still always open to new ideas. They also knew they wanted to have quality time with each child at some point every day, to discuss what the kids were learning. Evenings would be the best time, after Rick was home from work and after the dinner hour. They settled their three-year-old daughter nearby with her favorite coloring books, while they spent time with the boys, going over their daily activities together, discussing and commenting upon their day's projects. Some evenings the boys had science experiments they wanted to do, and they'd gather in the kitchen for those.

After spending a block of time with the boys, Rick and Tanya spent time with their teenaged girls, going over their day's projects. When there were questions on a math assignment or problems understanding a scientific concept, they helped the girls find the answers to the problems. Recently, their girls had taken an interest in creating their own glass beads and vintage-style jewelry. The girls especially enjoyed sharing their creations and their plans for future jewelry-making projects.

Tanya found that everyone was more content, more interested in learning, and the days went more smoothly for all of them. By discussing the day's learning each evening, as well as observing new interests and projects, both Tanya and Rick were able to see that the children were progressing and enjoying it.

Siblings as Role Models

In larger families, older siblings are usually influential in the younger children's lives and learning. The younger children want to emulate their older siblings and do lessons along with them. Older children often gain a new sense of importance and self-worth when they see their younger brothers or sisters learning from them. This can be a great source of satisfaction for older children and helps to reinforce their own learning, as well.

Let your older children know that you don't expect them to teach the younger ones. However, you would appreciate them interacting with the younger ones, continuing to extend goodwill and kindness toward their brothers and sisters. If they could help entertain a younger child while you help a middle child with a lesson, it could make parts of the day go more smoothly and allow more time for everyone at the end of the day.

Observe your older children to see how they take to this. You don't want to see them develop a grudge toward the younger children. At the same time, every member is an important part of the family unit, and it's important that everyone gets along and respects one another.

ALERT

There may be times when you need to sit down with each child and have a heart-to-heart talk. The chance to express oneself can be lost in the day-to-day action of family life. Let children know that you're always willing to listen to their concerns and feelings, and then share quiet times together when they feel free to talk with you.

Remember to show your appreciation to your older children, and never take them or their help for granted. In fact, reward them by allowing them some extra free time, or arrange a special time when they can just be with you, apart from the rest of the family.

If older children believe that they are being taken advantage of, or if they feel that they don't have enough time to themselves, take their concerns seriously. Try to create an arrangement that allows extra time for themselves and their friends. In most cases, they'll be happy to help out again in a few days, after they've had a break from the normal routine. Everyone needs a vacation now and then—even children!

Tips for Staying on Track

Even if you don't follow a strict schedule, most families have a framework they try to work within each day. This could be a loose unschooling format or an outline of what you want to accomplish during the day. In addition, you'll have your normal daily routine of meals, laundry, and housecleaning duties, so you'll want to keep those on schedule as well.

There are times, though, when an errant wind seems to blow through town, disrupting even the best-laid plans. And just like that, your good intentions for the day have been scattered. Try to not let it upset you. Understand that it's just one of those things that will happen occasionally, and tomorrow will be a better day.

Here are some ideas for helping your children stay on track:

- Print out guidelines for each child's weekly educational goals or lesson plans, post it on their door or bulletin board, and encourage them to achieve the goals.
- Pair children up when they share certain learning styles, then work with two or three children at a time.
- Bring out new games, puzzles, or books to entertain some of the children while you're working with others.
- Try the unit study methods or unschooling styles mentioned earlier, which can usually be adapted to most age levels.
- Consider a self-study program for some of the children if it seems to suit their learning style.

- Try to take field trips together as a family on weekends, or enjoy special outings or events together with the entire family.
- Set aside time every day when each child can have individual time with you (when others are napping, reading, or having quiet time).

Stress Busters and Mini-Vacations

Homeschooling can be stressful, even if you're homeschooling only one child. When you're trying to keep several children on track and taking care of a baby or preschooler at the same time, the stress can multiply. And this is something you definitely want to avoid.

Stress Reduction

Some of the main causes of stress in a homeschool are trying to do too much, planning to cover too much territory in a school year, and setting expectations too high for yourself and for your children. If you don't allow enough flexibility in your day, or you try to adhere too strictly to a schedule, this can compound the stress you're feeling.

Here are some ways to reduce stress in your homeschool:

- Don't try to be "SuperParent." When you overextend yourself, you over-stress your body.
- Cut back on extracurricular activities. Your children don't need to attend every class that comes along.
- Reduce the number of topics you're trying to cover. There's always next month or next year for covering those subjects.
- Guide your children in self-directed learning. Provide books and resources that will help them to learn on their own.
- Seek support from other homeschool families. They've often found great ways of reducing stress and achieving a more balanced lifestyle.

Simplify Your Days

Try different ways to simplify your day: simpler meals, simpler house-cleaning methods, more breaks during the day, more playtime. If nothing seems to be going right on a particular day, then stop while you're ahead and scrap the plans for today. Just as housework can always wait until another day, so can math or science.

FACT

Playtime is an important part of learning. Take time to relax and unwind, while allowing children to play. As children play, they explore and experiment, use trial-and-error, exercise choice and freedom in a fun and safe manner. So even as you relax and your children play, rest assured that learning is still taking place.

Nothing is as important as family and happiness within the family, so take the day off, go to the park or the beach with the family, and don't think another thought about homeschooling, lessons, or learning. Your mind needs a break and so do the kids.

Mini-Vacations

Vacations can be long or short, helping you to regain your energy and sense of balance within your life. Frequent mini-vacations can be especially beneficial. You can homeschool Monday through Thursday, then Friday can be free day. The children can select their own activities, and you won't need to create lesson plans for that day. It can be your free day as well.

Indulge yourself on your free Friday. Take your time sipping your morning coffee or orange juice in bed or on the porch, where it's quiet and peaceful. Don't make any plans for the day, except for those that you'll find enjoyable.

Getting Away

If it's a longer vacation you need, you can homeschool for three full weeks in a row, then take the fourth week off every month. Follow this cycle for twelve months, and you'll attain an average school year with thirty-six weeks. And you'll have a weeklong vacation, every three weeks.

You can take longer vacations when following a traditional nine-month school year, with two weeks off during Christmas holidays, one or two weeks off around the Easter holiday, and most of the summer off. For longer holidays such as these, you might want to plan on getting away for a while, spending a week at a lake or beach cottage, staying in a cabin in a national park, or visiting with relatives in another city or state.

When you've had a chance to get away for several days, it's a wonderful feeling to come back home. And the entire family is usually re-energized and ready to get back to their normal routine once again.

CHAPTER 16

The Single-Parent Homeschool

As a single parent, you can successfully homeschool your children. If time is a concern, you have several homeschool options available to you, including online schools, distance-learning courses, independent study programs, preplanned curriculum packages, and unschooling techniques. Children can, indeed, attain a quality education in a single-parent home. And your support network of family and friends will be there to offer help and encouragement, too.

Single-Parent Strengths

Single parents handle issues daily that are unique to their situation. The single parent doesn't have another adult in the home to share feelings or experiences with, bounce ideas off from, or to engage in conversation. Of course, there are times when two-parent families feel the same. The difference is that two-parent families know they *could* sit down and have a heart-to-heart discussion. The single parent, on the other hand, knows there's not another adult in the home on a regular basis. Single parents have learned to be strong, independent, and self-sufficient—all good qualities to pass along to their children.

Keys to Success

It can be difficult to work and keep the home, plus homeschool your children, spend recreational time with them, and attend homeschool support meetings or gatherings. Flexibility and balance are the keys to success. Avoid setting your expectations too high and overscheduling your days. Maintain a flexible routine that allows time for activities, recreation, and relaxation.

Remember that it's not imperative that you do everything. Set priorities, and don't worry about the little things that there's just no time for. Housework and yard work will always be there. Your children won't. Make your children, their childhood, and their home education your priority. Soon, they'll be grown and on their own. Then you'll have plenty of time to spend on that housework and yard work.

Your health and your state of mind are also priorities. If you don't take care of yourself, your health and happiness can suffer. You want to be able to enjoy your children while they're young, and to joyfully participate in their home education experience. Set time aside for yourself just for relaxing and rejuvenating. You'll be more valuable to your children when you have a refreshed and re-energized frame of mind.

Keeping the Other Parent Involved

If you're separated from your partner or spouse, hopefully he or she will be supportive of the decision to homeschool and eager to assist. Your former partner can spend quality time with the children while you're at work. He or she can encourage the children to share what they've studied and learned, help with lessons and ongoing projects, and contribute learning activities and ideas.

ALERT

If your former spouse has visitation rights every other weekend, and you rely upon weekends for homeschooling, try to arrange a more flexible schedule. Maybe he could have the children over during the week rather than on weekends. If not, perhaps he could follow the lesson plans, do science experiments, or arrange field trips that relate to current topics.

Strive to keep the lines of communication open with your former partner, so that you both can work together for the good of your children. Avoid letting any personal feelings intervene, add stress to your life, or disrupt your goals for your children. Stress and unhappy feelings deplete your energy and good intentions. Your top priority is the happiness and education of your children. Always keep that uppermost in your mind.

Homeschool Options

Remember that a wide range of homeschooling options are available. Home education doesn't require that you sit at a desk or kitchen table for hours each day, teaching the children. Unschooling, unit studies, or an eclectic style of schooling may provide the most flexibility for your lifestyle. Curriculum providers or schools may cost a bit more but can offer timesaving services, such as assignment preparation, grading, tests, evaluations, record keeping, and teacher assistance. Internet-based schools or online schools, distance-learning courses, or independent study programs may work well for some children, particularly if they're trying to achieve credits for high school graduation as they prepare for college.

Homeschooling Time

You might be required to keep attendance records showing that you homeschool 180 days per year, or 900 to 1,000 hours per school year. This works out to approximately five or six hours per day. Check with your state department of education to determine their homeschooling requirements. If your state has similar attendance laws, you should have little difficulty meeting the requirement.

For example, if you work during the day, you could spend two or three hours each evening, helping your children with new lessons and reviewing previous lessons, reading history books or biographies together, and playing educational games. While you're at work, your children can spend two or three hours a day on homework papers, finishing assignments, reading ahead to new lessons, and working on homeschool projects. A sitter, daycare worker, or family member could monitor your children to be sure they're doing their assignments and staying educationally entertained during the day.

ESSENTIAL

Let others know that you're homeschooling. When enrolling your child in community courses or clubs, inform instructors that your child is homeschooled. If there are special skills or knowledge they can convey to your child, tell them you'd be appreciative. If they spend a little extra time with your child, show your appreciation by rewarding them with small gifts of thanks.

Together Time

When the weekend comes, you can spend additional quality time on science experiments, hands-on projects, and real-life lessons. Some of the best learning takes place when you're running errands together, shopping, going to the zoo or museum, and other family activities. Together, you can experience these lessons, discuss them, and expand upon them, taking the knowledge or experience even further or in new directions to contribute to a comprehensive education.

Homeschooled children tend to experience more quality educational hours than do their conventional-school counterparts. This is mainly due to the fact that homeschool parents regularly capitalize on the educational opportunities that arise, seeing them for the knowledge or experience they can convey, rather than considering them a normal part of daily life. What may seem normal or mundane to us, may be new and exciting to our children. By making the most of everyday events, we help our children to understand and learn from these opportunities.

Year-Round Homeschooling

If your state requires a specific number of hours per homeschool year, and you can only homeschool a few hours per day, you can try the year-round approach to homeschooling. Since homeschooling is basically a way of life, you and your child shouldn't feel as if you're engaging in school all year long. Instead, you'll eliminate those boring days of summer when the kids think there's nothing to do. With challenging homeschool projects to do all year long, your family can enjoy daily activities that keep the kids busy, motivated, and learning.

Staying Within a Budget

As a single parent, you are the main breadwinner in your family, and it can be crucial to live within your budget. Therefore, you may feel that you don't have the extra money to invest in homeschooling. Contrary to what one might believe, it needn't be costly at all. Your children can receive a fine, quality education, even with limited funds.

Take advantage of these homeschool money savers:

- The library and all its wonderful resources
- Used-book stores, for buying and selling books
- Consignment shops, for buying and selling educational items
- Used-curriculum fairs and book sales
- Trading or sharing books and equipment with other homeschoolers
- Borrowing books, videos, or DVDs through homeschool support groups
- Free lesson plans and worksheets available on the Internet
- Household items for science experiments, art, and educational fun

Special Times with Children

Whenever you spend extra one-on-one time with your children, you and they will benefit. You'll become closer to your children and more in tune with their interests and thoughts. And they will develop a closer, stronger, more trusting relationship with you. In all likelihood, they will continue to open up and share their feelings more frequently as the months go by. Behavioral problems will most likely diminish, and a more mature and capable child will emerge.

Take advantage of the time you spend together at the dinner table. Children learn and retain information by talking about the things that interest them and by engaging in lively discussions. This is an excellent time to review topics studied during the week in an interesting, not drilling, way. You don't want dinnertime to turn into teaching or test time. Rather, you want to hear what your children gleaned from lessons in a casual way. This not only gives children the opportunity to expound upon their lessons or areas of interest, but allows you to observe and evaluate the progress they are making.

Weekend and Evening Homeschool

When dinner is over, the chores are done, and the day has been discussed, parent and child still have time to play games outdoors, read books together, do science experiments in the kitchen, work on educational projects, play board games or do puzzles together, look over assignment questions, or discuss concepts and subject areas for the next day. And it need not take all night to do this.

Evenings are also a good time to attend community classes and social events, such as art, music, sports, and concerts. Your child can attend one or two classes or events a week, when you're able to drop him off and pick him up. The other evenings during the week can be spent on educational activities at home. Weekends can be similar to your evening routines, but with more flexibility and free time for fun and recreation.

Don't feel that you should spend all your evening or weekend hours on home education. That's simply not necessary. If you're concerned that you're "falling behind" or there's a subject you weren't able to cover this past week, discuss the topic with your child, encourage her to think about it and share thoughts or feelings on it, and artfully weave it into an hour or two of your time together.

As mentioned throughout this book, homeschooling isn't school at home. You needn't stand in front of a desk and chalkboard to teach and instruct. Your role is to help your children learn, to be aware of what others their age are learning, and consider what you feel is important for your children to learn. Then you can provide the guidance, resources, assistance, and encouragement to start them on the road to an enjoyable educational experience.

Flexible Work Options

Even though homeschooling can work well for single parents, you might wish that you had more time to spend at home with your children. You could speak with your employer about a more flexible work schedule, consider telecommuting, or look into establishing a home business.

Support from Employers and Coworkers

If it's your hope to stay employed in your current job, speak with your employer about your career goals, as well as your educational goals for your children. Have a plan firmly in mind before approaching your employer. Stress your desire to continue contributing to the good of the company. Offer to arrive at work an hour earlier and work through your lunch hour. As a result, you could leave two hours earlier than normal and have extra homeschooling time in the evenings with your children.

Not surprisingly, the workplace can be similar to conventional schools. Much time can, unfortunately, be lost or wasted in a normal workday. What may take eight hours for some to accomplish can be done by an industrious person in four hours.

Time at work is often lost by waiting for others in meetings, taking breaks to chat about the previous day or night, gathering around the water cooler to discuss favorite television shows or movies. Each of these breaks interrupt the productive flow of the day. A worker who avoids these time-killers and focuses on work can accomplish as much in a four-hour day as the worker who spends eight hours at work, but who stops to talk or take breaks throughout the day.

Observant employers and coworkers can recognize the person who is willing to work hard, who focuses their mind and their skills on the job at hand, and who honestly does a good day's work. As a result, you'll often win their support and admiration when you can accomplish as much as you do in a day, and still manage to educate your children, too.

Telecommuting and Working from Home

If it's simply not possible to shorten your normal workday, suggest telecommuting or taking work home a few times each week. You may be able to work from home on Fridays, or even a couple days per week. If your place of business is computerized, you can access files from home via pcAnywhere, GoToMyPC, or other remote access programs. Imagine how much time you would have with your children if you had an extra day or two at home each week!

Taking Children to Work

Several homeschool parents have successfully taken their children to work with them. This works well for parents who have a separate office within the building. Your child can sit at her own workspace and complete lessons, occasionally asking questions or getting input from you. You can take your lunch break together and follow it with a nature walk before going back to the office. In the afternoons, she can read, draw, or work on homeschool projects. Depending on her age, she may be able to assist with simple duties around the office.

Flexible Job Possibilities

Your lifestyle may not be suitable to a regular nine-to-five job. If you'd prefer to have more control over your hours or to work at home, here are some moneymaking opportunities to consider:

- Home daycare
- Tutoring, music, or art lessons
- Substitute teaching
- Virtual assistant
- Graphic or web design
- Copyediting or proofreading
- Blogging or writing articles
- Marketing or advertising consultant
- Medical transcription or bookkeeping
- Home remodeling or design services
- Beautician or hair stylist
- Errand-running or catering service
- Home, party, or wedding organizer or planner
- Sewing, alterations, or laundry services
- Office cleaning service
- Home health aide

Talk with friends, family, and acquaintances to get their ideas on possible businesses you could start. They might just hire you as a tutor for their children or have freelance work they can pass on to you.

Support for Single Parents

Support from other adults is a major boost for single parent homeschoolers. When possible, set aside time to attend local support group meetings. The experiences, perspective, support, and understanding from other homeschool parents will center you, inspire you, and boost your morale. If you can't make it to all the group meetings, stay in touch via telephone or e-mail. A group of single homeschool parents may even want to meet separately on Saturdays or Sundays once a month.

A local homeschool cooperative could provide educational advantages and social contact for your children. Consult with other homeschool families in your community to see if they are interested in starting a co-op. If you're unable to participate during the week, offer to hold a science, art, or writing class for a couple hours on Saturdays, which their children could attend along with yours.

Help from Family and Friends

Relatives may be the first to say "Have you lost your mind?" when you tell them you're planning to homeschool your children. But they're often the first to boast to others about you and your children, and are soon eager to lend a hand. Don't be too proud to accept help from them.

Sometimes as a single parent, you may experience tight financial situations that require you to temporarily live with parents or friends. Although this arrangement may not be ideal, it enables you to have a closer circle of support around you and your children while you're getting on your feet. Try to make the best of the situation. While living with family or friends, encourage them to contribute their special abilities and knowledge to help further your children's education, or to take an active part in their home education.

Grandparents are wonderful sources of information, ideas, and inspiration for your children. They come from a time when they had to create their own forms of entertainment, learned beneficial skills at an early age, and have often experienced a half century of history, firsthand, that they can share with your children. The relationship your children develop with their grandparents may leave an indelible mark on their childhood that they'll always treasure.

Child-Care Solutions

The younger the child, the more challenging single-parent homeschooling can be. Older children or teenagers may be mature and responsible enough to stay alone for a short time during the day as they focus on their studies. However, always try to avoid leaving your child alone for very long, regardless of her age. Young children should, of course, never be left alone.

A viable and successful homeschool arrangement can usually be found, no matter your child's age. It may take a few tries to hit upon the best solution for your family, so don't give up. Since you're homeschooling your children, the thought of placing them in a daycare facility may not sit well with you or them. However, some daycare centers may be homeschool-friendly and understand your unique needs. Always research any daycare, speak to other families whose children attend, and see if daycare employees are open to supervising your children's homeschool assignments. Most are accustomed to making sure that after-school children complete homework assignments, so they should be able to do the same for your children.

An in-home sitter or relative is often the preferred choice for homeschool families. This person should also be open to helping your children with lessons or projects and making sure that they stay busy and challenged while you're away at work. You don't want your children sitting around all day watching television or playing video games.

Remember that homeschooling can work for you and your family. With a little creative inventiveness, and the understanding that homeschooling or unschooling is a natural part of everyday life, your children can enjoy the benefits of a quality education and a close family unit.

Resources for Single Parents

Visit *www.SingleParentHomeschool.org* for free information, helpful tools, and work-at-home ideas. This site includes examples of a typical homeschooling day for a single parent and encourages comments from readers, too.

CHAPTER 17

Working Parents Who Homeschool

If both parents have careers, you can still homeschool your children. With flexible work schedules or creative homeschool strategies, your children can enjoy the benefits of home education. It helps to remember that learning at home is a natural part of each day. You won't need to stand behind a desk and look over the shoulders of your children for six or seven hours each day. Here are some tips on combining work, family, and homeschool.

Sharing Responsibilities

When each member of the family helps out around the home, everything runs more smoothly. This is especially beneficial for families where Mom and Dad both work outside the home. To carve out the time you'll need for homeschooling (and it is much less than you might imagine), everyone can share the responsibilities and chores. Many working parents have successfully homeschooled their children, and, with a little help and insight, you can, too.

Sharing the Homeschooling

In the two-career family, you each have a partner who can help share the home education responsibilities. If Dad goes to work early in the morning and is home by 5:00 P.M., he can take over some of the homeschool activities when he arrives home and begins dinner. If Mom goes to work later in the morning and arrives home around 7:00 P.M., the family can have dinner together and discuss the homeschool projects that have been covered that day. After everyone has helped to clean up after dinner, Mom can sit down with the kids to read, go over lessons, or look over projects. The following morning, she can present lessons for the upcoming day, before she leaves for work around 10:00 or 11:00 A.M.

Consider the Age of Your Children

Of course, the schedule you establish will need to take the ages of your children into consideration. Younger children may require more one-on-one time as they learn new concepts, attempt to comprehend the lessons, and work on completing assignments. If you're not able to be alongside them throughout each step, you'll want to ensure that your partner, a relative, or sitter will be available to help them through the processes.

For instance, you might spend an hour in the morning before work, helping with an English or history lesson. Or you might have just enough time to introduce the math lesson and go over the necessary concepts, but you realize that your child doesn't grasp the lesson or needs additional practice before proceeding.

ALERT

Before heading to the sitter's home, leave a note for your partner that your child needs more help with his math lesson. Or, take the math book and note along to the sitter's home or daycare, and ask if they'd be able to help your child with the lesson. You can establish a relationship with the sitter or daycare ahead of time, so that they understand your home education schedule and are willing to help when possible.

Flexibility at the Office

Talk with your employer about a more flexible work schedule. Emphasize that you want to continue working for the good of the company, and you believe that you can do that, even while you educate your children. Devise a plan that would be beneficial to the company, as well as to your home life, and present it to your employer. Maybe you could go to work earlier and work through your lunch hour, then leave a couple hours early to spend time with your children.

When you have the company's interests in mind, employers can tell that you are sincere and hardworking. They will see that you're capable of accomplishing a full day's work in half the time it might take other employees. You have set priorities in the office and for your family.

Career Options

If it proves too difficult to keep your current career position and homeschool your children, other options are available. Perhaps you could move into another position within the company, where you can telecommute, work from home a few days a week, or work on computer files via a remote access program. When you take breaks from your office in your home, you can check on your children's lessons or spend your lunch hour on science experiments.

Flexible Work Schedules

Flexible work schedules can ensure that one parent is home while the other is at work. For instance, you may work from 10:00 A.M. to 4:00 P.M., and your partner may work the night shift from 11:00 P.M. to 7:00 A.M. In this way, a parent is always at home with the children, ensuring one-on-one time with the kids while overseeing the education process.

In this scenario, you may have some quiet time with your partner in the early mornings before the kids awaken. Then, after breakfast and before you go to work, you could start the kids on the lesson plans for the day. While you're away, your partner can help them with projects or questions, making sure they're staying on track. When you return in the late afternoon, you and your partner can spend more time with the kids, working on lessons and projects before it's time for the next work shift. This provides a great opportunity for children to have time alone with each parent, as well as time with both parents together each evening.

Of course, the parent working the night shift will need to sleep at some point during the day. If your children are mature enough to handle themselves properly while a parent is sleeping, they should be capable of completing lessons on their own with little supervision. If the children are too young to be on their own while the parent sleeps, they can go to a relative's or sitter's home, or to a daycare when you work the dayshift.

Homeschooling Dads

Dads are becoming more involved in their children's education at home. If they can't be home all day with the kids, then they take advantage of the learning opportunities during the hours they are at home. And in some cases, Dad stays at home with the kids while Mom goes to work.

FACT

Networks, conventions, and other helpful information for stay-at-home dads can be found at *www.AtHomeDad.org*. The stay-at-home dads site, *www.DadStaysHome.com*, provides support, ideas, and connections for fathers.

Steve's wife kept her career as an emergency room nurse when they made the decision to homeschool their children. Steve took over the main homeschool responsibilities and household duties. The arrangement worked perfectly for their family, and the kids enjoy the extra time they now have with their dad. When their mom comes home from work, they spend time with her while Dad, who enjoys cooking, prepares dinner for the family.

Involving Relatives

As busy as you are, you may overlook the benefits of involving grandparents, aunts, and uncles in your children's education. Grandparents can often provide firsthand knowledge of historical events that have occurred over the past fifty or more years. When you visit grandparents, encourage them to share memories of special events, the way life was when they were young, mementos from the past, or skills they have learned over the years.

Consider other relatives, too. Is your brother or sister a banker, computer wizard, musician, writer, attorney, or cattle rancher? Then they have knowledge and skills they could share with your children. Does your brother or sister have a knack for electronics, landscaping, painting, making speeches, or selling things? Encourage them to share their skills and talents with your children, broadening their horizons and illuminating them to the possibilities that await them in the world.

Dividing Responsibilities

It takes everyone in the family pulling their own weight to make each day a success. By the time a family decides to homeschool, it's usually a unified decision. In the beginning, it may have been Mom's idea, and she may have sought feedback from other family members. Or it may have been Junior's idea, and he may have had to work especially hard to convince Mom and Dad. It required research and homework, discussions and considerations.

One thing that may be overlooked in the initial stages, however, is the division of responsibilities in the home. No matter whose idea it was, the full weight of the homeschooling process shouldn't fall upon Mom (because it was *her* idea) or Junior (because it was *his* idea). If Mom happens to be able to stay home full time, she may have more time to be involved in the entire homeschooling procedure. But Dad can take part in the evening reading sessions, look over completed assignments, determine how the math skills are progressing, and take over the science classes in the evening or on weekends.

Taking Turns

If both parents work, each can take turns with the evening reading sessions. Then one parent may focus on English and history lessons, while the other may prefer to be in charge of math and science. Art, crafts, music, physical education, and life skills can be shared between the parents.

ALERT

When you first embark upon the homeschooling journey, be sure that everyone comprehends and agrees with the goals and what it will take to reach those goals. When *everyone* works toward a common goal, you'll have enough time for a quality education in the home, as well as time for family fun and recreation.

When both parents are working, each can also take turns with the daily household chores. Some people may be better suited for certain tasks. For instance, Dad may be the better cook, so he's the preferred chef each night. Mom may be more cognizant of the grounds around the home, thereby taking over the weekly mowing chores, planting, pruning, weeding, and outdoor upkeep.

Helping with Chores

Everyone's tasks go quicker when everyone pitches in to clean up the kitchen after the meals, to haul the trash to the curb, to set out or put away utensils and tools, to help parents, to help each other, and to pick up after one's self on a daily basis. The earlier this is learned (during preschool years), and the longer it is maintained (as long as people occupy the home), the more responsible, mature, and adept each child will become.

This does not mean that children should be servants within the home, nor does it mean that Mom or Dad should be subservient to their children or to each other. It only means that the people who live within a family should act in a proper and responsible manner, each contributing equal weight to the good of that family.

Chores can range from taking out the trash to meal preparations, mowing the lawn, or paying the bills and balancing the checkbook. Occasions may arise when the task-doer is incapacitated or out of town and can't complete his or her assigned tasks for a few days. You can make arrangements to cover for this person's chores, but, when possible, this person will need to return the favor in the near future.

Compiling a To-Do List

A lot of folks believe they can remember what needs to be done each day, and they don't need to write it down. That may be true. However, one of the major benefits of a to-do list is to free up space in your mind. When a dozen things are needling the back of your mind, they interfere with your focus and productiveness. Once you get those dozen items onto a to-do list, something surprising happens: Your mind immediately becomes clearer and more focused.

Your to-do list can be a small three-by-five-inch notebook that you keep in your pocket, purse, car, or by the phone. Or, your to-do lists can be written on slips of paper cut from scrap paper, then attached to the refrigerator with magnets or to a wall calendar with removable tape. Reminders jotted onto different-sized sticky notes can be adhered to computer monitors, telephones, cabinet door interiors, dashboards, calendars, or mirrors. Whatever your preferred method, getting those pesky to-do thoughts out of your mind and onto paper, where they are conveniently in sight, will enable you to think and focus more clearly each day.

Keeping a Daily Planner

A daily planner may be better than the to-do list for some. These usually provide separate spaces for noting appointments on a daily, weekly, and monthly basis; calls that need to be made; jobs that are due or deadlines to meet; bills to pay; birthdays, anniversaries, and special events; shopping lists; address and telephone numbers; and your own weekly goals, along with recreational plans.

Homeschooling at Night

If you and your partner must work an eight-hour day, then you'll probably want to homeschool in the evenings. Even if you're away from the home from 8:30 to 5:30, that's only nine hours out of a twenty-four-hour day. If you sleep for eight hours, you still have seven hours left to work in the time necessary for individualized homeschooling.

ESSENTIAL

The actual one-on-one time you spend with your child directly on lessons could range from one to two hours per day (kindergarten and early elementary) to three or four hours per day (middle to high school). A six-hour day requirement doesn't mean you must stand in front of your child, teaching for six hours straight. Learning occurs at all hours of the day.

You and your partner can spend a couple hours in the evening, working with children on their lessons and projects. Then, rather than having your children do homework in the evenings, as the schools do, your kids can do their assignments during the day while you're at work and when they're with relatives or a sitter. After their homework assignments are completed, they can work on other educational activities, such as reading, doing research, working on construction or art projects, or playing music or stimulating learning games. In this way, children easily attain the six-hour educational day that some states might require.

When the family is together again in the evenings and on weekends, you can all work together on projects: discuss them; contribute thoughts, ideas, and input; and brainstorm together on new ideas, themes, or unit studies to pursue. As a result, you'll stay in close touch with what your children work on each day. You'll encourage them, and you'll inspire them to think of new educational avenues to explore.

Weekend Learning Projects

Save those in-depth science experiments for the weekend. Then you can break out the chemistry set, lab equipment, Bunsen burner, microscope, and other science tools. You'll be able to spend hours on various experiments, learning and having fun at the same time. This is a great time to create volcanoes, landforms, erosion demonstrations, and study soil, rocks, and fossils. Grow crystals, construct a water cycle model, create a tornado in a bottle, or build electronic devices.

Keep science experiment books on hand or pick up new ones regularly from the library so you'll always have new projects to try. *The Everything® Kids' Science Experiments Book*, *Kitchen Science Lab for Kids*, and the *Science for Every Kid* books offer hundreds of experiments and projects.

FACT

Library Video, at *www.LibraryVideo.com*, carries science experiment videos, as well as educational videos on nearly every topic imaginable. The members of your local homeschool group may want to chip in to purchase a few and maintain your own video library.

Weekends are a good time to watch science or history videos, too. The *Tell Me Why* video series and the *Nova Adventures in Science* videos are fascinating. The *American Adventure* history videos, PBS documentaries, and National Geographic videos are also excellent. Check with your library on the videos they carry.

Fun Field Trips

Educational activities can be rolled into family field trips to museums, zoos, nature centers, aquariums, or planetariums. In addition to field trips to bakeries, restaurants, grocery stores, and other businesses, consider areas that welcome spur-of-the-moment field trips. Spontaneous stops could include visiting a honey bee farm, Native American craft shows, a medieval fair, log cabins, a fire lookout tower, a magic show, an eighteenth-century cemetery, wildlife sanctuaries, and an artists' colony.

Other places and events for educational field trips include:

- Military museums
- Railroad museums
- Historic homes or sites

- Blacksmith or woodworker shops
- Farms or orchards
- Ship or submarine tours
- Air shows or warplane tours
- Wildlife refuge or national parks
- Visits to nearby towns and communities

Local homeschool groups also hold field trips throughout the school year. Unfortunately, many of these are held during the week while working parents are on the job. Try to set up a few group field trips for the weekends when possible. Or arrange to work on a Saturday, so that you can take a day off in the middle of the week to participate in homeschool field trips.

ALERT

Keep field trips fun. You don't want to turn the event into a school lesson or threaten a quiz when the trip is over. Remember that learning occurs and lasts longer when activities are presented in fun, relaxing, and interesting ways.

When taking part in field trips, reinforce the educational aspects by discussing the destination in advance. Discuss any questions your kids may have and encourage them to research the areas you plan to visit. Take notebooks and sketch pads along on the trip. Children can draw maps to the destination, sketch the scenery or buildings you visit, and jot down thoughts and events as they unfold.

If you miss out on a few field trips, spend time with children taking virtual field trips on the weekends. See online field trips at *www.Exploratorium.edu*, *www.FieldTripZoom.com*, or those featured at *www.EverythingHomeschooling.com*.

Resources for Working Couples

For additional ideas on balancing work and family, see *www.BlueSuitMom.com* and *www.HomeSchoolDads.com*. The suggestions and help that you'll find on these sites will provide extra encouragement for your homeschool family.

CHAPTER 18

Homeschooling in the Early Years

Children love playing and learning. Through play, learning occurs naturally every day. Follow the joy and enthusiasm that bubbles from within your children each day. When they are running and tumbling, join in the fun as you sing alphabet and counting songs. When they're coloring and painting, encourage them to describe their creations and the different shapes and colors they use. When you run errands together, discuss the world around you, and enjoy the learning adventures that unfold.

Toddlers and Preschoolers

Parents sometimes ask how soon they should begin homeschooling their toddler. As soon as your baby is born, you're homeschooling. In other words, you're interacting with the new addition to your family, playing with him, and helping him to learn about the world around him. This process of interacting with children and guiding the learning process continues through the toddler years and through the teenage years. Homeschooling is simply a way of life.

Early Learning Activities

With babies and toddlers, you'll want to engage in visual, auditory, and sensory activities to stimulate all five senses. Include lots of music and dancing in your home, moving along to the rhythm of the tunes. Talk with your child as you go about your day, and carry on conversations, pointing out objects in the home or yard and describing the places you visit. Read to your child, no matter how young or old she is, and recite poetry, nursery rhymes, and lyrics to songs.

Toddlers learn quickly through simple songs and fingerplays. For lyrics and descriptions, visit *www.PreschoolRainbow.org* and click "Rhymes, Songs, and Fingerplays." For more fingerplays and rhymes, see *www.NaturalLearning.com* and click "Fingerplays."

Count out items on a daily basis; for instance: "One finger, two fingers, three fingers; one Cheerio, two Cheerios, three Cheerios; one block, two blocks, three blocks," and so on. Perform fingerplays with your young child, gently moving his hands and fingers for him in time to the rhythm of the song. Besides talking and interacting with your child, allow him to interact with himself in a mirror as soon as he's able to focus. He'll also enjoy looking at photos or picture books of babies and toddlers near his age, and may carry on conversations with their pictures.

You can also learn new activities to do with toddlers and preschoolers by attending mommy-and-me programs at community centers, or story time or puppet theaters at libraries or bookstores. Browse the local school-supply store or the educational section of the toy store, too. A multitude of ideas are available from these. You can also get ideas on how to make similar educational toys and games with household items at little or no cost.

Toddler Activities

As your child's ability to walk improves and he begins to explore his surroundings, his level of curiosity will increase. Provide texture boards or boxes for him to touch and respond to. Discuss the concepts of soft, hard, furry, and rough. He'll love to pour and fill items, so engage in these games with him, using plastic pitchers and balls. Count as the pitcher is refilled with balls, and count as he pours the balls into plastic bowls, mimicking the way you pour drinks into glasses.

Copying the actions of grownups or older siblings is one of the main ways that children learn. Babies and toddlers are fascinated by all the things that older siblings and adults can do. They constantly strive to be like you or an older brother or sister. Allow them to do the things you do, within reason and at their own skill level. Discuss the activities they work at or perform each day. Talking and discussion is just as important for reinforcing learning with babies and toddlers as it is with older children.

Active Learning

As your toddler's mobility increases, so will his desire for more activity. Help him develop his gross motor skills with rolling, throwing, and chasing soft rubber balls, climbing on pillows and cushions, and hopping and jumping, all with supervision, of course. Enhance his fine motor skills with finger-painting, roller-art, peg-style puzzles, fitting pieces into slots, and putting jumbo beads together. Remember to talk, count, and sing during these activities, to add more meaning to the learning process.

Books such as *The Everything® Toddler Activities Book, 2nd Edition*, by Joni Levine or *Preschool Play and Learn* by Penny Warner provide ideas and simple directions for games and learning activities for little ones. Or visit *www.First-School.ws* or *www.EnchantedLearning.com* for preschool activities and ideas.

Learning Through Play

Don't underestimate the learning benefits that result from playing. When a child is engaged in a playful environment where she's using her imagination, pretending, exploring, and discovering, she focuses her thinking and problem-solving skills on the moment at hand, inevitably learning from these firsthand experiences. This is true whether she's involved in fantasy play or building a LEGO village. When you remove her from this environment to sit her at a desk, you abruptly interrupt the learning process she is thoroughly engrossed in.

While her mind is in another realm, absorbed with the situation there, she's focused on problem solving and bringing resolution to the world she's playing within. When she is placed at a desk with worksheets to do, she feels suspended between two worlds where nothing makes sense for a few minutes. She has been torn from the world she was previously making sense of, only to have her imagination and creativeness suddenly turned off. Her brain must quickly readjust to this drastic change of events as it struggles to shut down its imagination process, its creativeness, and its problem-solving mechanisms. The child strives to comprehend what the worksheet in front of her has to do with the world she had so recently been captivated by.

Time for Playing

Even though lessons and worksheets may be important, there is a time and place for everything. It's imperative to your child's intellectual growth, as well as her physical, emotional, and social development, that she has plenty of time and space for playing. Set aside blocks of time each day for uninterrupted play, which will allow your child to explore her world, use her imagination and creativeness, and be an active participant in her own life.

Gently provide advance warning of when that playtime is about to come to an end, due to the need to work on lessons. When she has fifteen or twenty minutes to bring resolution within her world of play and draw things to a close, she'll be better able to make the transition from play to lessons.

Create a Stimulating Environment

A variety of activity centers will further your child's social skills, reading and language skills, and math and science skills. In your child's room or playroom, create areas that allow for dramatic or pretend play, a dress-up corner, a kitchen play area, music area, and a library or quiet corner. You can use cardboard boxes and the imagination to serve the purpose for these areas.

QUESTION

Can I use educational software with my toddler?
Some researchers believe that children age three and under should not spend time on computers. They feel that children in this age group learn best through movement, personal interactions, and using the senses. The sedentary aspect of using the computer is therefore not as beneficial to their development. However, three- and four-year-olds are generally ready to begin experimenting with age-appropriate, educational software.

The presence of stuffed animals or dolls allows for the care and nurturing of animals and infants. Arrange other toys and hands-on manipulatives appropriate for your child's age on shelves that are accessible to him. Make learning activities available that stimulate the sensory, visual, and auditory senses, such as physical touch, reading, playing, singing, dancing, and talking.

Create a place for arts and crafts projects, painting, clay, puzzles, and games. Display the artwork your little one creates on a bulletin board in the kitchen or hallway. Hang colorful pictures or educational posters where your child can see them. Discuss the pictures on the posters from time to time; point out and read the words, too.

Spend lots of time together, looking through picture books and discussing what your child sees. Include your child in daily outdoor activities, such as walking the dog, feeding the birds, getting the mail, or planting and weeding a garden. You'll round out your child's daily education and enhance his mental, social, and physical growth by including dramatic play, music, reading, art, discussions, and recreational play each day.

Socialization Concerns

Young children may go through a shy stage of "stranger suspicion," where the only people they are comfortable with are their parents or siblings. They may resist making eye contact with others, pull back from others' touch, or hide behind Mom or Dad. Most children will outgrow this stage, so there's no need to force your child to interact with those she's presently not comfortable with.

Rather, allow your child to observe friends or relatives from a safe distance, until she's ready to venture forth at her own pace. When she watches the way you interact with others, how you meet and greet people, the way you smile or laugh, and the comfortable and natural relationship you have with others, she'll begin to open up and mimic your positive, friendly, and sociable behaviors.

Arrange to attend story time at libraries or bookstores and mommy-and-me programs where she can simply watch, rather than participate. Provide opportunities for her to observe other children at play in the park or in preschool or kindergarten groups. Over time, the reticence and suspicion she feels will begin to subside, and she'll become more relaxed and able to enjoy, and look forward to, opportunities to socialize with others of all ages.

Kindergarten Readiness

Many preschool activities carry over into kindergarten, but with emphasis upon strengthening various skills, comprehension levels, and reading readiness abilities. Continue to talk with your child about everything going on around him, engage in discussions about topics of interest to him, and encourage him to always ask questions about anything on his mind.

ESSENTIAL

For kindergarten ideas, consult books such as *Ready for Kindergarten!* by Deborah Stewart and *What Your Kindergartner Needs to Know* by E.D. Hirsch and John Holdren. Or you can visit *www.KinderStart.com* for learning activities and crafts.

As with preschool children, repetition is an important tool for learning. Kindergarten children still enjoy hearing rhymes, songs, and stories repeated over and over. Due to their unique sense of humor at this age, they often like to switch the lyrics or stories around in a silly manner, just to see if you can catch the discrepancies.

Learning Readiness Skills

By now, children will need to know critical information about themselves, their families, and their homes, such as full names, addresses, and telephone numbers. Their ability to communicate is a high priority, not only for communicating with family members, but with sitters, doctors, police officers, and other adults. Yet, they must be cautioned against talking with strangers.

They need to be able to follow simple directions, then increasingly complex directions suitable for their age. Manners and showing respect are important, along with proper social skills. They should understand how to take turns, share, and that hurting others is not acceptable behavior.

You'll want to help your child improve his fine motor skills, such as handling pencils, cutting and pasting, and tying shoes. You'll also want to encourage him to practice gross motor skills, such as hopping on one foot, pumping a swing, or riding a bike. Emotional growth shouldn't be overlooked, either. Outbursts or temper tantrums need to be curbed, as well as whining or crying when things don't go one's way.

Reading Readiness Skills

Reading readiness includes the ability to listen attentively to stories, tell or retell stories, make the connection between words on a page and the story they tell, understand that letters create words, and identify signs and labels in the community. You can help your child prepare for reading by surrounding him with picture books and storybooks, reading to him regularly, and asking him questions about his thoughts or feelings on stories.

Read to your child from anything that has words on it: the cereal box, milk carton, labels on cans or jars, newspapers, calendars, posters, or anything else around the home. Show him the letters that spell "Cheerios" or "milk." Repetition in this manner will help him make the connection between the item, the letters printed on it, and the spoken word.

Reading Field Trips

When you're running errands, continue to point out letters and words on signs, logos, and at the grocery store. It can be helpful to engage in reading field trips on a regular basis. Walk or drive around, pointing out the letters and words on signs and in grocery stores. Then go to the library and sit down at a table with a few favorite books, and continue to point out the letters and words in books. Back at home, read a favorite story and, again, point out familiar letters and words. He'll soon see that words are everywhere, and reading is an important skill to possess.

Show your child how you can write a simple short story, using letters and words that he may be familiar with. Allow him to watch you create this short story on paper. Then read it back to him. He'll make the connection that he, too, can put letters and words on paper, then read them to you.

Varied Learning Rates

Of course, not every child will learn to recognize letters or words, or learn to print or read, at the same time. Not every child learns to walk or talk at the same age, nor learns to ride a bike or tie his shoes at the same age. If your child does not show interest in letters or words, don't force him.

You don't want to exhibit frustration or associate negative feelings with reading or writing. Simply continue to read and point out words and signs, but don't quiz him on them or force the issue. As long as you make reading an enjoyable activity, it's only a matter of time before he eventually makes the connection.

Educational Activities

In a traditional school during kindergarten and first grade, a report card will cover social and emotional capabilities. Areas they cover include the ability to pay attention in class, listen well to the teacher, play well with others, stay on task, and exhibit self-control. Cognitive skills on a report card can include the ability to recognize or print the alphabet and numerals, count objects, associate sounds and letters, use appropriate vocabulary, and demonstrate problem-solving skills. As your child matures, she will continue to work on these skills as they become increasingly more challenging.

You can help your child work toward similar goals by continuing to talk and read to her daily, sing and recite rhymes together, tell and retell stories, and create and print your own stories. Play educational board games and recreational games together, visit the library and check out a variety of books and tapes, and go on field trips and various places of interest on a regular basis.

ESSENTIAL

Worksheets for preschool and kindergarten skills are available at web-sites such as *www.KidsLearningStation.com* or *www.Kindergarten Worksheets.net*. You can print the pages for your children to complete, color, and display. Some of the worksheets are free; others are available through an online subscription, usually for a minimal fee.

For busywork, judge your child's interest in kindergarten-level to second-grade-level workbooks or worksheets. You may want to purchase a reading workbook and a math workbook that interests your child. If you have Internet access, you can download and print age-level worksheets from children's websites.

Kindergarten Activities

The following activities will help enhance fine motor skills, visual discrimination, auditory discrimination, classification skills, sequencing skills, reading readiness, and math readiness.

- Recognizing and matching colors and shapes
- Cutting and pasting shapes and puzzle pieces
- Tracing straight and curved lines and letters
- Determining same and different
- Determining same sounds and rhyming words
- Determining what comes first, second, and last
- Recognizing upper- and lowercase letters
- Counting and adding objects
- Measuring and estimating size and distance

First Grade Activities

The following activities will help to improve fine motor skills, printing and composition skills, phonics and decoding skills, independent reading, and math skills.

- Matching shapes and patterns
- Using charts and graphs
- Counting, adding, and subtracting

- Measuring objects and counting money
- Telling time and using calendars
- Printing short sentences
- Organizing ideas and sentences logically
- Creating and printing stories
- Reading and comprehending short stories
- Making inferences and drawing conclusions

Length of Homeschool Days

The time you spend on formal learning activities will depend on your child and her abilities and attention span. Once her fingers have grown tired of holding a pencil, or her mind can no longer grasp the concept of adding objects, it's time to quit for the day. Next week, she may better understand the concept of addition. Or, next month, she may have attained better control of the pencil and will have an easier time printing sentences.

For now, if ten minutes is all she can spend on tracing letters or printing sentences, that's fine. If ten minutes is all she can spend on listening to a story, recalling some of the details of the story, and summarizing it for you, then that's enough. If ten minutes is all she can spend concentrating on the name of community helpers, maps of your neighborhood, or safety rules, it's time to allow her a much-deserved break.

Be happy with all she's absorbed in thirty minutes today. She's actually learned a lot and practiced important skills during that time. The rest of the day, she can continue learning through play—independently, with you, or with siblings or friends. Tomorrow will offer plenty of opportunities for additional learning, practice, and playtime.

Resources for Early Learning

See Preschool Rainbow at *www.PreschoolRainbow.org* or the "Preschool Place" at *www.EverythingHomeschooling.com* for educational activities that young children will enjoy. Activities range from fun crafts for toddlers and preschoolers to reading, math, and science experiments on themes such as birds, animals, communities, and more.

CHAPTER 19

Homeschooling in the Elementary Years

The elementary years are some of the most exciting and inspirational of the homeschool experience. Children are full of curiosity and eager to explore, experiment, and excel. It's a fun time for learning in the home, whether your child is in the first grade or the fifth. Whatever the age of your child, you can be sure that exciting adventures await you just around the bend.

Teaching Your Child to Read

With practice and patience, you can teach your child to read. It's not as difficult as you might think. These tips and suggestions will soon have your child on the road to reading success.

Phonics versus Whole Language

Much debate has occurred in the past over the use of phonics versus the whole-language concept in teaching children to read. The phonics method of sounding out and deciphering words provides beginning readers with the tools they need to sound out a multitude of words. When a child has learned the sounds of the consonants and vowels, and is able to sound out the word *cat*, she will be able to sound out a dozen more words rhyming with the *at* sound. When this method clicks in your child's mind, and she realizes the key to reading is to sound out words, there will be no holding her back.

FACT

My Reading List, a keepsake book by Emily Ellison, includes charts for your child to keep track of books she has read, along with reward stickers. In addition, the book provides reading and writing activities, information about books and their authors, plus suggested reading lists for beginning readers through advanced readers.

Of course, there are certain words that defy logic and the rules of phonics. You have *ate* and *eight*, and *through* and *though* and *trough*. The pronunciation of sight words such as these will be learned in time, with practice and with patience. Good reading skills result from good reading habits. The more a child reads and becomes familiar with sounding out words, and the more she recognizes words that don't adhere to basic phonics rules, the more adept she'll become at reading.

Reading to Your Children

Once your children become good readers, don't slack off reading to them. Continue reading aloud every day from favorite books, classics, bestsellers, biographies, or textbooks. Continue reading bedtime stories, as well.

Even after children have learned to read, they will pick up proper pronunciation of words, voice inflection, the sound of dialogue, and add to their vocabulary skills as you read aloud to them.

Continue to expand your child's world of books and reading. Visit the library often to select books at your child's current reading level and to determine her abilities with higher-level books. While at the library, sit down together and have her read a few lines from the selection of books. In this way, you both will be able to determine if the books are too easy for her or whether she's ready to move on to the next reading level.

Mastering Math Skills

Basic math, or arithmetic, includes counting, adding, subtracting, estimating, measuring, and calculating. As your children progress through the elementary years, additional mathematical skills will be introduced. When your child has grasped the basics, you'll be able to help him build upon a solid mathematical foundation.

Take Time for Math

Unfortunately, the math skills introduced in traditional schools move along so quickly that if a child doesn't catch them the first time around, they've often lost that window of opportunity. In the homeschool, however, if you see that your child is still struggling with basic subtraction, for instance, you won't want to move ahead to more complex problems until he has mastered the basics. Fortunately, you can spend weeks practicing basic concepts in your homeschool if necessary. There's no specific timeframe your child must stay within.

ALERT

Math programs or textbooks can incorporate methods unique to its principles. Research each carefully and compare notes with other homeschool families. Most importantly, consider your child's learning style. A math program could work well for one family, but the methods might be in direct contrast to your child's learning style.

When your child has achieved true comprehension of subtraction, along with the ability to perform the calculations flawlessly, then he can move on to the next lessons. You will know without a doubt that he has truly mastered the skills he needs before moving ahead. With this solid foundation, he is ready for multiplication and division, fractions and decimals, estimation and measurement, problem solving, and more challenging mathematical equations.

Math Manipulatives

By using concrete examples of math problems, children will better understand the abstract concepts that are introduced. You can use any objects for counting, adding, and subtracting, from buttons to beans to plastic animal counters. You can also use an abacus or counting frame with plastic beads.

Educational supply stores carry a wide variety of math manipulatives. However, you can often make your own. From poster board or construction paper, you can create coin-sized counters, pattern blocks, fraction circles, fraction bars, cardboard clocks, and mathematical charts. You can also make rulers, number lines, geometric boards, play money, and flashcards. And your children will enjoy the cutting and creative activities, too.

Everyday Math

Textbooks and math programs are one way to learn and practice skills. But everyday situations present excellent ways to put those skills to regular, logical use. In a normal day, your family can practice telling time as the minutes and hours go by. You and your children can estimate, then measure ingredients when cooking on a daily basis.

FACT

Activity books such as *Fabulous Fractions* by Lynette Long, *Hands-On Math!* by Frances McBroom, *Math Wise!* by James Overholt, *Real-Life Math Problem Solving* by Mark Illingworth, and *Real-World Math for Hands-On Fun!* by Cynthia Littlefield, all provide interesting, down-to-earth activities that help your child understand and relate key math skills to everyday life.

Practice counting and money skills by setting up a store in your home. Have children put prices on items gathered from the pantry or on toys or books gathered from their room. Make purchases, have children add up the total costs, pay with play or real money, and have children count out your correct change.

When you're grocery shopping, children can keep running tabs of the items you're purchasing and see how close they come to the actual total. At the gasoline station, they can calculate the cost of your tank of gas. Then, based upon how many gallons of gasoline are in the tank and how many miles your car gets to a gallon, they can determine how far this tank of gas will go. Every day offers mathematical problems that can be fun to solve, clearly showing children the importance of learning and applying math skills in real life.

Living History

For decades, children have complained about reading long, dry chapters in history textbooks, then answering the even drier questions at the end of the chapter. There are no fascinating experiments to do, no stimulating challenges, and little creative license allowed with the lessons. It's just facts, and more facts, which can quickly take on a dull, repetitive tone, with little correlation to the child's life today.

Dramatizing Historical Events

Now is a good time to bring dramatic play back into lessons. If you're studying the era of the Revolutionary War, for instance, along with the signing of the Declaration of Independence, enlist the help of the local children's librarian. Seek colorful books written about that era or biographies about prime characters, such as George Washington, Thomas Jefferson, and John Hancock.

Then have your children bring the historic period to life by dramatizing the events. Each family member can take a part, speaking the dialogue and adding to it as they further develop the performance. They can use their creativeness to design their own costumes to the best of their ability. If they don't have boats or a nearby stream to illustrate Washington's crossing of the Delaware River, they can make a cardboard skiff and place it upon blue bed sheets spread upon the living room floor, representing the river. If they don't have powdered wigs or quill pens lying around to use when signing the Declaration, cotton batting can adorn their heads and a feather can be inserted into their pens.

Advantages of Re-Enactments

Nearly all historic events or periods can be dramatized, and children are generally eager to recreate those periods, using whatever props they have at hand. Such props, no matter how simple, can pull children into a particular era, making them feel as if they're actually living the events. Not only does this manner of recreating history inscribe the events into their mind better than simply reading about them, but it provides the opportunity for children to memorize and deliver parts of important documents or speeches, such as the Declaration of Independence, the Gettysburg Address, the Mayflower Compact, the Magna Carta, and many more.

ESSENTIAL

Encourage children to create a short book on their historical presentations. They can write and illustrate the steps they took in researching, designing, and performing parts of the living history lessons. They can also include the script they developed and followed for the performance. Bind the book with string or staples, and add it to their portfolio of homeschool memoirs.

Re-enactments need not only cover historic events, but everyday colonial life as well. Children can dress and perform in the manner of early pioneers and craftsmen they've read about. They can relive the adventures of early explorers, sail the Mississippi River, and traverse the Oregon Trail. History provides thousands of events to recreate, dramatize, and instill in their minds.

Exploring Science

History can easily be carried through into science lessons, as both are intricately intertwined. Scientific and medical discoveries, inventions and machines have all contributed to the progression of historic events in our world. One can hardly learn about the invention of the telephone, light bulb, or radioactivity, for instance, without learning the history of Alexander Graham Bell, Thomas Edison, or Marie Curie.

Backyard Science

Engage in science experiments and hands-on projects several times a week. Take advantage of your backyard, your region, and your seasons and climate. It may be the time of year when mushrooms, fungi, and spores are prolific and available for observation. Flowers and fruits may be blossoming or ripening, or leaves may be falling and plants going into hibernation.

FACT

The Exploratorium at *www.Exploratorium.edu* provides virtual visits to the Antarctic, the Observatory, Sports Science, Brain Explorer, and Math Explorer. Visit Questacon at *www.Questacon.edu.au* for science shows, illusions, activities, and puzzles. Science and math lessons are also featured on Discovery Education's site at *www.DiscoveryEducation.com*.

It may be the rainy season or the dry season, offering insight into the season's impact on soil, crops, gardens, leaves, harvests, streams and rivers, and heat and humidity. Birds and rabbits may be making nests or teaching their young ones to fend for themselves. All of nature, throughout the seasons, offers opportunities for hands-on learning and projects right in your own backyard.

Science Experiments

Science books can provide knowledge, methods, theories, and principles for the topics you study. These are helpful for establishing the background or foundation of experiments your children will conduct. But it's the actual experiments or hands-on projects that provide real understanding of the reasons and results of the projects, or the cause and effects of the experiment. They bring scientific principles to life, making them tangible and concrete for your children, easy to explore and easy to comprehend.

Science Biographies

Short biographies on scientists and inventors help children zero in on the person and their accomplishments. Such biographies sometimes include suggestions on scientific experiments that children can explore at home. The relation between the scientist, the experiments, and that period in history help to pull events together in a logical way. When a child thinks of an experiment she did involving a battery and a light bulb during a study of Thomas Edison's life, she's more likely to remember the fact that Edison was nearly deaf, lived through the Civil War era, and not only developed the incandescent light bulb but also the phonograph and movie projector.

Creating Art and Music

In some traditional schools, art and music programs have begun to suffer due to a lack of funding or mismanagement of school budgets. Yet, art and music are fundamental parts of even the earliest education. Rhythmic moving and dancing come naturally to youngsters as soon as they are able to stand in their crib, swaying to the music they feel within their bodies. Coloring and doodling are the first exercises that children attempt when they pick up a crayon, whether they have paper before them or not.

Art and music are an integral part of human beings, helping to enhance thinking skills, creativeness, and imagination. Such skills should, therefore, never be discounted or relegated to one or two days a week. Rather, they should be an essential part of every day.

Artistic Creations

Art brings out the creativeness and inventiveness in children, as well as provides ways for children to illustrate, convey, and communicate feelings and perspectives from their point of view. You'll want to focus on the creative process of hands-on arts and crafts projects rather than the outcome of the project. It's the involvement and action of creating art that makes it so enjoyable. Being overly concerned with the end result can extinguish the creative spark before it ignites.

Harmonizing Body and Mind

It's fascinating how we can remember the words to a song we haven't heard in twenty years, yet we can't remember what we wanted to pick up at the grocery today. Perhaps we should set our grocery lists to music.

ESSENTIAL

Creativity involves many areas of the brain! Encourage children to do something creative every day: draw a scene outside their window, compose their own music, make a new scrapbook page, create art from items in a drawer, build a small device that actually runs. For daily creative ideas, see the Creative Writing ideas at *www.EverythingHomeschooling.com/creative.aspx.*

Similarly, children can have difficulty learning the alphabet, the months of the year, or the countries of the world, but put them to music, and suddenly they can sing them in the correct order. Music has this ability. Music brings the mind and body together in a splendid harmony of sound, rhythm, words, and brainwaves. Research has shown that music increases spatial-temporal reasoning skills, which are especially helpful in grasping some mathematical concepts.

Even if your children are not necessarily musically or artistically inclined, they will still reap the benefits of artistic creation and the sound of music. Welcome both into your lessons every day.

Testing and Assessments

Testing can be a testy subject with some homeschoolers. In schools, testing has been a way to determine what each child has learned, or, as some say, how well the teacher has taught the child. Due to the close, one-on-one interaction in a home-based education, parents can clearly see how well their child is progressing and what areas may need additional attention. They also understand that the mere idea of a test can set anyone on edge, which can result in adverse or misleading test results.

However, some states require testing as part of their evaluation process, so it may be something that your child will need to deal with at some point. The good news is that homeschool-friendly testers are usually available to administer the tests. These are certified teachers who are authorized to give tests, and many of them are also homeschool parents.

When you have a friendly, state-certified tester in your home, administering the test to your child at the dining table—and allowing your child to take breaks, go outside for fresh air to clear the mind, and have lunch or a snack in the middle of the test—it makes for a less stressful test environment and truer test results. Some homeschoolers prefer to gather in one location and have the test administered as a group. Again, breaks from the testing and a more casual atmosphere will enable children to be more relaxed and perform better. Check with your local homeschool support group regarding standardized tests in your region.

Socializing with Others

Children in this age group, from six to twelve years of age, usually have little trouble making friends and socializing. In most cases, they've already developed friendships with other children in the community through play dates, church events, or by taking part in baseball, gymnastics, or similar activities.

To broaden their circle of friends, you can join the local homeschool support group, where you can attend regular gatherings and take part in picnics, field trips, bowling, miniature golf, and similar group activities. Invite homeschoolers near your child's age to your home and allow your child to visit their home.

Enroll your six-year-old in swimming lessons, your eight-year-old in violin lessons, and your ten-year-old in sculpture classes. Next semester, enroll the children in skiing lessons, voice lessons, and painting classes. In addition, sign the kids up with a theater group, musical band, sports team, or 4-H to encourage group interaction and teamwork. Not only will your children learn new skills and improve upon previous skills, but they'll continue to meet new and old friends, as well.

Resources for Lessons and Activities

The Weekly Lessons for Grades K–12 at *www.EverythingHomeschooling.com* provide fun learning activities for courses such as Language Arts, Social Studies, Math, Science, Life Skills, and Arts and Music. In addition, you'll find science experiments, hands-on projects, and weekly challenges for all grade levels.

CHAPTER 20

Homeschooling in the Middle Years

The middle-school years are often a harbinger of change. As your child enters these years, her educational, emotional, and social skills will take on deeper meanings. The high-school years are just around the corner, the emotional and physical changes of adolescence are on the horizon, and closer alliances are formed with friends. Through homeschooling, you can make this transition time a smooth and enjoyable experience for all.

A Perfect Learning Pace

In the homeschool, your child should be allowed to move at a pace that remains challenging, yet allows for thoroughly grasping concepts and skills. Unlike a traditional school, it's not necessary to keep all lessons moving along on the same time schedule. In other words, you needn't feel that you must complete a history lesson in thirty minutes, a science lesson in thirty minutes, math and English each within a thirty-minute time frame, then repeat the process again tomorrow.

If your child can do his English lesson in thirty minutes, that's fine. But if he has difficulty in math, struggling with ratios and percents, for example, then the time allotted for math class may need to be extended. In fact, there's nothing wrong with spending a couple hours learning a new concept, as long as your child is inclined to do so.

If he simply cannot make sense of the lesson today, then it's okay to set it aside and work on it another day. A couple weeks from now, he may be able to comprehend the relationship of ratios and percents more easily.

Strengths and Weaknesses

If you've homeschooled your child for a number of years, you have a good understanding of her strengths and weaknesses. Because you've been in tune with her, you have been able to help her overcome most of her weaknesses over the years. However, if you've recently withdrawn your child from school, you may notice gaps in her education.

Some weaknesses may be a part of your child's unique personality. Some people are better talkers than others, some better writers, some better at math, and some better artistically. There are some things you can't change.

Other weaknesses are a result of gaps in the education process or of your child missing certain nuggets of information. When you're homeschooling your child, you'll quickly see where she needs extra assistance. Together, you can focus on the weak areas and turn them into strengths.

If your child isn't as strong in math as her brother, father, or mother, then it's probably a trait that is unique to her character. She may possibly be stronger in art, science, or music than her brother, father, or mother. Everyone has strengths and weaknesses, some of which can be improved, and some which cannot. Knowing that you've done your best and knowing that your child will be a success, thanks to the many other strengths she possesses, will be reward enough.

Comprehension Skills

One of the best things you can do for your child is to continue encouraging his interest in reading. As children approach their preteen and teenage years, their focus begins to shift. They may interact with their peers more and want to be more like them, which means developing new interests in music, movies, or the latest fads. With their attention focused elsewhere, they may think that they don't have enough time to read anymore. However, reading, literacy, and comprehension should remain a top priority in the homeschool.

Choosing to Read

In the homeschool, your child may spend two to three hours each day on school topics, but during the rest of the day, he is free to think, read, and learn about the things that genuinely fill him with enthusiasm. As a result, he has more time for reading and is more likely to choose to read books on subjects that interest him, to research and to read related topics on the Internet, and to visit the library and bookstore more often.

When reading and research are a result of a child's own interest in a subject, he doesn't feel as if he's being forced to do something that has little meaning for him. Therefore, he's more likely to read magazines, newspapers, or the latest fiction book, just for the pleasure of it. When you resist the temptation to force the reading issue, you'll often be surprised by the positive results.

Encouraging Reading

If your child's interest in reading still seems to have waned, invest more time in reading, yourself. Avoid nagging your child to read. Instead, casually turn off the television and radio, pick up a book from the collection you keep on the side table or bookshelf, and spend an hour quietly reading. It can be helpful to spread a few books or magazines on a coffee table, too.

Sometimes, reading can seem like too much of a chore to a child. If this appears to be the case, get things moving by reading the first chapter of a book to your child, or take turns reading chapters aloud. Even though they are now middle-schoolers, kids still enjoy being read to, whether they want to admit it or not.

Reading for Pleasure

When reading for pleasure, you don't want to drill your children on what they've read. However, it's helpful and interesting for everyone in the family to discuss books they're currently reading. When children hear you describe a special passage from a book, the events unfolding in a novel, or the surprise ending of a mystery, they're intrigued. As you continue to comment upon the story day after day, the characters and events take on a more realistic quality. Your kids can see how wrapped up you are in the story, how deeply it affects or excites you.

When they, too, become engrossed in a book, they'll be more likely to share the story or events with you, just as you shared your comments with them. Make the discussion of books and stories as normal and routine as discussing a movie or television show.

By relating what they've read in a book and how it made them feel, children are demonstrating their comprehension skills. And by listening to your book discussions, they have a better idea of the themes that can run through a story, the inferences that can be made, clues to watch for in stories, conclusions that can be drawn, and how events in books can relate to real life. These are critical reading and comprehension skills that can be applied across the curriculum in all subject areas.

Writing Skills

The middle years are great years for pursuing special interests and exploring educational topics together, doing research together, writing reports together, and learning together. When your child sees you select a book to read and to write a report on, she's more likely to select her own book and write a report on it, right alongside you.

ESSENTIAL

For middle school book report ideas, browse the suggestions at the Web English Teacher website, *www.WebEnglishTeacher.com*. Your child can try alternatives to standard book reports, create a 3D book report, have a book party, or design her own style of book report.

If your child doesn't know how to write a report or the bibliography page, and you've forgotten, you can both research it together. When it's time to stand up and give the book report from notes, you can do it together, in front of family, friends, or relatives. Learning together helps a family stick together.

Interests, Talents, and Hobbies

During the middle school years, children may need to spend an average of two to three hours per day on core curriculum subjects. Some days may require more; some may require less. The remainder of your child's waking hours should be spent on exploring, thinking, reading, playing, discovering, creating, composing, and exercising both the mind and body.

Finding One's Niche

Always encourage your child's current interests or hobbies. If your daughter is presently fascinated by computer art, for instance, allow her to attend computer art classes and experiment with digital art software. She may enjoy reading numerous books and articles on three-dimensional computer animation, and spending hours creating her own computer art or animated clips. She might also enjoy visiting local artists or graphic design businesses.

If your son loves taking apart computers, printers, or small engines, and putting them back together again, give him plenty of opportunities to do so. He can have access to the many discarded computers that end up at recycling centers and work on rebuilding them. He can use his special skills and instruction manuals to help him repair your DVD player, the lawn mower, or water pump. He would no doubt enjoy visiting computer-repair businesses or small-engine repair services in your area.

Making the Most of Talents

If your daughter loves music, allow plenty of free time for practicing the piano, guitar, violin, and any other instruments that interest her. In school, she would probably be able to choose *one* instrument to learn to play. At home, she can choose to play the flute, *and* the clarinet, *and* the trumpet, *and* the drums. And she will have the time to become accomplished on all four instruments, as well as the time to compose her own music and record her compositions.

FACT

At this point in their lives, as they approach adolescence, children begin to search for themselves. Psychologists refer to this as *identity formation*. It's an integral part of making the transition from child to adult. When children seek independence and focus on things that interest them, it is the natural order of things.

If your son is captivated by politics, is stimulated by debates aired by political analysts, often has his nose buried in political science books, and speaks strongly of his own views and platforms, he may be headed toward a legal or political career. He may be energized by debates he witnesses, driven to deliver rebuttals on viewpoints expressed by others, and feels the most alive when he can listen to facts and opinions supporting diverse viewpoints, then articulate his own feelings. He will need plenty of time to absorb these areas of interest, reflect upon them, hear your views on them, and consider his own feelings regarding them.

Turning Hobbies Into Careers

When children are able to devote much of their time to special areas of interest, they are actively developing their skills for the career that awaits them. The child with an interest in computer art may become a graphic artist; the interest in putting together computer parts may result in a computer-repair business; the musically inclined child could become a musician or open a recording studio; the politically motivated child could become a state representative, working for the good of the people.

Self-Directed Learning

It may be difficult for some people to understand that children naturally teach themselves. As a parent you can share information, share your own experiences, provide guidance, answer questions, and suggest ideas, but you can't get inside your children's minds and take over the way they process, absorb, or retain information. You can help them, you can be of assistance, you can observe the ways in which they seem to learn best, but you can't force them to learn according to your own styles or timetables. Forced learning will usually result in a lack of learning.

Children acknowledge, absorb, and retain information through their own experiences, research, and discoveries. When they have some control over what they're learning, and have the freedom to delve into ideas and concerns that interest them, they have a sense of purpose and identity.

Self-directed learning, or freedom to pursue their own interests, is one way to help children begin to acquire their independence. The desire for more freedom in self-directing their learning should be supported and encouraged by parents, who can keep a watchful eye on their children and guide them when they need assistance.

Socialization Skills

These are the years when children begin to go through emotional and physical changes, and socialization can take on more importance. It's a good time to reinforce proper etiquette, social skills, morals, and values. Children may begin to be away from home more than they've been in the past, visiting with others, going to a movie or to the pizza parlor. Your children will need to select friends based upon the values and character education you have passed on to them during their homeschool years. And they'll need to make informed decisions based on the solid moral training you've provided.

Here are some wonderful books for reinforcing and improving manners and moral behavior:

- *365 Manners Kids Should Know* by Sheryl Eberly
- *Building Moral Intelligence* by Michele Borba
- *Modern Manners* by Dorothea Johnson
- *Rules to Be Cool* by Karla Dougherty
- *Teach Your Children Well: Helping Kids Make Moral Choices* by Don Otis

Extracurricular Activities

As your child's social life begins to pick up, he may become more active in art or drama clubs, writing or book clubs, youth groups, environmental groups, sports, bands, or other organizations. His circle of friends will expand along with his interest in hobbies and community events. These are important social times for him, allowing him to interact with others, use his social skills and manners in real situations, work as a team on projects, and use his logical reasoning and problem-solving skills in the real world.

As your child matures and spends more time with friends or in extracurricular activities, continue to be there for him. Keep the lines of communication open, answer any questions he may have, observe his behavior and his friends' behaviors, and help him find ways to resolve conflicts he may encounter. As much as he wants independence, he also needs to know that he can always turn to you for support.

Community Involvement

Volunteerism brings a sense of responsibility to one's community and to the world we live in. Volunteering in libraries, churches, nursing homes, senior citizen programs, daycare centers, or animal shelters offers insight into situations and lifestyles that your children might be unfamiliar with. The experience can broaden their vision of different lifestyles and cultures within their community.

Children might also want to volunteer in a business or service that parallels their passions: computer, art, music, or bookstores; woodshops or repair shops; science or nature centers; museums or libraries; summer camps or after-school programs; political headquarters or newspaper offices. Volunteering in certain businesses may eventually lead to a part-time, paying job. And what a thrilling and motivating experience that is for a youngster—being paid for something she already loves to do!

Resources for Weekly Learning

The Weekly Lessons for Grades 7–9 at *www.EverythingHomeschooling.com* provide activities for language arts, social studies, math, science, life skills, arts and music, and computer skills. In addition, the daily homeschool activities, science experiments, and weekly challenges will keep children interested in learning each day.

CHAPTER 21

Homeschooling in the Teen Years

Congratulations! You've reached the teenage years in your homeschool! Or perhaps you're just beginning your homeschool odyssey with the teen years. Either way, it's sure to be a voyage that you'll remember and treasure. Of course, you'll want your teen to remember and treasure these special years as well, so read on.

Life with Teens

Some parents might dread the teenage years. But, surprisingly, home-schooled teenagers often seem to escape many of the stereotypical problems associated with these years. They are excited about the direction their lives are going, the things they're learning and pursuing, and the activities they're involved with. They're overflowing with ideas, plans, and goals for their lives. It's a joy to see and feel such energy and happiness from these young adults. Their boundless excitement is positively contagious.

FACT

For help on raising teens in today's world, consider these books: *10 Best Gifts for Your Teen* by Patt and Steve Saso, on maintaining strong relationships and providing guidance; *Parent's Guide to the Teen Years* by Susan Panzarine, about teen pressures and the importance of support systems; and *Parenting Teens with Love and Logic* by Foster Cline and Jim Fay.

Yes, there may be times of moodiness or irritability, which, as you may well recall, are all a part of the teenage years. Hormones are still fluctuating, occasionally wreaking havoc physically as well as emotionally. In many ways, you're sharing your life and your home with another adult now—a young adult, who may still waver between behaving as an adult and behaving as a child.

These can be challenging years, but they can also be exceedingly wonderful years. Enjoy, treasure, and savor these years, for when they're gone, your child will be off and away.

Handling High-School Courses

Yes, you can teach high-school courses. As this book has noted several times before, teaching in the homeschool is a form of *guiding* your child and assisting him in finding the answers and resources he needs to help him learn. It's important that your child experiences and understands the concept of *learning to learn*. Just as he must learn to be responsible for his actions, he must learn how to learn on his own. This is a major skill that will benefit him for the rest of his life.

Educating Oneself

Today's fast-moving technology and way of life demand that children, young people, and adults all be capable of learning new skills, enhancing their own knowledge base, and continually expanding their education. A child who has sat through school, expecting others to teach him what he needs to know, or who expects that the education process is over after high school or college, may not advance as far in the workplace as the person who has learned how to educate himself.

ALERT

Teens may become more secretive and touchy about others prying into their lives, so be careful how you approach them. Most important, keep the lines of communication open. Though they may have nothing to say for days on end, when they know you're there for them, the floodgates can open at any moment, and a deluge of thoughts and feelings may stream forth.

As you progress through the high school years, you'll want to reinforce the importance of learning on one's own while still helping to guide your child through his studies. Now is the time for your child to keep track of his grades and credits earned, particularly if he's planning to attend college. He should keep a list of books he's read each year, the daily learning log complete and up to date, his portfolio of assignments completed, book reports, essays, science projects, and proof of other activities he's involved with.

Correspondence Schools

Keep in mind that your child can attend independent study programs or correspondence schools as he works toward his graduation. Some of the schools that offer diplomas include the following.

- A Beka Academy: *www.AbekaAcademy.org*
- Alger Learning Center: *www.Independent-Learning.com*
- Alpha Omega: *www.aop.com*

- American School: *www.AmericanSchoolOfCorr.com*
- Clonlara High School: *www.clonlara.org/home/highschool*
- CompuHigh: *www.CompuHigh.com*
- Indiana University High School: *https://IUHighSchool.iu.edu*
- Keystone National High School: *http://keystoneschoolonline.com/high-school*
- Laurel Springs School: *http://laurelsprings.com/high-school/*
- Oak Meadow School: *www.OakMeadow.com*

Courses Required for College

As your child prepares for college or a career, it's a good idea that she take four years of English courses (including grammar, composition, and literature) during her high-school years. In addition, she should take three years of math (including algebra and geometry); three years of science (including biology, physical science, and lab experiences); and three years of social studies (including U.S. history and government and economics). If she's applying to college, she'll also need two years of a foreign language, a computer technology course, and at least two years of electives.

Many of these electives are actually life skills that every parent would want their child to learn. Most can be studied and experienced in six- to eight-week courses at the local parks and recreation department or community college. The number of credits your child may need for electives can add up quickly.

Fun with Electives

Electives are the fun part of school. These can include art, music, dance, drama, filmmaking, broadcasting, sculpting, computer science, computer programming, accounting, business practices, business law, journalism, speech, agriculture, forestry, woodshop, auto shop, drafting, mechanical engineering, electronics, health and nutrition, cooking, family living, parenting, philosophy, and psychology, among others.

Handling Difficult Subjects

Along with the fun subjects, the high-school years can hold some challenging subjects, as well. It may have been a while since you took Algebra I or Algebra II, and you didn't like it the first time around. How, you may wonder, will you be able to help your child with those subjects? There are several ways.

The Saxon Math books are excellent. They are designed for the user to teach herself by reading easy-to-understand lessons, building upon previous lessons, and continually practicing and refreshing her skills. Their set of math textbooks (ranging from basic math to pre-algebra, advanced algebra, advanced math, calculus, and physics) may not be for everyone, but they have worked wonders for some homeschool math programs. Of course, you can also supplement the textbooks with math games and software, logical reasoning skills, problem solving, and working with basic, everyday math problems.

ESSENTIAL

Educational math software, such as MathMedia, *www.MathMedia.com*; Math Tutor, *www.MathTutor.com*; and Math Tutor DVDs, *www.MathTutorDVD.com*, provide learning and practice in geometry, algebra, and advanced math skills.

Many other math programs are also available, as well as videos that clearly explain and illustrate math concepts and exercises. Library Video, at *www.LibraryVideo.com*, carries numerous videos on nearly every mathematical topic. If your homeschool group has several homeschoolers approaching the high-school years, you may want to pitch in and purchase a few videos to share over the upcoming years. If your group has a couple of parents who are especially interested in math, they may want to work with a group of teens on weekends. This type of group learning, use of videos, or educational software can be helpful in any of the subject areas: foreign languages, government and economics, biology, or electives.

Help from Tutors and Mentors

Sometimes you just can't teach certain things to your child. If you took French in high school or college, you may not be the most helpful when your daughter decides she wants to learn Russian. When certain subjects prove to be too difficult for your child, it can be a good idea to seek a well-trained and experienced tutor.

Colleges and libraries often keep a database of tutors, along with their specialties, such as foreign languages, calculus, chemistry, and physics. If you're still unable to find tutors or mentors in your community, don't forget your local school district. They will have a list of tutors who may be able to help your child.

Driver Education Courses

Getting one's license is a huge milestone in a teenager's life. It's the moment when he may feel he's attained true independence. Now he can experience one of those privileges that adults get to enjoy. But, as we all know, everyone must earn that privilege and follow the rules in order to keep that privilege. An obvious level of maturity, responsibility, and consideration for others must be displayed before a child can get behind the wheel of a car.

Contact your local department of motor vehicles to determine your state's driver education requirements and restrictions, as they will vary from state to state. Some states allow homeschooled children to enroll in a high-school driver education course. Or they may require that your child enroll in a driving school. Some states require teens to take a drug and alcohol awareness program, which is usually offered locally, before they can obtain their learner's permit or enroll in a driving course.

Social Activities and Events

During these high-school years, teens have busy lifestyles. Social events take on even greater importance, and many teens volunteer their time, serve apprenticeships, or work part-time jobs. They might begin to experience more stress as they take on more responsibility, have fuller schedules, and work hard to complete their high-school studies.

As she ventures further into the world, your child must realize that the choices she makes during these years can have lasting results. If she chooses the wrong group of kids to spend her time with and that group gets into trouble, she could feel reverberations from her unwise choice for many years to come. If she chooses to spend her spare time on college prep courses, and she's able to enroll in college a year early, this, too, can have an impact on her life. As she teeters on the threshold of adulthood, she must understand and accept the relevance and responsibility of preparing wisely for this important phase of her life.

Decision-Making Skills

To help your teen with decision-making skills, you'll need to remain steadfast in your own beliefs and morals. When she comes to you for support, you can help her see both sides of an issue. If she chooses this path, *this* could happen. But if she chooses the other path, *that* could happen. You can share which path you would choose to follow, based on your personal beliefs and experiences.

Yet, you don't want to force your feelings upon her; rather, you want to help guide her in finding the right decisions. This helps her work through the decision-making process, keeping your beliefs in mind while considering her own. The day will come when she is on her own and will have to make her own decisions. Now is the time to help her work her way through the process.

New Challenges and New Joys

New opportunities and experiences will present themselves during the teen years. In addition to boyfriends and girlfriends, dates and dancing, working and socializing, teens still need to focus upon their studies, possibly more than they have at any time in the past. Prospective employers or college administrators will be interested in seeing proof of capabilities when meeting with the young adult. Your child will need to have a solid background to present to them.

Volunteerism and Apprenticeships

Volunteering is an excellent opportunity for your child to meet and interact with others, and work as a team on projects. A tremendous sense of satisfaction and personal achievement can be derived by making a difference in the lives of others. If your teen has special interests or hobbies, he may want to volunteer in an area that corresponds to that interest. For instance, if he loves books and reading, he may want to volunteer to read to seniors in a nursing home. If he loves animals, he could volunteer at the animal shelter, nature center, or wildlife refuge.

FACT

Teens face new challenges, rocky relationships, and difficult decisions as they approach adulthood. These books provide insight and guidance for teens on their journey: *The 7 Habits of Highly Effective Teens* by Sean Covey; *Life Strategies for Teens* by Jay McGraw; *Teen Esteem* by Pat Palmer and Melissa Froehner; and *Think Confident, Be Confident for Teens* by Marci Fox.

Encourage your teen to call or visit places that interest him. He can express his enthusiasm and offer his time and desire to help the facility or business. If they currently don't need extra assistance, have him check back from time to time. Watch your local newspapers for notices regarding volunteer groups and opportunities, too.

Volunteering in Businesses

Your child might want to volunteer his time and help in a special business. At age thirteen, Brad volunteered to help in a comic-book shop, and eventually became a paid employee and store manager. While working there, he spent time improving his artistic skills and went on to become a book illustrator. Heather loved fashion and jewelry design and chose to help the owner of a clothing consignment shop; she then opened her own boutique while taking fashion design courses. Amanda volunteered to run errands and do filing in a newspaper office at age fourteen. She soon began writing articles and is now a newspaper reporter. Volunteerism can help your child obtain real-life experience in the retail or business world, or it may even lead to a lifelong career.

Apprenticeships and Internships

Apprenticeships aren't as popular in the United States as they are in some countries. However, colleges or vocational schools often try to match up students with employers in apprenticeship or internship programs in many regions of our country. Many communities and organizations, such as 4-H, YMCA, or the Boys and Girls Club, offer work experience or mentor programs.

Part-Time Jobs

Your child's first paying job is another milestone in her life—another step toward independence and becoming an adult. In addition to earning her own money, she experiences a new form of satisfaction when helping others run a business or service, which enhances her self-esteem. She takes on the responsibility of exchanging her skills and time for money, while agreeing to put her best efforts into her work.

ALERT

Working ten to fifteen hours a week is usually enough for a teenager. As she nears the end of her high-school years, she may be able to increase her work hours or switch to a job that offers more hours and advancement opportunities.

Whether she works in a fast-food establishment, a video rental store, or a gift shop, this is a great experience for a teen. She learns how to meet others' expectations by delivering what she promised when taking on the job, being punctual, and getting along with supervisors, coworkers, and customers. At the same time, she will need to continue her studies as she works toward college or her career. Just because she now has a job, it doesn't mean she can slack off on her educational responsibilities.

Preparing for College

If your child is planning to attend college, the early high-school years are the time to begin preparations. He'll want to focus on the subjects that are required for college, as well as his grades and credits earned. His volunteerism and part-time jobs also come into play. Most colleges recognize the benefits of real-life experiences, so your teen will want to document all these experiences and include them with his college admission package.

College Entrance Exams

Your teen will also want to begin preparing for SAT or ACT tests if he plans to take them. These are only given at certain times of the year, so he'll want to be prepared well in advance and register ahead of time. To find out when and where the tests will be given in your area and how to register, contact your local school district. They can also advise you on ways to prepare for the test, the costs, and any other information you may need. Although there are no age restrictions, students usually take the SAT or ACT tests during the eleventh or twelfth grades.

Scholarships and Financial Aid

Many books and websites are devoted to helping you locate scholarships or financial aid for college expenses. You needn't pay a service to do this research for you. However, you do want to be on the lookout for scams regarding scholarships and aid. Once again, look to your local school district and library to help guide you in the best directions for information and advice on applying to colleges.

QUESTION

Are college scholarships available for homeschooled children?
Yes, many scholarships are designed especially for homeschooled students. For a list of homeschool scholarships, see *www.HomeschoolScholarships .org*. Financial aid and student loans are available, as well. For information on applying for student aid, visit *www.FinAid.org* and *www.StudentAid .ed.gov*.

High-School Transcripts

For homeschoolers, the high school transcript is an important tool for gaining entrance into college. You or your child will want to keep track of all the subjects he covers, his grades, and credits earned from the ninth through twelfth grades. This information will be recorded in the high-school transcript that many colleges require.

Generally, a half credit is earned in a subject in one semester, providing your child with a full credit for a year's study in that subject. For instance, one semester of science can equal one-half credit; the second semester earns another half credit. By the end of the freshman year, your child will have earned one full credit in science.

As indicated earlier, your teen will usually need twenty-two to twenty-four credits to meet traditional graduation requirements. These credits can easily be attained in each of the core subject areas and electives during the four years of high school. For examples of high school transcripts, as well as blank transcripts to print out, see the "Homeschool Forms" page at *www.EverythingHomeschooling.com.*

High-School Graduation

When your child is ready to graduate from your homeschool high school, you can have a celebration that equals the graduation festivities from a traditional public school. In many ways, it can even be more enjoyable for everyone. You can arrange a schedule that is convenient for everyone attending, it can be much less formal, there will be no huge crowds, everyone will know each other, and everyone will be more relaxed and, consequently, will enjoy themselves more.

QUESTION

How can I issue a diploma to my child?
You can order a diploma, issue it in the name of your child, and award it to him from your homeschool on graduation day. A diploma, certificates, graduation invitations, caps and gowns, and even class rings are available from the Homeschool Diploma website at *www.HomeschoolDiploma.com.*

While your child's graduation can be a private affair, many homeschool organizations also hold graduation ceremonies, complete with invitations, commencement speeches, caps and gowns, the handing out of awards and diplomas, and yearbook signings and class rings. Homeschoolers can enjoy their moments in the sun just as much as any other child, and, often, they even enjoy them more!

Resources for Teen Education

Lesson plans for grades 10 to 12 at *www.EverythingHomeschooling.com* provide weekly learning adventures in language arts, social studies, math, science, life skills, arts, and music. In addition, the Teens' Place page has lessons for teens who enjoy teaching themselves. Subjects include algebra, calculus, trigonometry, biology, physics, chemistry, government and economics, foreign languages, and more.

For graduation needs, visit *www.HomeschoolDiploma.com*. There, you'll find caps and gowns, class rings and medallions, diplomas and certificates, graduation invitations, and more. They also have articles on issuing a homeschool diploma and on making the graduation ceremony memorable.

CHAPTER 22

Children with Special Needs

Individualized attention in a safe, caring environment is wonderful for every child, and especially for children with special needs. In a home environment, you can help your child benefit from learning at his own pace, on his own terms, and in his own style. Whether your child has special needs, special gifts, or learns differently, the following resources can help you homeschool your precious child.

Learning Disabilities

Labels such as "learning disabled" or "intellectually challenged" are placed upon children quite readily these days. When a child learns at a slower pace or learns differently from others, it doesn't necessarily mean that he's learning disabled. It's one thing to diagnose a child with special challenges; it's quite another to unfairly label or categorize a child. Always seek second or third opinions from professionals regarding your child's abilities.

QUESTION

How can I instill self-confidence in my child?
Allow your child plenty of opportunities to do things on her own, no matter how trivial they might seem, so that she frequently feels a rewarding sense of accomplishment. Exhibit a great depth of patience with your child, and cheer her on with meaningful statements that tell her she can do it and that you have faith in her abilities.

The Learning Disabilities Association of America, *www.ldaamerica.org*, provides information on homeschooling children with learning disabilities. The site also offers resources, articles, and updates on various types of learning disabilities, including ADD/ADHD, dyslexia, reading disorders, and speech and language disorders.

Learning Challenges

Sometimes, all that mildly learning-challenged children need is someone who can understand their style, who is in tune with them, and who can help them make the most of their learning styles. In the homeschool, you have the ability to focus on your child's unique abilities, you can progress at his own pace, and you have the flexibility to work with him when he is at his best. Some children with special needs require more structure than others. You can provide the amount of structure they are comfortable with, while remaining flexible enough to take advantage of special learning opportunities as they arise.

If your child's learning challenges are more complex or difficult for you to handle on your own, ask your child's pediatrician to recommend a therapist or special-education expert. Seek their advice and suggestions on improving your child's learning skills and ways to help you make the most of your home education program.

ALERT

Some states could have certain regulations on homeschooling a child with special needs. Check with your state department of education to see what regulations, if any, might apply to you. Access to special-needs services also varies from state to state, so check the availability of such services within your local school district.

Input from Your Child

Every child and every family is different. What works for one may not work for another. A professional therapist and special-education program may be perfect for your child, or it may be frustrating and unproductive for your child. Most important, you want your child to be happy and to learn in an environment that is comfortable for him.

If he's not happy with the environment he's in, is frustrated by the activities he's trying to do, or feels he's not learning the way that best suits him—whether it's through you, a therapist, or a special-education program—listen to what he has to say. Knowing that you care enough to listen can make all the difference to him. Ask for his input and what he'd like to learn, and how he'd like to learn it.

Talk with other families, speak with the experts, and contact organizations dealing directly with your child's situation. Then apply all you've researched and learned toward determining what you feel is best for your child.

Creating Your Curriculum

You can create your own curriculum by determining your educational goals and objectives for your child. Based upon your goals, you can then design an educational program as discussed earlier. When designing a curriculum, consider your child's individualized needs, learning style, and his special areas of interest. Steer the curriculum and activities toward those areas. For additional learning opportunities, contact community centers, museums, libraries, and bookstores about classes or events they offer.

You'll also want to consult with your child's pediatrician, therapist, or special-education teacher to consider their advice and suggestions on working with your child. They have the training, knowledge, and experience to help you assist your child with his learning. In some cases, the school system may provide speech therapists, physical therapists, or occupational therapists to help with your homeschool program. Continue to closely monitor your child to determine the learning style that seems to work best for him, how well he's adapting to the educational program, and the progress he's making.

ESSENTIAL

An IEP (individualized education program) is used by special-needs teachers to create a curriculum for a child, record the objectives and goals for that child, and to document any specific programs or instruction he may require. To learn more about IEPs, check the articles at LD Online, *www.ldonline.org/indepth/iep.*

Ask for Input

As you incorporate an educational program in your home, do so at a pace that is comfortable for your child. Allow him time to adjust to this new routine and method of learning. He may become distracted or disoriented if there's not enough structure in his day. Or he may become overly anxious and stressed if he senses pressure, or if there's not enough free time to enjoy the things he likes to do.

Every few weeks, have another heart-to-heart discussion with your child about his learning program and encourage him to continue sharing his feelings. His feelings on the program may change as he learns and matures. The way he learned six months ago may no longer feel right to him, and he may be ready for something more stimulating, or perhaps he needs something less challenging for a while. The beauty of homeschooling is the ability to change and adapt according to each child's learning styles and preferences. This can be especially beneficial for your child.

Family Support and Resources

Support from others is extremely beneficial. No one knows what you're going through better than another family in circumstances similar to yours. Support groups for families with special needs can provide insight, encouragement, and strength as they share their personal experiences.

Online forums or message boards can provide support to parents, and some can put you in touch with families in your community. Those with experience in homeschooling special-needs children can help with the process or share particularly useful resources they've tried with their children.

Resources for Children with Special Needs

Check the following companies for resources that may be helpful to you or your child.

- Do2Learn, *www.Do2Learn.com*, provides resources, tools, and products for children with disabilities.
- Don Johnston, *www.DonJohnston.com*, carries books, software, and other products for children with learning disabilities.
- ISER (Internet Special Education Resources) has a page of links to special education products, *www.Iser.com/specialproducts.html*, including auditory tools, videos, reading helps, and books on working with your children.
- Wrightslaw, *www.WrightsLaw.com*, provides information on homeschooling rights and special-education needs.

Books for Homeschooling Special Children

These books provide guidance for families of children with special needs:

- *Home Schooling Children with Special Needs* by Sharon Hensley
- *Homeschooling the Child with ADD* by Lenore C. Hayes

- *Homeschooling the Child with Autism* by Patricia Schetter and Kandis Lighthall
- *Learning Differences Sourcebook* by Nancy Boyles and Darlene Contadino
- *Right-Brained Children in a Left-Brained World* by Jeffrey Freed and Laurie Parsons

Understanding ADD/ADHD

Children with ADD/ADHD are better understood and treated today than in previous decades. One of the leading nonprofit organizations, Children and Adults with Attention Deficit Hyperactivity Disorder (CHADD), provides support, guidance, and up-to-date information for families. They discuss multifaceted treatment approaches, which incorporate parent training, educational and behavioral modifications, and medical treatment. You can visit their website at *www.CHADD.org* and click on your state to locate a chapter near you.

FACT

Teaching LD, *www.TeachingLD.org*, has articles and information on reaching children with learning disabilities in reading, writing, and math. They also offer links to lesson plans, discussion forums, and other helpful resources.

The Attention Deficit Disorder Association, *www.ADD.org*, provides coaching guidelines as a way of helping those with Attention Deficit Disorder. They cite research suggesting that current methods of treating ADD/ADHD individuals, such as behavioral, psychological, and medical treatments, aren't always successful. They include an in-depth look at ADD coaching, how it works, and the principles behind it.

Dyslexia Help

Dyslexia becomes apparent through single-word decoding difficulties. Usually, no other types of developmental disability are evident. The

International Dyslexia Association's website, *www.eida.org*, offers updates, research, a message board, and links to branches throughout the United States and Canada. Techniques for overcoming reading and writing difficulties are included on the Davis Dyslexia Association International website at *www.Dyslexia.com*, along with learning strategies, articles, and a forum for networking with other families.

Autism Assistance

For many families, the calm, comfortable surroundings of home make homeschooling the preferred educational alternative for their autistic child. When parents are able to discover their child's unique learning styles, homeschooling becomes fun and the child begins to blossom.

The Autism Society also includes information on educating children with autism, as well as treatment options. They list state resources and support groups on their website at *www.Autism-Society.org*. Families for Early Autism Treatment (FEAT) offers support for families, along with field trips, gatherings, and other events within their state chapters. Visit their website at *www.Feat.org*.

ESSENTIAL

If you decide that you'd prefer to try a local private school or individualized program dealing specifically with your child's learning challenges, ask your child's pediatrician or therapist for their recommendations. They may even know of an in-home tutor specializing in special needs, which may better suit your child.

Down Syndrome Support

The National Challenged Homeschoolers Association Network (NATH-HAN) got its start when the mother of a Down syndrome child contacted the mother of another child with Down syndrome in an attempt to find support for those with learning-challenged children. The NATHHAN website at *www.Nathhan.com* includes experiences from parents of children with

Down syndrome, autism, hearing and vision impairments, and other physical handicaps and challenges.

Vision and Hearing Concerns

The National Organization of Parents of Blind Children, *www.nfb.org*, provides the Homeschooling and Blindness Network for families, along with a magazine, seminars, and workshops. A website for homeschool families with deaf or hearing-impaired children, Another Path at *www.DeafHomeschool.com*, provides articles, tips, and resources for homeschooling your child.

Gifted Children Resources

Gifted children look at things from a different perspective, learn and process information differently, may read or do math at a higher level, and/or seem mature for their age in some situations, yet childlike in others. They realize they have different abilities, and they, like any child, need to understand that it's okay to be different.

When homeschooling a gifted and talented child, you'll want to locate educational resources that meet her level of interest and will continue to stimulate and challenge her. Gifted children are creative, innovative, and enjoy brainstorming and exploring. They're good at self-educating themselves, due to their curiosity and interest-driven desire to know more. The challenge in the homeschool is to ensure that your child remains enthusiastic about her areas of study and that she's continually motivated to use her talents.

Resources for Homeschooling the Gifted

Check these websites for educational games, books, and materials designed for gifted children:

- Gifted Education Press, *www.GiftedEdPress.com*, carries books on teaching and parenting gifted children.
- Hoagies Gifted Education, *www.hoagiesgifted.org/shopping_guide.htm*, has a page of links to educational games and toys.

- Prufrock Press, *www.Prufrock.com*, offers activity books on enhancing thinking skills, math, science, and reading abilities.
- Stanford University's Education Program for Gifted Youth, *www .giftedandtalented.com*, offers online courses for students.

Associations for the Gifted

The National Association for Gifted Children, *www.nagc.org*, lists enrichment programs and schools, along with state associations for the gifted. The National Society for the Gifted and Talented, *www.nsgt.org*, provides resources and articles for parents on gifted education.

Books for Homeschooling the Gifted

These books provide guidance for families of gifted children:

- *Creative Homeschooling: A Guide for Smart Families* by Lisa Rivero
- *Gifted Teen Survival Guide* by Judy Galbraith and Jim Delisle
- *Helping Gifted Children Soar* by Carol Strip and Gretchen Hirsch
- *Helping Gifted Children Succeed at Home and School* by James Carroll
- *Homeschooling Your Gifted Child* by Lee Wherry Brainerd

Resources for Special Needs

The National Association for Child Development, Inc., *www.NACD.org*, helps to design individualized home education programs for learning-challenged children and adults, including those with Down syndrome, Tourette syndrome, and Rett syndrome, as well as ADD/ADHD, dyslexia, autism, cerebral palsy, and other developmental and physical conditions.

CHAPTER 23

Veteran Homeschool Parents

As a veteran homeschool parent, you could probably write your own book on homeschooling! Or maybe you still have a few years of homeschooling ahead of you, and your initial spark is beginning to burn out. It could be time to try different methods, to broaden your horizons, and to make changes not only in your homeschool, but in your lifestyle. Change can help you keep growing and lead to many happy years of exciting, rewarding homeschool experiences.

Regain Your Enthusiasm

If you've gone from burning with enthusiasm to burnout, it's time to rekindle that fire. Try to determine what has lost its appeal. Perhaps you are bogged down by record keeping and constant updating of learning logs. If your children are old enough to print, hand that duty over to them. You may need to spend a few days helping them record their activities, but they'll quickly get the hang of it. As you're preparing the next lesson or activity, they can update their learning logs and reading lists.

Streamline Record Keeping

If your children are unable to handle the updating of the learning logs, streamline the record-keeping process. You might be keeping records because your state requires it or because you want documented proof that your child has covered certain materials. But this doesn't mean you must write daily essays on your child's homeschool experiences. Imagine a teacher writing descriptive analyses for each of her thirty children every day! Simply write the chapter or page numbers of textbooks you used that day in social studies, jot down the Cuisenaire rods math lesson, the Super Spellicopter spelling game in language arts, the nature walk in science.

Reduce Lesson Planning Time

Are you spending too much time preparing lessons? This can cut deeply into the best part of homeschooling: the fun, interactive learning activities. You really shouldn't have to keep a lesson plan book *and* a daily learning log. If you keep a lesson plan book but don't get around to that lesson, erase it and move it to another day. If you do something in place of that lesson, jot that down.

Rather than developing in-depth lesson plans, note what you hope to cover and what you plan to use to cover it. The point of a lesson plan book is to help you be prepared, saving time over the long run. Use an hour or two on the weekend to think about the topics you'd like to cover in the upcoming week. On your next trip to the library, check out books that cover those topics in interesting ways. Jot them down in your lesson plan book. Skim through your homeschool idea books and your favorite websites on the Internet for supporting activities and experiments. Jot them down, and you're ready for the week ahead—plus you've got your learning log filled out in advance!

Prevent Burnout

Burnout can occur after ten years of homeschooling, or it might happen after just two years. Parents may feel that they have exhausted all the ideas that once seemed so fabulous and endless. After a few years of homeschooling, the kids might not be as excited about the homeschool experience as they were in the beginning. Trying to get them to open a book or finish an assignment seems like a losing battle.

Eliminating Stress

Stress is one of the main causes of burnout. Parents may find themselves trying to fill two full-time roles in the home—as a parent and as a schoolteacher—which adds unnecessary stress to their lives. As mentioned previously, learning is a natural part of living, and homeschooling should be a natural part of your family's lifestyle. You needn't turn it into school at home or make it more difficult than it should be. Homeschooling your children is simply a part of everyday parenting.

ESSENTIAL

A picture is worth a thousand words. Keep your camera handy and snap photos of ongoing lessons, activities, and projects. These can reduce the need for in-depth documentation in the learning log, remind you of projects you've done, and be placed in your child's portfolio.

Burnout can also result from setting expectations too high, then trying to reach them, day after day, and finding yourself falling short. Your expectations may be emotional ones, intricately interwoven with how well your children are learning. If you feel you'd be a better teacher if your children were ready for learning every morning at 8:00 A.M., dove into their lessons with glee each day, stayed on task throughout the morning and afternoon, achieved

100 percent on all their papers, and were able to deliver the Gettysburg Address over dinner, then you're only setting yourself up for disappointment.

If you, on the other hand, feel you're accomplishing your goals when your children enjoy most of their lessons, like to delve into things that interest them, are learning new information and skills each week, and can deliver the Gettysburg Address by the end of a school year, then you and your kids are probably enjoying the homeschool process, and you won't be as likely to burn out.

Lowering Expectations

As they say, an ounce of prevention is worth a pound of cure. Lower your expectations for yourself and for your children, and you will lower your feelings of stress and chances of burnout. It's true that you'll want your children to attain certain goals, so you naturally have some expectations of them. Just remember that you have an entire year to reach those goals. And then there's next year, too, and the year after that.

ALERT

If your children are exhibiting signs of boredom, then they may not be challenged enough. Raise the learning bar a little higher for them—just enough to entice them to try a little harder. But not so high that they become frustrated, which will lead to feelings of frustration and burnout for everyone.

When you begin to get that nagging feeling that maybe you're not doing enough in your homeschool, or you read or hear about the fantastic adventures of other homeschool families, take some moments to step back and look at your own family. Consider the happiness and well-being of your own children. Consider how much they've grown, how much they've learned since you began homeschooling.

Less Structure and More Flexibility

Remember that childhood is a time for being a child, not for squeezing hundreds of extracurricular activities into their lives. Remind yourself that childhood is a time for being curious and explorative, for daydreaming and thinking, playing and learning, having fun and being happy. The child who has plenty of time for these simple activities will grow into a happy adult who enjoys the freedom and fun of learning.

Stay Excited and Inspired

When you stay genuinely excited, motivated, and enthusiastic about home-school, your children will stay motivated, interested, and enthusiastic, too. However, the time may come when the wind has gone out of your sails and you begin slowing down and not billowing with as much enthusiasm as before. Your children are quick to pick up on this, and they could begin losing their enthusiasm, too.

ALERT

For a child to remain enthusiastic about learning and education, they must enjoy the *process of learning*. Avoid using motivational reward systems that focus on end results, that is, reading to appease a parent, completing an assignment as quickly as possible, or striving to get the best grades on a test.

When learning has meaning and is enjoyable, your children will be inspired to continue learning. Here are some strategies to help motivate your children to learn:

- Have children think of new ways to promote learning, using games, arts and crafts, hands-on projects, recreational pursuits, and field trips.
- Allow children to choose the topics they'd like to study and the ways in which they'd like to learn.
- Provide plenty of free time for children to become deeply involved in the learning activities that interest them.
- Be sure that learning activities have real meaning to your children and are genuinely interesting to them.
- Encourage children to follow those areas of interest that branch off from the path they're currently traveling.

- Pursue family hobbies or studies you might never have considered as a way to stimulate new interest and goals.
- Praise children for specific skills they've developed, information they've learned, and efforts they have made.

When a child enjoys the learning process and has the desire to learn, very little can hold him back. His curiosity will abound, his knowledge will increase, and his desire to continue learning will expand. This desire to learn is a form of self-motivation. Because there is something that he wants to learn, he will learn. Motivation and enthusiasm are key ingredients in successful learning.

Reconsider Curriculum Choices

If you've been using a certain type of curriculum or teaching style, but you've noticed a lack of interest in your child or an obvious resistance to home-schooling, it's time to make a change. Try unit studies for a while (these are lots of fun for everyone) or explore the concepts of unschooling (a wonderfully natural way of living and learning). Your children will love it, and they'll be bubbling over with excitement once again.

ESSENTIAL

Try an eclectic approach to learning by using a textbook from one publisher; a couple of activity books from another; unit studies for certain topics; learning games from the Internet; board games, construction sets, and hands-on projects; and lots of books from the local library for inspiration and ideas.

It can be difficult to release your hold on a curriculum (whether it's one you designed or a prepackaged plan) and adopt an unschooling form of education. It can be difficult to trust your children to learn in their own way. But it can be done—and done successfully.

Evolving into Unschooling

In our personal homeschool experiences, we did a lot of pigeonholing of activities as we tried to follow a specific course of study. We'd decide that this learning activity could be classified as science, that one as social studies, another as logical reasoning skills, and yet another as life skills. Finally, it clicked. They are *all* life skills, logical reasoning skills, social studies, and science, because they are *all* a part of life, and *life is made up of all these skills*. When the light finally came on, when that connection finally clicked, the need for pigeonholing every activity and fitting it into a specific subject area no longer seemed as important. That's when unschooling, or natural learning, became a normal part of everyday life.

For us, it wasn't a conscious decision to unschool. It just evolved that way, and it suddenly made the most sense. When I first heard of unschooling, I didn't give it a lot of thought. It seemed like a very unusual way to get an education, and I gave it no further consideration at the time.

Trusting Interest-Led Learning

As things evolved in the unschooling direction, and I eventually realized that ours was, indeed, a form of unschooling, I was past the point where I would have had doubts. I was already in the process of seeing the actual results of my son's learning and improvements in all areas of his education through his own style of unschooling, or interest-driven learning.

Today, Devin is a professional computer programmer and owns his own web development company. As a homeschooler who evolved into an unschooler, he developed the desire to learn, to follow his true interests, and to self-educate himself—a skill that will benefit him the rest of his life.

FACT

Unschooling may not work for every child or family. However, a modified version may work for yours. Test the waters by incorporating certain aspects of unschooling, while relying upon your main curriculum as a foundation. *The Unschooling Handbook,* by Mary Griffith, provides hundreds of examples of unschooling experiences from dozens of families.

Looking to Your Child for Direction

Relinquishing your dependence on a curriculum can be difficult. If your child is truly motivated and stimulated by the program you're using and is enjoying the learning process, there may be no need to change directions. But do keep in mind that children will not be following curricula the rest of their lives.

How well they'll learn and how productive they'll be in college will depend upon them and their desire to learn. No one will be helping them through a packaged curriculum at that point or leading them through pre-established guidelines. Their success in college and beyond will depend upon their level of self-motivation, fostered by their enjoyment of learning.

Therefore, even if your homeschool curriculum still works for your child, strive to introduce interests and learning challenges not included in the current homeschool program. Most important, encourage your child to explore areas that interest her, to follow the many paths that may branch out from those areas, to spend plenty of time learning on her own and in ways that work best for her.

Explore New Ideas

If you just can't make the switch to an unschooling or unit studies method of learning, you can still add renewed enthusiasm to your homeschool program. By now, you've probably incorporated some of the tips noted earlier on motivating your children and helping them to regain the joy of learning. You've encouraged them to pursue new hobbies, follow new directions of interest, create new ways of learning, and to spend plenty of time exploring their areas of interest.

Provide new resources and/or unusual tools for learning. Seek out different or more advanced scientific experiments to try. Select interesting books for learning ideas or to read aloud. Investigate new toys and games, or try new music styles and artistic techniques. Take part in more field trips, community events, and local festivals.

If these suggestions don't necessarily excite your child, he'll usually come across something in the process that leads to a different area of interest that neither you nor he had considered. As a result, he'll achieve a new or special interest, which can lead to further interest-driven learning, self-motivation, and self-education—the skills that are necessary for continuing education throughout his life.

Handle Unexpected Challenges

What if your child loses his interest in learning? What if he becomes resistant to homeschooling? Try the motivation strategies mentioned earlier. If that doesn't work, sit down and talk about the situation. As always, ask for his input and suggestions. What does he not like about his lessons? What would he rather be doing? How can the two of you come to a resolution on his feelings?

QUESTION

How can I trust my child to teach himself?
Your child's ability to teach himself is one of the most pleasant surprises of homeschooling! Give him the freedom to learn, and look to your child for direction and guidance. Observe his style of interest-led learning, self-education, self-motivation, and learning enjoyment. He will delight in sharing the things he's learned with you and the rest of his family.

If your child is bored with his lessons or no longer has interest in them, tell him that's okay and set them aside for a while. You can always go back to those lessons later. In the meantime, brainstorm new and different ways of learning that are more real to him, or focus on current interests that truly excite him.

Resisting Learning

If your child is resisting the home education process, hand it over to him for a while. Tell him that you understand his need to be in charge of his own learning and that you admire that in him. Jot down a few topics or skills you have planned for the next few weeks, such as learning about the kingdoms of classification; studying the Mayans, Aztecs, and Incas; plotting coordinates on a graph; and composing music on a staff. Then ask him to devise a new and innovative way to learn those skills in a way that is enjoyable to him.

Your child could find this challenge exciting and freeing. Or maybe he'll realize that he prefers the guidance you've provided in the past. Perhaps he'll find that a little of both is just right: freedom in learning his own way with some guidance and suggestions from you.

Flavorless Lessons

If your child has lost his desire for some of his lessons, find out why. What is it that he doesn't like about them? Answers you may hear could include: "They're boring; too easy; too hard; there's no reason to learn those things; they have nothing to do with *real* life."

Take what he says to heart. If a lesson is too boring, jazz it up. Better yet, ask *him* to help you jazz it up. If it's too easy, then it's definitely time to move on to the next level. If it's too hard, then it's time to back up and refresh previous skills. If refreshing skills is too boring for him, find *real life* ways to sharpen those skills. Then he'll see how those lessons apply to his life, how they make sense, and how there is a reason to learn them, after all.

Tired of It All

If your child has simply had it and doesn't enjoy anything at all about learning at home, have him share his reasons. Maybe it's not what he thought it would be. Ask him what he thought it would be like, then agree to try those ideas.

Maybe he'd rather be fishing instead of homeschooling. Then go fishing. When homeschooling or daily life becomes uninteresting for your child, it's time to make changes. It's important to find at least one thing that interests him. If fishing truly is the only thing that sparks his enthusiasm, then fishing it is. Learn about life together on the bank of a bubbling stream.

If cooking is the only thing that interests him, spend time together in the kitchen, concocting seven-course meals and seven-layer desserts. The time spent together—doing, talking, sharing, laughing—results in quality learning experiences, helping to bring both parties closer together, in a greater understanding of each other.

Share Goals with Children

You'll get better results, and children will learn more, when you explain the goals of each lesson, what the learning outcome is to be, and the steps required to reach the goal. For instance, the purpose of a specific geometry lesson could be to determine the perimeter and area of a room, knowledge that is useful and understandable to children. Geometry is a study of shapes and space. Our world is made up of shapes and space, and geometry helps us to better visualize those shapes, measure the space, and see two-dimensional objects in 3D.

When children understand *why* they are studying a specific subject, or how it relates to the real world, they'll learn and absorb information more thoroughly. When they understand what can be gained from learning about a topic, their mind is better focused on real goals and objectives.

Take a Break

A break is great for everyone. And that's one of the benefits of homeschooling—being able to take breaks when it best suits you and your family. Do you need an extra day off each week? Then have a Fun, Freaky Friday or a Mild, Mellow Monday, where everyone does what they want that day (within reason).

Maybe you want to homeschool for four or six weeks at a stretch, then take an entire week off. Knowing that you have a week off every month or two helps you maintain a better frame of mind during the homeschool weeks.

If you prefer to keep your schedule closer to that of regular schools, then have a Wild, Wacky Week every four to six weeks. That week can still be a homeschool week, but it can be quite different from your normal schedule. During that week, your children can be in charge of lesson plans, or they can take on the role of teacher, or together, you come up with a fun, unusual way of learning.

You can also simply stop homeschooling for a while. Schedule a vacation for a couple of weeks from now (so that you have time to look forward to it!) and tell everyone that school will be out for a two-week period. No teaching, no lesson plans, no attendance logs, nothing but free time.

Happy, Successful Homeschooling

Do something special each day with your children and your partner. And do something special for yourself, as well. When you lie down at night, you'll feel much more satisfied and happy with the way your day turned out.

If you didn't get to Lesson 12 in the math book as you had hoped, but you *did* play tag with the kids this afternoon and joined in their laughter and joy, then this makes your day worthwhile. If dinner wasn't on the table at six o'clock sharp because you spent an hour sitting with your partner, engaged in meaningful conversation, then your day was still a great one. If you didn't finish the laundry, but you were able to relax in a bubble bath for twenty minutes, then you felt renewed and rejuvenated, ready for another day.

There will always be another day for laundry, for fixing dinners, for doing math lessons. But for today, and for every day, your children, your partner, and your self should take priority. You will be happier, your children will be happier, and a happier homeschool is a more successful homeschool.

Resources for Fun Homeschooling

Use the wide variety of hands-on activities, along with weekly challenges and lessons, at *www.EverythingHomeschooling.com* to keep children interested in learning. For homeschool projects, see *www .project-based-homeschooling.com*. For science activities to keep children enthralled, see *www.ScienceMadeSimple.com*. When children enjoy what they're doing, they learn quicker and retain the information longer.

CHAPTER 24

College and Beyond

Your child will have a wide range of choices available to her as she steps into the world. Consider her goals, personality, and life principles, as you help her find the college that will be most beneficial to her. Of course, not every young adult wants to attend college. Many are more interested in teaching themselves. They're eager to continue with their self-directed studies in the way that has served them well in the past. Now they're ready to embark upon their next journey.

College for Homeschoolers

Many colleges today not only welcome home-educated students, they actively seek homeschoolers. Impressed by the level of maturity, independence, well-rounded education, and self-directed study habits of homeschoolers, more universities continue to open their doors to homeschoolers.

Homeschool-friendly colleges include Auburn University, Florida State University, Georgia Tech, Indiana University, MIT, Princeton University, Stanford University, and hundreds more, large and small. For more colleges open to homeschoolers, see *www.TheBestSchools.org* and search for homeschool colleges.

If your children are set on going to college, they can usually get into the college of their choice by planning ahead, taking the recommended courses during high school, preparing for the college entrance exams, and obtaining scholarships.

Searching Online

To begin your college search, try some of the following websites. College Week Live hosts virtual college fairs at *www.CollegeWeekLive.com*. The National Association for College Admission Counseling (NACAC) provides information on college fairs held around the country. Check NACAC's list of fairs, locations, dates, and times at *www.nacacnet.org*.

Many Christian colleges are especially open to homeschoolers. The Christian College Guide at *www.ChristianCollegeGuide.net* allows you to search for colleges and read about life at college. Additional listings of Christian colleges and general college information for the homeschooler are included at *www.AaronAcademy.com/aacollege.html*.

College Preparations and Selections

The preparations begun during the high-school years should culminate in a solid college application package. And the real-world experiences of the homeschooled years should make an outstanding impression on the college admissions officer. As your child begins to prepare for college, speak with him candidly about his expectations and goals for college.

Take a Tour

Encourage him to speak with others who have attended and graduated from the college he's interested in, as well as acquaintances who are currently attending. Contact the admissions office to arrange a visit to the college and take a tour. Your child might find these books helpful reading as he considers the college life that awaits him: *ABC's of College Life* by Vicki Salemi; *Making the Most of College* by Richard Light; and *Orientation to College Learning* by Dianna Van Blerkom.

Subject Requirements for College

Most colleges require that your child take four years of English courses, which should include grammar, composition, and literature, during his high-school years. In addition, he should take three years of social studies, including U.S. history and government and economics; three years of math, including geometry and algebra; three years of science, including biology, physical science, and lab experiences; two years of a foreign language; a computer technology course; and at least two years of electives.

ESSENTIAL

The College Board, *www.collegeboard.org*, provides information on planning ahead for college, considering careers, selecting courses, choosing majors, SAT preparation, how to apply to colleges, seeking financial aid, and much more. CollegeNET, *www.CollegeNET.com*, offers information on scholarship searches, financial aid, college fairs, college searches, and college preparation tips.

Colleges often have their own specific subject requirements. One college may require only one year of a foreign language, while another may require two years. Still other colleges may require particular math, history, science, or lab courses. If your child is set on a certain college, find out well in advance what subjects that college requires your child to take. Also determine if the college requires your home-educated student to meet any other special requirements in order to attend their school.

Transcripts and Documentation

During the high-school years, your child will want to collect and document the materials that are generally requested with the college applications package. Of course, you'll want to keep her high-school transcript up to date, along with her portfolio and daily learning log. Most colleges can provide you with a transcript form to fill out. Many make them available on their websites for downloading and printing, or you can contact the colleges that interest your child and ask for a blank transcript form.

FACT

If a college requires that your child have a General Equivalency Diploma (GED), she might be able to take the exam upon completion of her high-school years. States have varying age restrictions. Check with your local school district to find out what age restrictions apply in your state.

Your child will want to assemble letters of recommendation from mentors, teachers, tutors, and people she has worked for or apprenticed with. She'll also want to write and polish her personal admissions essay to include with the package. This essay can include her reasons for selecting that college, as well as the career or field of study she's chosen, along with information on her interests, hobbies, abilities, and goals.

Read More about It

These books might help you and your child make decisions regarding a college education:

- *And What About College?* by Cafi Cohen
- *Choosing the Right College* by John Zmirak
- *College Credit without Classes* by James L. Carroll
- *HomeScholar Guide to College Admissions and Scholarships* by Lee Binz
- *Teenagers' Guide to School Outside the Box* by Rebecca Greene

Entrance Exams and Interviews

Your child will want to begin preparing for the SAT or ACT exams if he plans to apply to colleges that require these test scores. Students usually take the SAT or ACT tests during the eleventh or twelfth grades, although there are no age restrictions. The exams are only given at certain times of the year, so your child will want to register ahead of time and be well prepared for them. To find the location of test sites and dates in your area, and how to register, contact your local school district or college. They may also be able to advise you on how to prepare for the test, the test fees, and related information.

ALERT

If your child expresses an interest in attending college, it could be beneficial for him to occasionally take a standardized test. This can help to familiarize him with test taking, determine his comfort level with tests, and monitor how well he performs on exams.

Many colleges and universities do not use SAT or ACT scores for admission decisions. Be sure to check ahead to see what they require for your homeschooled child, though. To view a list of over 300 of these schools, visit the FairTest website at *www.FairTest.org*.

Getting College Credit

The College Level Examination Program (CLEP) provides college credit for students based upon information they've learned and how well they perform on the test. The CLEP exams can be taken at various testing sites. Contact your local school district, community college, or university for more information.

College Admissions

A meeting with the college admissions officer is especially important for the homeschooled student, as they base much of their evaluation on the face-to-face interview. You'll want your child to prepare well for the interview.

Admissions officers are accustomed to meeting with thousands of students over the years. They can tell if your child is somewhat nervous during the interview, and they won't hold that against him. However, in preparation for interviews—not only with college officials, but also with potential employers—you can work with your child on improving his self-confidence, communication skills, pleasant personality, and positive attitude.

In addition to the interview with your child, admissions officers will consider the real-world experiences your child has had, volunteerism, internships, work opportunities, and community involvement.

Financial Aid and Scholarships

Scholarships are available for homeschooled students, but it can take some searching and perseverance in locating them. Check with your local reference librarian or school district to help guide you in the pursuit of scholarships and student loans. Scholarships are often awarded based upon SAT and ACT scores, so be sure to look into those exams before the junior or senior year. For a list of scholarships available to homeschoolers, visit *www.HomeschoolScholarships.org*. For information on financial aid, see *www.FinAid.org* and *www.StudentAid.ed.gov*.

Online and Distance Learning

Many well-known colleges and universities offer online classes or distance-learning courses. Some could require on-campus time for a few weeks out of each year or at some point during the enrollment period. If your child has done especially well with distance-learning courses or independent self-study programs during her homeschool years, distance-learning or online courses may be perfect for her.

CollegeDegree.com provides a list of colleges and universities that offer degrees through distance learning. Check their website at *www.collegedegree.com*. The Distance Education Accrediting Commission, *www.deac.org*, maintains a list of accredited degree programs and certificates for specialized training.

Life after Homeschool

The transition from homeschool to real life is generally pretty easy for the homeschooler. Homeschoolers are already in tune with the ebb and flow of their days, have an established routine that revolves around their daily life-style within the home, and have developed hobbies and activities that fill their days with interest.

The homeschooled teen has been acclimating himself for the day when his high-school obligations no longer take top priority. He can now focus wholeheartedly on the interests he's developed over the years, the fields of study he wants to pursue further, and the adventures and projects he's ready to undertake. He may still intend to enroll in college at some point, after he's taken time to investigate his options, desires, and dreams. He may even want to travel before he makes a commitment to attending college in a particular city or state.

Rather than travel or pursue higher education, the homeschool graduate may be eager to put his skills to good use right away in the job market. Whatever he chooses to do, you can be sure that he will most likely continue to hone his skills, seek ways to further his knowledge and education, and strive to be the best he can be in the areas that fascinate him today and in the future.

Options, Internships, and Travel

Homeschooled graduates can be anyone or anything they want to be. Most already know this from firsthand experience during their homeschool years. By this point in their lives, many have experienced a wide range of fulfilling ventures, from acting on the stage to helping injured animals to building boats to playing trumpet in the community band.

ESSENTIAL

When our youth know that they can be anything they want to be, life takes on deeper meaning for them. Each day has purpose; each day holds promise. They are not floating in midstream, with no direction to their lives. They've already tasted what life is about, and they're eager to get on with it and live it to the fullest.

Most homeschoolers have special interests that were never put down, never discouraged, or never set aside due to lack of time. They have, instead, pursued their interests heartily and woven them into the very fabric of their lives. They have goals and dreams to achieve, and they know how to go about achieving them. Life is a great adventure, and they are thrilled to play their part in it.

But what if your child has so many interests she's undecided which to follow first now that school is over? Or, what if she knows what she wants to do, but is unsure of how to go about it? Here are some options she may want to consider.

Internships

Internships allow your child to work in areas that interest her before she has the actual experience to be hired as a full-time employee. Internships are most often offered during the summer or for a few weeks out of the year. The position may be paid or not, but the experience and contacts in the business are invaluable.

In many cases, the intern may be asked to come back again, and the temporary position can evolve into an actual paying job. The company may even offer to pay for training courses that keep skills up to date and help workers continue being an asset to the company. Help your teen make calls to businesses she is interested in to see if they offer an internship or on-the-job training program.

Travel Adventures

A simple change of scenery can help you view your daily life in a different light and from a fresh perspective. Travel to another region of the country or to an entirely different country helps you to view life from a very different angle. Your homeschooled graduate may feel the pull of the oceans, the call of the mountains, and the undeniable desire to roam and explore this world before him. If he's determined to strike out on his travels, you can help him find the assistance he needs.

Your child can contact organizations such as the American Youth Hostels, *www.hiusa.org*, and Volunteers for Peace, *www.vfp.org*. Adventure travel programs, such as Earthwatch, *www.earthwatch.org*; Outward Bound, *www.OutwardBound.org*; Pacific Challenge, *www.PacificChallenge.org*; or Westcoast Connection, *www.WestcoastConnection.com*, offer trips geared to young adults. Many of these have age and group size limits, so check any restrictions that might apply.

Learning Abroad

Once your teen has been bitten by the travel bug, he may decide to postpone that trip back home. He might not have wanted to attend college at home, but the allure of studying at the American University of Paris is too enticing to pass up. Education in another country not only improves one's knowledge of geography and foreign language, but also of new cultures, life and business styles, social skills, history, art, literature, and music. It can, indeed, open one's mind to a brand new world.

The Council on International Educational Exchange, *www.ciee.org*, provides additional information on exchange programs and study programs abroad. You can also search Peterson's list of programs at *www.Petersons.com* or Study Abroad's site at *www.StudyAbroad.com*.

Military Adventures

The military offers some of the greatest adventures for young people. The branches of the military provide the opportunity to travel, learn a life-long career, and meet people in all corners of the world. To enter a military school, your child will need to take a military entrance exam. A high-school diploma from an umbrella or satellite school, or other distance-learning or private school, is also helpful. Without a diploma, the student will need to score higher on the entrance exams. If your homeschooler is interested in serving his country, contact your local recruiting office for details.

Careers and Continuing Education

Your child may know exactly what she wants to do with her life, but has no intention of sitting in a classroom or doing lengthy assignments day after day. She wants to be an active participant, rather than reading about life. She's ready to take off with her life and her life's work.

Yet, there may be just a few things she'd like to learn as quickly as possible, before she takes flight. For example, she might need to learn C++ in the shortest amount of time or how to create streaming video for websites. Short courses such as these are offered at many sites on the Internet, along with Microsoft Certification courses, Java Certification, HTML Certification, and similar courses.

Vocational Training

Book learning is all well and good, but some people thrive on hands-on learning. Tearing apart a car engine, rebuilding computer printers, wiring an alarm system, raising sheep, training seeing-eye dogs, building a house with their bare hands, or growing organic vegetables is what drives these hard-working young people. For them, the local vocational, trade, or technical school provides the additional knowledge they need in a fairly short amount of time. Many of these schools offer night classes, as well as full-day classes. The schools nearly always strive to match their skilled students with an internship program, or they assist students in finding jobs locally.

Alternative or Creative Careers

To learn more about careers available for those not wanting to spend four years in college, check out these books. They can provide ideas and food for thought as young adults consider their futures:

- *America's Top Jobs for People without Four-Year College Degrees* by J. Michael Farr
- *But What If I Don't Want to Go to College?* by Harlow G. Unger
- *Career Guide for Creative and Unconventional People* by Carol Eikleberry
- *Creating a Life Worth Living* by Carol Lloyd
- *Great Careers in Two Years* by Paul Phifer
- *Uncollege Alternative* by Danielle Wood

After the Nest Is Empty

Once you have homeschooled a child, truly educated that child, spent days and months and years of your life homeschooling, it's difficult to imagine life any other way. When you make the most important realization that home-school is not school at home, it becomes life itself. It's just life. There's really no other way to explain it.

Yet, life is continually changing, and the day comes when it's time for the young ones to spread their wings and leave the nest. Most parents with grown children can empathize with the feelings associated with the empty-nest syndrome. Many parents who also homeschooled their children feel it even more intensely. Not worse, mind you, but more intensely.

A house that was once full of homeschoolers, lesson plans, learning logs, dioramas, artwork displays, LEGO inventions, tumbling stacks of library books, fingerpaints, modeling clay, construction paper, math books, *papier-mâché* solar systems, chemistry sets, computers, musical instruments, and portfolios—now seems quite stark. And a bit sad.

FACT

Homeschoolers learn at an early age that education is a natural part of everyday life. Having taken responsibility for much of their learning through the years, it seems unnatural to *not* be learning. They learn at an early age how to be lifelong learners—a skill that will benefit them all the years of their lives. You can be quite proud of how you helped your children grow, learn, and live life to the fullest.

Take comfort in knowing that you have made a profound impression upon your child's life. Your home may feel a little empty, but his life, his successes, and his future more than fill that small void. True, you may not know what to do with yourself now, or with all that time you now have on your hands. But you, like him, know how to keep learning, how to keep finding new interests, how to stay busy, and how to expand your mind and your spirit. After all, you're the one who helped guide him to where he is today.

Ideas for a Full and Happy Life

If you need a little prodding, here are some ideas to help you get started as you consider the many possibilities that yet await you:

- Set up and pursue your own self-directed educational program.
- Return to college and get a degree in education.
- Volunteer or substitute in schools or child-care facilities.

- Establish a daycare service for homeschooled children of working parents.
- Offer specialty classes or mentorships for homeschooled children.
- Start a tutoring service for children and adults.
- Teach in a private or charter school.
- Learn how to ski, skydive, surf, or sail.
- Travel to new and exotic lands.
- Become a state-certified, homeschool-friendly teacher who can work with homeschoolers, reviewing portfolios, administering exams, and inspiring other homeschool families.

The world is your oyster, just as it was and continues to be for your children. They are shining. They are sparkling. Now it's your turn. Get ready to shine!

Resources and Websites

EDUCATIONAL MATERIALS	
Back Pack	www.thebackpack.com
Educational Innovations, Inc.	www.teachersource.com
Home Training Tools	www.hometrainingtools.com
Kidware	www.kidwaresoftware.com
Laurelwood Books	www.laurelwoodbooks.com
Library Video	www.libraryvideo.com
MathMedia	www.mathmedia.com
MathTutor Educational Software	www.mathtutor.com
MindPlay	www.mindplay.com
MindWare	www.mindwareonline.com
Education.com	www.education.com
Owl & Mouse	www.yourchildlearns.com
School Express	www.schoolexpress.com
Smart Kids Software	www.smartkidssoftware.com
Special Interest Videos	www.sivideo.com
SuperKids Educational Software	www.superkids.com
Virtu Software	www.virtu-software.com
FREE EDUCATIONAL MATERIALS	
Note: Most of these websites offer many free materials. Some sections of a few sites might require a fee for additional resources.	
ABC Teach	www.abcteach.com
ChildFun	www.childfun.com
Education Place	www.eduplace.com/edugames.html
Enchanted Learning	www.enchantedlearning.com
Everything Homeschooling	www.everythinghomeschooling.com
Free-Ed.net	www.free-ed.net
FunBrain	www.funbrain.com
Gamequarium	www.gamequarium.com
KinderStart	www.kinderstart.com
Kindergarten Worksheets	www.kindergartenworksheets.net
Learning Page	www.learningpage.com

Preschool Rainbow	www.preschoolrainbow.org
School Express	www.schoolexpress.com
Tampa Reads	www.tampareads.com
TeAchnology	www.teach-nology.com
TLS Books	www.tlsbooks.com

RESOURCES AND MATERIALS FOR SPECIAL-NEEDS CHILDREN

Another Path	www.DeafHomeschool.com
Autism Society	www.Autism-Society.org
Do2Learn	www.Do2Learn.com
Don Johnston	www.DonJohnston.com
Davis Dyslexia Association International	www.Dyslexia.com
Families for Early Autism Treatment	www.feat.org
ISER (Internet Special Education Products)	www.iser.com/specialproducts.html
LD Resources	www.ldresources.com
Teaching LD	www.teachingld.org

RESOURCES AND MATERIALS FOR GIFTED CHILDREN

Gifted Education Press	www.giftededpress.com
Hoagies Gifted Education	www.hoagiesgifted.org/parents.htm
Prufrock Press	www.prufrock.com
Stanford University's Education Program for Gifted Youth	www.giftedandtalented.com

FAITH-BASED SUPPLY RESOURCES

Behrman House	www.behrmanhouse.com
Christian Book Distributors	www.christianbook.com
Heritage Catholic Curricula	www.chcweb.com
Torah Aura Productions	www.torahaura.com

FREE LESSON PLAN IDEAS

Discovery Education	www.discoveryeducation.com
Education World	www.educationworld.com/a_lesson
Everything Homeschooling	www.everythinghomeschooling.com
Lesson Plan Search	www.lessonplansearch.com
Lesson Plans Page	www.lessonplanspage.com
Lesson Planz	www.lessonplanz.com
PBS Learning Media	www.pbslearningmedia.org
Teachers Corner	www.theteacherscorner.net
Teachers.net	www.teachers.net

CORRESPONDENCE AND ONLINE SCHOOLS

A Beka Academy	www.abekaacademy.org
Alger Learning Center	www.independent-learning.com
Alpha Omega	www.aop.com
American School	www.americanschoolofcorr.com
Calvert School	www.calvertschool.org
Christian Light Education	www.clp.org/christian_light_education
Chrysalis School	www.chrysalis-school.com
Citizens' High School	www.citizenshighschool.com
Clonlara School	www.clonlara.org
CompuHigh Online	www.compuhigh.com
Griggs International Academy	www.griggs.edu
Heritage Home School Academy	www.heritagehomeschool.com
Indiana University High School	https://iuhighschool.iu.edu/
Internet Home School	www.internethomeschool.com
Keystone School	www.keystoneschoolonline.com
Kolbe Academy	www.kolbe.org
Laurel Springs School	www.laurelsprings.com
Malibu Cove High School	www.seascapecenter.com
Oak Meadow School	www.oakmeadow.com
Seton Home Study School	www.setonhome.org
Sycamore Academy Home School	www.sycamoreacademy.com
Texas Virtual School	www.texasvirtualschool.org
University of Missouri	http://cdis.missouri.edu
Wilostar3D	www.wilostar3d.com

COLLEGE RESOURCES

Council for Christian Colleges & Universities	www.cccu.org
College Board	www.collegeboard.org
College View	www.collegeview.com
CollegeDegree.com	www.collegedegree.com
CollegeNET	www.collegenet.com
FairTest	www.fairtest.org
Federal Student Aid	www.fafsa.ed.gov
FinAid	www.finaid.org
HSLDA Homeschool Scholarships	www.hslda.org
National Association for College Admission Counseling (NACAC)	www.nacacnet.org
Student Aid	www.studentaid.ed.gov

PUBLICATIONS	
Home Education Magazine	*www.HomeEdMag.com*
Homeschool Fun	*www.HomeschoolFun.com*
Homeschooling Today	*www.HomeschoolToday.com*
Practical Homeschooling	*www.Home-School.com*
Teaching Home	*www.TeachingHome.com*
DRIVER EDUCATION	
Driver Ed in a Box	*www.driveredtraining.com*
Driver Ed to Go	*www.driveredtogo.com*
DriversEd.com	*www.driversed.com*
I Drive Safely Drivers Ed	*www.teen.idrivesafely.com*
National Driver Training	*www.usdrivertraining.com*
VIRTUAL FIELD TRIPS AND MUSEUMS	
Exploratorium	*www.exploratorium.edu*
Field Trip Zoom	*www.fieldtripzoom.com*
Field Trips Online	*www.everythinghomeschooling.com*
Questacon	*www.questacon.edu.au*
Smithsonian Institution	*www.si.edu*
Virtual Dissections, Labs, and Field Trips	*www.accessexcellence.org/RC/virtual.html*
TRAVEL	
American Youth Hostels	*www.hiusa.org*
Council on International Educational Exchange	*www.ciee.org*
Earthwatch	*www.earthwatch.org*
Outward Bound	*www.outwardbound.org*
Pacific Challenge	*www.pacificchallenge.org*
Peterson's	*www.petersons.com*
Study Abroad	*www.studyabroad.com*
Volunteers for Peace	*www.vfp.org*
Westcoast Connection	*www.westcoastconnection.com*

Curriculum Providers and Programs for Homeschoolers

A Beka Book	www.abeka.com
Alpha Omega	www.aop.com
Bob Jones University Press	www.bjup.com
Charlotte Mason	www.simplycharlottemason.com
Christian Liberty Academy School System	www.homeschools.org
Core Curriculum of America	www.core-curriculum.com
Covenant Home Curriculum	www.covenanthome.com
Curriculum Services	www.curriculumservices.com
Design-A-Study	www.designastudy.com
eTutor	www.e-tutor.com
Excellence in Education	www.excellenceineducation.com
Explorer's Bible Study	www.explorerbiblestudy.org
Five in a Row	www.fiveinarow.com
Heart of Wisdom	http://heartofwisdom.com/blog/
K^{12}	www.k12.com
KONOS	www.konos.com
Moore Foundation	www.moorefoundation.com
Robinson Curriculum	www.robinsoncurriculum.com
Trisms Curriculum	www.trisms.com
UnitStudy.com	www.unitstudy.com
Waldorf education	www.steinercollege.org

National Homeschool Organizations

Catholic Homeschool Support	www.catholichomeschool.org
Considering Homeschooling Ministry	www.christianhomeeducation.org
Family Unschoolers Network	www.unschooling.org
Home School Legal Defense Association	www.hslda.org
Latter-Day Saint Home Educators Association	www.ldshea.org
Muslim Home Education Network	www.muslimhomeschool.net
National Association for Gifted Children	www.nagc.org
National Challenged Homeschoolers Associated Network	www.nathhan.com
National Society for the Gifted and Talented	www.nsgt.org

Index